▼▼▼▼ # Understanding I/O Subsystems

Foreword

Microcomputer systems initially had simple designs with performance limited by processor speeds. During years of relentless processor, cache, and bus improvements, I/O subsystem performance clearly emerged as an equally crucial consideration for system and network performance. Simply stated, bad I/O kills system performance every time regardless of system MIPS or bus speeds.

Today's I/O subsystems are increasingly complex since they interact with hardware, software, and firmware architectures. The architectures range from processor and memory subsystems, to operating systems, to I/O subsystems. Hardware ranges from network controllers, storage devices, device controllers, system buses, to caches. Software includes device drivers, file systems, network protocol stacks, and system BIOSs. Firmware includes peripheral device, host adapter and processor microcode. While other literature addresses each element in isolation, this book integrates them allowing readers to achieve an integrated systems perspective about high-performance I/O.

Integrating these various topics is difficult because the architectures and subsystem elements are individually complex in their own right. So, it is understandable that their collective complexity and interactions at various levels and times present significant challenges in achieving maximum system performance. Effectively integrating the architectures to obtain maximum system performance is a process that is genuinely rewarding, but equally harsh and unforgiving when done poorly. The task is complicated by an innovation-driven industry that presents constant evolution. In other words, the job is never finished.

Adaptec is the leader in providing high-performance desktop and server I/O solutions. To achieve the broad perspective and expertise that leading system-level performance designs require, Adaptec continually participates in all microcomputer technology, architecture, and bus standards efforts. This enables Adaptec to develop IOware™ products that span all industry standards—from SCSI, EIDE, and PCMCIA, to ATM, infrared, IEEE 1394, SSA, and Fibre Channel. These products enhance performance and connectivity for high-performance workstations, desktop systems, department and enterprise servers, and mobile computing environments.

This book discusses many considerations associated with I/O sub-systems. We have tried to make the material readable and present the relationships between individual topics. A gradation of technical depth is provided. The intent is to illuminate the total scope of issues involved in high-performance I/O subsystems. Our goal is to help you improve overall systems performance.

F. Grant Saviers
Chief Executive Officer, Adaptec
January 1996

Dedicated to the people who pay our salaries:

Our customers

▼▼▼▼ Contents

5 Hard Disk Controllers   83

6 Other Rotating Storage   97

7 SCSI Primer   113

8 IDE, EIDE, and ATAPI Device Interfaces   133

9 Serial SCSI Protocols   153

10 PC I/O System Software   195

11   Performance Assist Considerations   253

From the Authors

Thank you for taking the time to read this book. We hope you find the first edition useful. It is the result of many folk's efforts here at Adaptec. Reviewers included Karen Ammer, Michael Arellano, Vince Bastiani, Tom Battle, Randy Berger, Mark Bradley, Julene Casamayou, Mary Corcoran, Barbara Dali, Debbie Horen, Diana Lovelace, Tom Martin, Ted Matsumura, Mike McMurdie, Jack Newman, Joe Repac, Valarie See, Grant Saviers, Dr. Robert Selinger, Tom Shea, and Chris Simpson. External reviewers were Dr. Richard Gardner of Seagate Technology, and Dr. David W. Hunter of IBM Corporation. Mike Riggle, one of the disk drive industry's legends, heavily edited the chapters on disks and disk controllers. Jim Gast of Novell Corporation thoughtfully provided NetWare® material as we approached deadline. Bill Knight and Connie Michael drew the illustrations. Jean Jacobson Knight formatted the text. While the many reviewers and copy editors have done excellent jobs within their time constraints, any remaining errors or possible improvements remain the responsibility of the authors.

You may find the book's material a bit uneven in depth because of the book's breadth, very complex individual topics, and finite heartbeats allocated for the immense undertaking. Adaptec constantly strives for improvements and we hope to fix this in later editions. If you find any serious omissions, we would enjoy hearing your thoughts for future editions because refining our products is part of our daily work.

If you find any errors, we would appreciate hearing from you so we can fix them. In fact, you probably should introduce yourself to our Human Resources department at the same time. Be assured, Adaptec's management is fabulously bright, the support employees are fantastic, the engineering intellect exquisite, the sales representatives dedicated, and customer service tireless. It is a seriously wonderful place to work and my only disappointment is not connecting with Adaptec sooner—particularly since Adaptec has been profitable for more than 45 consecutive financial quarters. Please check us and our products out, you'll be glad you did.

W. David Schwaderer
Senior Digital Media Engineer
Milpitas, California
January 1996

Andrew W. Wilson, Jr.
Senior Performance Analyst
Milpitas, California
January 1996

About the Authors

W. David Schwaderer is an internationally recognized author on a broad range of computing subjects. He has written *Modems and Communications on the IBM PC*; *C Wizard's Programming Reference*; *IBM's Local Area Networks*; *C Programmer's Guide to NetBIOS, IPX and SPX*; *The Adobe Acrobat™ Handbook*; and *Digital Image Processing by Example* (published summer of 1996 by Addison Wesley). He has a Masters Degree in Applied Mathematics from the California Institute of Technology and an MBA from the University of Southern California. He has produced numerous products, programming for over 30 years in a variety of languages and system architectures. Many of his written works are internationally published and some personal achievements have been noted in *Data Communications* magazine. A veteran of EDS, IBM, and three hard-core Silicon Valley start-ups, his summer 1996 vacation plans include bicycling the entire Oregon coast in six and one half days, staying in Mongolian yurts at Oregon state parks. At Adaptec, he is a Senior Digital Media Engineer, working on strategic development efforts with significant performance advantage.

Andrew Wilson has a BA from Pomona College, an MSEE from the University of Arizona, and a Ph.D. from Carnegie Mellon University. He has worked with computers since 1968 when he took an IBM 1401 assembly language programming class in high school. He has since used, programmed, or designed hardware for a variety of microprocessor, minicomputer, and mainframe systems, as well as IBM compatible PCs. He has authored over a dozen publications, and conducted leading edge research in extensible shared memory multiprocessor architectures, developing a patented hierarchical cache coherency design incorporated in two prototype systems. Delighted with his current position as Manager of Performance Analysis for Adaptec's IO Technology Department, he is involved in advanced product exploration. When not occupied with computers, he is busy with his wife, camping, and model railroading. All things equal, he'd really rather be working on a laptop while riding on a train.

Introduction and Overview

What This Chapter Is About

This brief chapter presents the data hierarchy present in most computers. This hierarchy gives a brief glimpse of the considerations popular desktop computing systems use to insulate high-performance processors from slower supporting components. We begin by examining the data hierarchy found in contemporary desktop systems.

Data Storage Hierarchy

Some system performance enhancement strategies attempt to stage data optimally for CPU execution unit processing while others reduce transit time between staging areas. From highest to lowest performance, data staging points typically include:

- Processor instruction pipelines
- CPU registers
- CPU on-chip first-level cache
- Second-level (L2) cache
- System memory buffering
- Host adapter cache/buffer
- Hard disk controller hardware cache/buffer
- Hard disk
- Archive storage (e.g., tape or optical devices)

In every sense, these elements exist to deliver data to processor execution units. Their individual cost varies, for example, memory prices vary from \$40/MByte for DRAM to \$600/MByte for second-level cache memory and their presence or absence is usually evident. Benchmarks clearly indicate systems with a second-level cache can outperform their counterparts without them by as much as 25 percent.

Interfaces between hierarchy levels (e.g., system busses and main memory or, adapters and disk drives) exist to couple one component to another. In an ideal system, the hierarchy elements:

- Completely anticipate processor needs

- Seamlessly coordinate data processing with data-staging activities

- Provide processors the illusion of instantaneous access to data located anywhere

But system processing peaks and troughs present varied data access patterns which defy anticipation. Even in the best circumstances, staging data by moving it temporarily closer to the processor introduces serious side effects, requiring considerable forethought and system resources to resolve. It's therefore no surprise that new systems often incorporate industry-standard, incremental improvements. These improvements address the most serious predecessor system design problems, and may not even be performance-related.

Moreover, the best chance for maximum performance *only* occurs when system designs simultaneously characterize *all* possible hardware and software alternatives and, using systems perspectives, optimally select, integrate, and apply them to well-defined objectives or specific application requirements. Some people refer to this as a *Zen* systems approach, others as impossible. But design cycles and customer financial resources are finite. Hence, component exploration involves compromise, since it is not feasible to characterize all hardware and software combinations.

For example, in some simple situations, numerous possibilities may exist for each system component. In these cases, it is tempting to select components in isolation, based on single attributes. Doing so usually produces overall system performance suboptimizations. In other situations, only one choice exists for given components. When the components are later upgraded to new versions, small differences in the newer parts may irreparably suboptimize or otherwise change performance for the worse. It follows that maximum system performance remains elusive, and systems necessarily embody compromise. Likewise, system designs that maximize one application's performance usually degrades other application performance due to differing system requirements.

Benchmarks

It is traditional to compare systems using benchmarks that supposedly represent typical workloads. But, because benchmark activity requires arbitrary consistency, it is inflexible. Its artificial nature can provide crude and incorrect metrics. Because system configuration is complex, benchmark administrators may inadvertently fail to enable system performance enhancing features, thereby invalidating benchmark integrity. Even with the best intentions, inadvertent but serious errors regularly happen, sometimes in prominent industry testing labs (much to everyone's chagrin).

The remainder of this book examines performance element considerations with an attempt to interrelate them from a historical and systems perspective. We hope the journey is both enjoyable and informative, leaving a sense of how to judge components and how to anticipate what combinations are most likely to exhibit the performance you seek.

This material has overlaps because topics do not divide cleanly. As a single example, there is a chapter on hard disks and one on disk controllers though most disks now embed controllers. You do not have to read every chapter to understand all later chapters, though it helps. For example, you can read the start of Chapter 4 and then skip to later chapters if you are not concerned with how disks are built. For a thorough reading, you may likely want to read Chapters 1 through 8, 10, and 11.

Chapter Questions

1 Good hardware designers know how applications access data and optimize designs to the access pattern.

   a True
   b False

2 Typically the lowest performance element within the data storage hierarchy is

a A hard disk

b Processor instruction pipelines

c Archive storage

d None of the above

3 Typically the highest performance element within the data storage hierarchy is

a A hard disk

b Processor instruction pipelines

c Archive storage

d None of the above

4 It is difficult to test all applicable combinations of hardware and software because

a There aren't that many summer intern employees available

b Some components go out of production and new components appear every month

c No one could afford it

d All of the above

5 Most benchmarks

a Are always realistic, hence relevant

b Are never performed incorrectly

c Are flexible

d None of the above

❒

Original PC Motherboard Design—A Historical Perspective

What This Chapter Is About

To understand I/O trade-offs and performance evolution, we begin with early IBM PC model designs since they set early evolutionary directions and many of their legacies remain. Figure 2-1 provides a simplistic overview of a typical PC systems unit. Referring to Figure 2-1, a typical desktop PC system contains:

- A processor (CPU)
- System I/O space for I/O port reading and writing

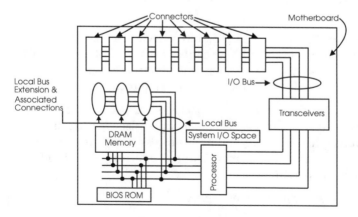

Figure 2-1. Typical PC System

- System memory space containing DRAM and a ROM BIOS

- An I/O bus of varying design

- Expansion slots with connectors housing various adapter cards

- Peripheral devices such as hard disks, diskette drives, and CD-ROM drives (Not shown in the figure)

- Optional local bus extension and associated connectors

Because the CPU performs most processing, system designers attempt to maximize CPU performance within stringent, industry-competitive, economic constraints. To this end, PC motherboards incorporate additional hardware considerations, not illustrated, to minimize device and memory latency effects. This chapter expands on PC motherboard designs and explains the PC boot sequence, including how adapters containing their own BIOS support are activated during the boot sequence.

Ground Zero

The initial 1981 IBM PC and the subsequent IBM PC-XT variation motherboard featured:

- An Intel 8088 microprocessor as the system processor and an optional 8087 as a numeric processor

- 40 KBytes of ROM, comprising system BIOS support and resident Microsoft, Inc. BASIC implementation

- 64 KBytes of Read/Write DRAM memory (256 KBytes for the PC-XT)

- Five (eight for the PC-XT) 62-pin card edge sockets (slots) for optional expansion adapter cards. One special slot's specifications differed from the other general purpose sockets and was specifically designed for an expansion box connection adapter

- A configuration dual-in-line package (DIP) switch that users manually set to specify system memory size, diskette drive count, whether an 8087 numeric processor was installed, and monitor type (color or monochrome) information to the PC-DOS 1.0 operating system

- 60 watt switching power supply

IBM functionally divided the motherboards into the following systems:

- Read/write memory subsystem
- Read-only Memory (ROM) subsystem
- Processor and processor support subsystem
- I/O channel connecting adapter slots to the motherboard

In addition, IBM also superimposed I/O port allocation and memory usage considerations on the 8088's architectural capabilities. The original design considerations are included because they provide the foundation and concepts which today's designs still observe, at least partially.

Read/Write Memory Subsystem

The Intel 8088 processor had 20 address lines which allowed it to address 1,048,576 (2^{20} bytes or one MByte) memory locations, collectively referred to as the PC *Memory Space*. The PC designers reserved the first 655,360 (640 KBytes) locations (zero through 655359) for parity-checked Random Access Memory (RAM). The original PC motherboard contained four 16 KByte Dynamic RAM (DRAM) banks, allowing the motherboard to provide 64 KBytes total. The PC-XT motherboard contained four 64 KByte parity-checked DRAM banks, allowing the motherboard to provide 256 KBytes total.

With DRAM, all processor reads erase the accessed location's contents. To preserve a memory location's contents following a read requires an immediate write to replace the original value read which the circuitry automatically performs, sometimes with clever approaches. In addition, because values are stored in capacitors that slowly leak their electrical charges, stored values eventually disappear unless they are periodically read, forcing an immediate write to preserve their values. To preserve DRAM values, the PC regularly *refreshed* each DRAM location. In other words, the PC performed this read/write operation. While the 8088 processor was not directly involved in this activity, refreshing required its bus which was then not available to the processor for fetching either program instructions or data. As a result, DRAM refreshing activity produced an approximate 6.5% processing overhead. Fortunately, today's DRAM controllers and motherboards often successfully hide DRAM refresh times (provide *hidden refresh*) so this general concern has essentially disappeared.

Users could install additional memory in both machines, using memory expansion cards that plugged into an I/O bus slot. However, the 8088 took longer to access such memory due to the additional I/O bus delays, so higher performance programs operated faster when residing in the first 256 KBytes. This performance penalty continues today for I/O bus accessed memory which is why, along with the availability of high capacity memory modules, motherboards now allow up to 256 MBytes or more motherboard memory.

In addition, in both the PC and the PC-XT, the RAM access speed was 200 ns (a nanosecond is one billionth or 10^{-9} seconds). This meant that memory produces requested data 200 ns after the processor generates the request. However, if the processor immediately generated another request for data located within the same memory bank, the access time became 345 ns to allow the internal circuitry to refresh the previously accessed, and subsequently destroyed, location's contents. Successive requests to the same memory bank are typical, since programs were small, forcing both program and data to reside in the same memory bank.

While these access times are slow by today's standards, PC 8088 processors could only generate bus requests every 840 ns, so slow RAM access times did not present a problem. However, with current processor speeds, these access times became unacceptable. Increasing processor speeds eventually forced designers to isolate processors from main memory delays, giving rise to faster RAM components, caches, clever memory designs, and different memory types such as static RAM, static column RAM, page memory RAM, and RAM-Bus. Actual use by PC designers still hinged on whether benefits exceeded the extra costs.

Read-Only Memory (ROM Subsystem)

The original PC and PC-XT contained 40 KBytes of Read Only Memory (ROM) in two modules. ROM is memory that processors read but not alter. It retains its data even when no power is available. ROM allows PCs to operate after a power-on by providing the programming necessary to begin power-on self-testing (*POST*) and initialization operations, or *boot* as it is termed. One 32 KByte PC ROM module contained the PC's resident BASIC, originally referred to as *cassette BASIC* before the PC-XT abandoned cassette support. The other 8 KByte module contained the PC's booting logic and

Input/Output (*I/O*) handling, collectively called the *Basic Input/ Output System* or *BIOS*. The PC BIOS provided interface programming support for the system's:

- Diskettes

- Keyboard

- Parallel Printer Ports

- Serial Communication Adapters

- Monochrome and Color Video Screen

The PC ROM access cycle time was 250 ns. Since ROM data is unchangeable, there was no additional cycle time delay for same-bank requests as with DRAM. However, as DRAM components became faster, dramatic performance differences developed between DRAM and ROM access times, favoring DRAM. Because of this, most present PCs copy essential ROM routines to DRAM, called *shadow* RAM, for improved performance.

I/O Port Usage Considerations

In addition to its one MByte memory address space, the Intel 8088 had 16 I/O address lines which could address 65,536 (2^{16} or 64 K) I/O *port* locations. These port locations, collectively referred to as the *I/O Space*, each have a unique location address ranging from zero to 65,535 which could each contain an I/O port. Device controllers for diskettes, display adapters, keyboards, communication adapters, and other I/O devices consume manufacturer-selected addresses (which in many instances owe their current locations to the original selections for the IBM PC and PC-XT).

While other machine architectures use Read/Write memory locations to communicate with I/O devices, called *memory mapped I/O*, Intel elected to provide a different space and instruction set to manipulate I/O devices to maintain compatibility with previous Intel controllers. IBM also used memory mapped I/O to provide an address space for display screen data by reserving a 16 KByte area for the monochrome display adapter and a 16 KByte area for the color graphics display adapter. Programs made screen data appear on the display screens by moving data into these reserved memory-mapped I/O areas.

Finally, IBM reserved the first 512 addresses for motherboard and other uses, from zero to 511, and left the remaining for adapter card use. IBM also allocated several port addresses for manipulating IBM printers, serial devices, diskette drive adapters, etc. For cost reasons, early IBM adapters only use the lower 10 bits of the 16-bit port values, ignoring the six high-order I/O address bits. This effectively limits the addressing range to ten bits or 1024 values since, for example, an address with a hexadecimal value 13F8 is equivalent to the hexadecimal value 03F8 (the high-order "1" is ignored since it is not within the range of the lower 10 bits of addressing). This initial cost saving caused long term I/O space ambiguity and product addressing collision problems. The legacy of this shortsightedness remains today, requiring special handling and complexity. Consequently, since the available I/O space was so much smaller, adapter manufacturer port allocations within the remnant I/O space often conflicted, causing significant user installation problems.

Memory Space Usage Considerations

As you can see by referring to Figure 2-2, IBM allocated the 8088's memory space as follows:

- Contiguous DRAM occupied the first reserved 640 KBytes from hexadecimal address 00000 through 9FFFF. Some DRAM could be on the motherboard while other would reside on memory expansion adapter cards plugged into I/O bus slots. Lower memory address locations (*low memory*) contained interrupt vectors, BIOS work areas, PC-DOS, and user programs.

- The monochrome display adapter (MDA) occupied 4 KBytes within a reserved 16 KByte range form hexadecimal address B0000 through B3FFF.

- The color graphics display adapter (CGA) occupied 16 KBytes within a reserved 16 KByte range from hexadecimal address B8000 through BBFFF.

- BIOS and resident BASIC occupied the upper (*high memory*) 64K addresses from hexadecimal address F0000 through FFFFF.

IBM reserved the remaining memory fragments mysteriously labeling the 192 KByte address range from hexadecimal address C0000 through EFFFF *ROM Expansion and Control*. This is the area

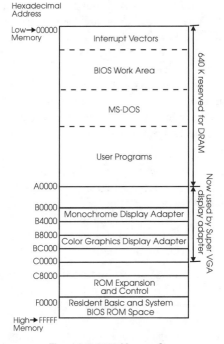

Figure 2-2. 8088 Memory Space

intelligent adapters such as fixed disk adapters use for their ROM BIOS logic. How the actual BIOS ROM address is selected varies by adapter and may controlled by adapter jumper settings, programming logic, DIP switches, etc.

When there were few products available, this approach of mapping expansion BIOS into system memory was suitable, though it limited flexibility. Since the area is finite, adapter manufacturers inevitably tried to use the same addresses, giving rise to additional user installation problems arising from conflicting overlaps.

Processor Subsystem and Processor Support Subsystems

Crystal Oscillators (Clock Crystals)

Crystal oscillators provide constant frequency pulses that keep system components synchronized and ultimately determine machine performance. For TV screen output compatibility reasons, the original

PC used a 14.31818 MHz clock which hardware divided by three to generate a 4.7727267 MHz clock speed, usually rounded to 4.77 MHz. A clock pulse is often referred to as a *clock tick*, and an 8088 processor requires one or more clock ticks to complete processor instructions. The 8088 processor had an *instruction prefetch queue*, sometimes referred to as an instruction *pipeline*, which allowed the processor to fetch another instruction while it executed one. This somewhat insulated processors from memory access delays, though the benefit was as small as the pipeline size—three bytes.

To underscore the importance of the crystal oscillator speed in machine performance, the IBM PC-AT initially used a pluggable 12 MHz processor crystal oscillator which hardware reduced to 6 MHz for its Intel 80286 processor. But many users quickly replaced the crystal oscillator with a 16 MHz crystal oscillator or an even faster one, realizing 33% performance increases or more using processors not certified for the higher clock speeds.

Thereafter, IBM soldered crystal oscillators to the motherboard and inserted "golden bullet" clocking speed tests in its BIOS boot sequence to prohibit booting machines using faster crystals than originally supplied. IBM cited the technical and operational risks that can occur from such *over clocking* including unreliable operation and component overheating. Determined users then resorted to external clocking switches that allowed them manually to select clock speeds after booting their systems.

Current designs use high frequency crystal oscillators but the entire system is designed to operate at the higher speed. Nonetheless, some unscrupulous vendors are removing processor labeling and relabeling processors as faster (and more expensive) processors. These processors may eventually burn out and completely fail. In its December 12, 1995, issue (p. C-1), the *San Jose Mercury News* reported that Intel Corporation now uses a new *overspeed protection* manufacturing process that installs *governing circuitry.* This circuitry protects the processor from operating at higher rates than the processor is rated at.

Interrupts

Interrupts provide a handy way to invoke system service routines. There are three types of interrupts:

- *Software*—Interrupts that occur as a result of executing an *interrupt* (or *int*) programming instruction

- *Maskable*—Interrupts that occur as a result of a hardware signal that the processor can block (*mask*)

- *Non-maskable*—Interrupts that occur as a result of a hardware signal that the processor cannot mask

All interrupt routines have a unique numeric value from decimal zero through 255. Each interrupt routine is registered in the system *interrupt vector table* located in the first 1024 bytes of low memory. This table has 256 four-byte entries, numbered zero through 255. Table entries usually contain the address of an associated interrupt routine but sometimes point to system data placed earlier in memory such as diskette drive characteristics. Since memory is empty after a PC powers on, the trick is to fill in this critical table before it is needed and we will see how that is accomplished later in this chapter.

When an interrupt occurs, the processor:

1 Saves information necessary for it to resume processing where it was interrupted.

2 Determines the interrupt number.

3 References the interrupt table to determine the correct starting address.

4 Begins executing at the correct memory location.

When an interrupt routine completes processing, it resumes the interrupted programming at the instruction following the interrupt instruction using the information automatically saved by the processor.

Software Interrupts

Software interrupts allow programming to invoke service routines provided by other software. The service routines may be BIOS routines, operating system routines, I/O driver routines that control specific devices, etc. For example, application programs usually generate interrupts for data file access services such as open, read, write, and close. When the operating system file access interrupt routines begin executing, they usually issue BIOS hard disk interrupt routine requests which may issue yet even more BIOS interrupts to actually perform disk reads and writes for the application requests. After BIOS routines complete processing, they return control to the

operating system routines which return control to the application
program.

Hardware Interrupts

Interrupts allow peripheral devices to temporarily defer on-going
processor activities, notifying processors to perform predesignated
activities before resuming the interrupted processing activity. The
activity usually involves some peripheral device housekeeping task
such as error checking or device controller post processing.

For example, the PC's predesignated timer interrupt routine maintains the system's clock, which in turn maintains the date and current time of day. Original IBM PC hardware divided its 4.77 MHz
clock by four, producing a 1.19318 MHz clock. The system's Intel
8253 Timer component divided this clock signal by 65,536 to produce approximately 18.2 timer clock ticks every second.

Each timer clock tick caused an interrupt, which the timer interrupt
routine handled by updating the timer information field values.
After the update, the timer interrupt routine exited, allowing previous processing to resume at the interruption point. Because these
timer interrupts may disrupt time-sensitive operations, they introduce subtle timing variances into performance benchmarks. This
virtually guarantees performance measurements vary on the same
machine, typically requiring extended or numerous averaged runs
to obtain accurate data.

The Intel 8259 Programmable Interrupt Controller

The 8088 receives peripheral interrupt requests on its *maskable* interrupt request line. In the PC, only one hardware device, the Intel 8259
Interrupt controller, directly interrupts the processor. Programs can
temporarily delay the interrupts by instructing the processor to
mask, the interrupt line signal. The processor later senses pending
interrupts when a program instructs the processor to *unmask* the
interrupt line. Other peripherals connect to the 8259 using their individual interrupt request (IRQ) lines (Figure 2-3) and the 8259 can
selectively mask these individual interrupts as well under programming from the processor.

The 8259 has eight interrupt lines numbered zero (for IRQ0) to seven
(for IRQ7). Having interrupters transmit an interrupt signal to the
8259 allows the 8259 to prioritize simultaneous interrupts and keep

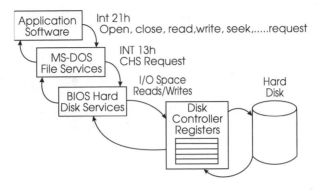

Figure 2-3. IRQ Lines for Peripherals Connected to the 8259

lower priority devices from interrupting higher priority devices. In the PC, IRQ0 has the highest priority, IRQ7 has the lowest priority, and PC BIOS 8259 initialization routines specify that higher priority interrupts can interrupt lower priority interrupts.

IBM's PC designers ignored Intel reserved interrupts and assigned various IBM devices and adapters specific interrupts as follows:

- IRQ0: Timer Interrupts (18.2 per second)

- IRQ1: Keyboard Interrupts (keystrokes)

- IRQ2: Enhanced Graphics video adapter (EGA), PC Network Local Area Network Adapter, General Purpose I/O Bus (GPIB) adapter

- IRQ3: Alternate Serial Communication Adapter (COM2), Synchronous Data Link Control (SDLC) communications adapter, Bisynchronous communications (BSC) adapter, Cluster Local Area Network adapter, PC Network Local Area Network Adapter, GPIB adapter

- IRQ4: Primary Serial Communication Adapter (COM1), SDLC communications adapter, BSC communications adapter, GPIB adapter

- IRQ5: Hard Disk Controller Interrupts, GPIB adapter

- IRQ6: Diskette Controller Interrupts, GPIB adapter

- IRQ7: Printer, GPIB adapter

The duplicated adapter assignments show that early IBM adapter designers recognized that limited interrupt numbers caused coexistence problems. They usually provided means for installers to select the interrupt number on the card which required a matching software parameter specification when running the adapter's software. This provided yet another well-exercised opportunity for user confusion and installation problems. (Finally, because IBM ignored Intel reserved interrupts, subsequent PC compatible motherboard designs were never able to use the Intel 80186 processor which combined a 8086 processor with several peripheral circuits into one economical chip).

Interrupt Invocation, Collisions, and Sharing

The original PC only contained eight IRQ lines but only IRQ2 through IRQ7 appeared on the bus for adapter use. As more peripherals became available, they competed for these few lines, causing collision problems and incompatibilities. The PC-AT partially remedied the situation by introducing a second 8259 *slave interrupt controller* that connected to the first *master interrupt controller*. This provided eight new interrupt IRQ levels, IRQ8 through IRQ15, but consumed IRQ2 in the process. (Because processors only have one interrupt line, the additional IRQ lines fed another interrupt controller whose output fed (*cascaded*) into the original interrupt controller via IRQ2. This preserved the original PC design but required cascaded interrupt processing for the additional interrupts.)

A second solution allows multiple routines to share a given interrupt level, though only one is identified in the interrupt table. Thus, when a new sharing routine installs itself, it notes and remembers what routine address the table entry contains before replacing it. When an interrupt occurs, the new routine obtains control. If the incoming interrupt is not for its device, determined by inspecting its associated controller, it passes control to the routine that previously controlled the interrupt. If the interrupt is not for that interrupt routine's device, it passes control to the routine that previously controlled the interrupt, and so on.

This cooperative approach works as long as all interrupt routines cooperate. If one does not, then it must be the first installed so that it is at the end of the control chain. In the competitive PC industry such cooperation was sometimes difficult to achieve, and user problems abounded. Sharing is also complicated by the PC's use of *edge-sense* versus *level-sense* interrupts as the next chapter discusses.

DMA

DMA is an acronym for Direct Memory Access. The PC's Intel 8237 DMA controller allows peripherals to transfer data directly into and out of computer memory, eliminating the need for the system processor to fetch every byte from the peripheral controller, place the byte in memory, and then wait for the next byte. The processor first initializes the DMA controller, instructs the peripheral controller to begin data transfer, and then proceeds with other activities until the peripheral controller signals transfer completion.

For example, suppose a program needs to read data from a disk. First, the application makes the request to the operating system. Eventually, the disk's *I/O driver* routine (that knows the target disk's characteristics and how to fetch individual data chunks) receives a very specific request from the operating system specifying the disk chunk size and data location. This I/O routine first instructs the processor to tell the DMA hardware where to place the data in main memory, and how much should arrive. It then instructs the disk's controller to signal when it is ready to deliver data.

As the disk controller produces each data byte, it signals the DMA hardware. The DMA signals the 8088 processor to stop using (*release*) the I/O bus. When the processor signals that the bus is free, the DMA hardware generates the correct memory address, and signals the controller to emit the data on the I/O bus—placing the data in memory at the correct location. When the transfer completes, the controller generates a hardware interrupt, allowing the system to check for successful data transfer completion

While this achieves minimum processor data transfer involvement and is six times faster than having the original PC's processor handle the request directly, it's not necessarily the highest performance approach now. Today's processors are dozens of times faster than the original 4.77 MHz 8088 PC processor. The time it takes to initialize the DMA processor now often exceeds data transfer times. In the original IBM PC's BIOS, the processor waited for the transfer to complete. Current multitasking trends and device driver BIOS bypass these performance bottlenecks by providing minuscule individual request delays in exchange for substantial system performance increases that stem from overlapping I/O operations on different devices.

Finally, DMA was a major source of user installation frustration. The Intel 8237 DMA controller contained four independent DMA facilities (referred to as *channels*) numbered DMA channel zero through DMA channel three. These channels were prioritized with DMA channel zero having the highest priority. Only one transfer could occur at a time and higher priority transfers temporarily suspended lower priority ones. Since IBM reserved channel zero for DRAM refresh operations, only three channels were available for OEM expansion card use. Various peripheral products inevitably collided while trying to use these scarce resources.

The PC-AT partially remedied the situation by providing a second DMA controller with four additional DMA channels. Because the 8237 was slow, innovative DMA schemes arose that eclipsed ordinary DMA. Advanced adapters now provide their own DMA circuits which generate their own memory addresses. This is known as *bus mastering*. This reduces DMA set-up time while maintaining DMA transfer performance advantages.

For a DMA bus master transfer, the CPU initiates transfers between system memory and the I/O device, but the DMA controller handles the actual data transfers and their completion. At data transfer conclusions, the I/O device interrupts the CPU to indicate completion. With what is referred to as *second party* DMA transfers, the CPU calculates buffer sizes, manipulates page boundaries, other perform support issues for the DMA controller which requires more CPU activity than bus master transfers.

Programmed I/O (PIO)

PIO transfers provide an alternative to DMA transfers. In PIO transfers, the CPU uses *in* or *out* instruction (or the *instring/outstring* equivalent for multiple operation activities) and uses interrupts. Devices can provide several different transfer speeds, so BIOS POST procedures now query PIO devices to determine the optimum transfer speed for the motherboard processor.

Processor Memory Data Organization

For cost reasons, the initial IBM PC used an inexpensive Intel 8088 processor, an 8-bit external data bus variant of the Intel 8086 processor.

Other than an I/O bus interleaving performance delay, the programming considerations for the 8088 processor were identical to the Intel 8086. One of the more controversial aspects of these processors is the way they store data in memory, referred to as *little-endian*.

With little-endian data organization, two and four byte values are stored in contiguous memory with the low-order values occupying the lower address positions. This means that a hexadecimal value of 11223344 appears in memory as hexadecimal 44, followed by hexadecimal 33, followed by hexadecimal 22, followed by hexadecimal 11. Visually looking into memory from memory address zero up, the data looks backwards. But, this has no computing performance penalty over *big-endian* organization which stores data in the opposite order.

Processor Data Alignment Considerations

Internally, the 8088 is a 16-bit processor and used on-board circuitry to translate 16-bit (word) requests to two sequentially-interleaved 8-bit (byte) external I/O requests, each minimally requiring four bus cycles. The IBM PC-AT's 80286 later provided 16-bit bus support for all memory accesses, even single byte accesses. This remedied the 8088's two data fetch operations for single memory words, but only for even address data words. Fetching *misaligned* data words (two adjacent bytes beginning on an odd-numbered address) still required two 16-bit fetches:

First fetch obtained:

- The even-numbered address byte (which was discarded) preceding the first target byte
- The adjacent, first target byte

Second fetch obtained:

- The second target byte located on an even-numbered address location
- The odd-address byte (also discarded) following the second target byte

In this instance, fetching discarded data consumed 50% of the bus bandwidth because the first fetched byte was not located on an even-numbered address—resulting in measurable processor performance degradations. So, early programmers were very careful to *address align* heavily referenced data fields. In general *data alignment* considerations remain an on going consideration for machine designers and performance-oriented programmers.

Finally, because the PC's eight bit memory access bus was relatively narrow and very slow, instructions that executed in one or two cycles often outran the bus, emptying the instruction prefetch queue, causing what is referred to as an instruction prefetch queue *stall*. In this instance, the processor temporarily ceased execution until another instruction was available.

Subsequent PC-compatible designs use wider and faster buses as well as processors with deeper prefetch queues, but alignment remains a continuing consideration. For example, the December 1995 issue of *BYTE* magazine (pg. 25) reports a serious problem with its BYTEmark benchmarks. The text reads in part:

> A problem with the BYTEmark benchmarks has been located and corrected. Specifically, the logical unit (LU) decomposition test ... behaved erratically under certain OSs. One unfortunate outcome of this problem resulted in *BYTE*'s publishing low benchmark numbers for Intel P6 processors. ... the resulting scores for the P6 [Pentium Pro] were sometimes low (which yielded an index of 1.7) and sometimes high (yielding an index of 3.6). The test showed its worst behavior under Windows NT.
>
> The problem concerned data alignment. The LU [logical unit] decomposition algorithm ... processes data ... while making numerous 8-byte fetches. ... The decomposition algorithm calls the library routine malloc() ... malloc() always returns data that is aligned to 4-byte boundaries. However, it doesn't always return data that is aligned to 8-bit boundaries.
>
> Nonaligned memory accesses are always slower than aligned accesses. Consequently, whenever malloc() returned a non-8-byte aligned array to LU decomposition, the algorithm proceeded more slowly than when it received an aligned array. ... We apologize for the confusion this has caused ...

BYTE magazine promptly updated its BYTEmark program. *BYTE* magazine's immediate disclosure of the problem and its consequences is evidence of outstanding publishing ethics. Once again, benchmarking systems proved to be a complex undertaking, even for experts.

Boot Up Sequence

When the Intel 8088 is reset or powered-on, the processor waits for the power supply to signal that power levels are correct. The processor's internal circuitry automatically begins executing at hexadecimal address FFFF0. The original PC's BIOS instruction at that location jumps to the BIOS power-on, self-test (POST) routine which sequentially:

- Tests the 8088 processor for possible internal errors

- Checks the 8 KByte BIOS ROM modules for data errors

- Determines how much memory is installed

- Tests the 8237 DMA channels

- Tests installed DRAM for parity errors

- Initializes the 8259 interrupt controller

- Initializes the BIOS interrupt vectors

- Determines the display adapter type, initializes, and tests it

- Tests the 8259 interrupt controller

- Tests the 8253 timer chip

- Tests the keyboard

- Initializes the 8259 hardware interrupt vectors by copying a ROM table into the interrupt vector table

- Initializes the resident BASIC interrupt vector

- Tests for an expansion box

- Tests installed DRAM memory for possible parity errors

- Checks the 32 KByte BASIC ROM module for errors

- Tests to see if a diskette drive is attached

- Initializes the printer and primary serial adapter if present

- Attempts to load an operating system by reading the first data sector on the first diskette drive's diskette

- If the diskette drive times out, issues the start resident BASIC interrupt to start resident BASIC

Because current systems usually support legacy devices, they must also perform similar procedures as well as additional ones for newer devices such as Plug and Play devices. It is now rare for ROM programming to execute from ROM. Most ROM modules are copied to DRAM and execute there.

PC-XT Hard Disk BIOS Extension Installation

When the IBM-XT designers developed the IBM-XT, they designed an adapter which contained a 16 KByte ROM BIOS extension. This BIOS resided at PC memory hexadecimal address C8000. When invoked during the power-up sequence, the BIOS set-up routine sequentially:

- Moved the diskette interrupt from interrupt vector 19 to interrupt vector 65

- Installed a new interrupt vector at interrupt 19 that optionally invoked interrupt 65 for diskette requests based on the request's specified device number

- Specified drive number (zero and one for diskettes, hexadecimal 80 and 81 for disk drives)

- Identified the drives and initialized a drive parameter table

- Installed a new boot interrupt vector

When the I/O requests drove interrupt 19, the hard disk adapter obtained control to determine whether the request was for itself or for a diskette drive. If it was for a diskette drive, the fixed disk BIOS simply issued an interrupt 65 and returned when it received control from the diskette routines. Now, the pertinent question is: *just how did the disk controller's routine get invoked?* Answer: By slightly changing the original PC BIOS for the PC-XT BIOS version.

Immediately after testing the installed DRAM for parity errors, the PC BIOS author inserted a small test for optional BIOS ROM modules installed in hexadecimal addresses C8000 up to F4000. The system BIOS checked address C8000 for a 55 hexadecimal value and address C8001 for a AA hexadecimal value. If these values were present, the BIOS checked the ROM for errors using a size value located at address C8002. If the value exhibited no errors, the system BIOS called the optional BIOS extension module beginning at address C8003, which is the beginning of the fixed disk adapter's set-up routine. When the fixed disk BIOS routine returns, optional ROM searching continues after the end of the located optional BIOS extension. When an optional BIOS extension is not found, testing continues 2 KByte locations after where the last test failed. Testing stops at hexadecimal address F4000.

Note that this allows adapter designers to install an optional BIOS extension or even DRAM at any 2 KByte address boundary within the available 176 KBytes (192 KBytes less 16 KBytes for the fixed disk BIOS) range. Again, competing manufacturers quickly consumed this finite space and inevitable collisions commenced, providing users additional installation headaches.

Finally, it is interesting to note that the IBM PC Network Local Area Network adapter captured the resident BASIC interrupt when invoked during the optional BIOS scan process. This allowed the PC Network adapter to detect that all possible boot options (disk and diskette) had failed and that it should try to boot off the network before passing control to resident BASIC. This clearly illustrates that boot options extend well beyond fixed disk and floppy diskettes.

Conclusion

As compared to many systems, the original PC and PC adapter designs provided a well-documented, open computing environment. In hindsight, their designs also introduced the following potential conflicts and limitations for designers and their customers:

- Few adapter slots

- Few DMA channels

- Reduced I/O space size

- Limited memory addressing

- Complicated DIP switch and jumper settings

- Few IRQ levels, sometimes requiring shared interrupt programming logic

- Limited ROM BIOS expansion and control address range

- Error prone manual configuration requirements using jumper pin settings, DIP switches, and matching program parameter specifications

Eventually, users discovered BIOS errors and various hardware design errors. Follow-on models and OEM designs attempted to remove these limitations. But some proved intractable, such as the PC's constrained I/O space size. Subsequent PC products offered incremental improvements and more powerful processors.

The Intel 80286 provided a 16 MByte address space and memory protection mode that was widely disparaged within the industry. The Intel 80386 processor fixed the memory protection problems and added a 4 GByte virtual address space along with support for multiple simultaneous 8088 address space emulations. The Intel 80486 processor added a numeric coprocessor and on-board cache. The Intel Pentium continued the evolution with multiple execution units. Meanwhile component integration levels also progressed allowing various corporations to combine system I/O chips and memory controllers.

In the final analysis, history discloses that the only real error the IBM PC group made was the common error of underestimating their phenomenal future success. With a fledgling initial product, this small engineering group redefined computing. The subsequent industry now produces as many PCs per week as IBM originally forecast would ever be built.

Chapter Questions

1 The two original Intel address spaces are

 a ROM Space and I/O Space

 b Memory Space and I/O Space

 c Register Space and I/O Space

 d None of the above

2 Executing program instructions from contemporary ROM components is usually faster than from DRAM.

 a True because ROM does not require refresh

 b True because the interrupt vector table interrupts DRAM data alignment operations

 c False, and answer b is mega-hogwash

 d None of the above

3 Clock Crystals

   a Melt at temperatures above 120° F, requiring system unit cooling fans

   b Are hard substances that coat microprocessors for protection

   c Provide the system heartbeat

   d Answers a and c

4 Interrupts

   a Occur with each Clock Crystal heartbeat

   b Can always be masked

   c Only occur 18.2 times per second in the IBM PC

   d Introduce subtle timing differences into benchmarks

5 Interrupt Tables

   a Queue interrupts for processing

   b Designate what routine handles what interrupt

   c Are for hardware devices

   d All of the above

6 Sharing interrupts

   a Is complicated

   b Is a system consideration that is difficult to retrofit

   c Desirable where possible

   d All of the above

7 DMA speeds up I/O operations

   a Always

   b Never

   c It depends

8 Data alignment considerations

   a Are no longer important because ROM speeds have significantly increased

   b Eliminate processor pipeline stalls

c May increase with wider buses and processors

d None of the above

9 In the PC, interrupt controllers

   a Prioritize interrupts

   b May cascade

   c Do not control the NMI

   d All of the above

10 A PC interrupt controller can

   a Handle four high priority interrupt lines and two low priority lines

   b Divert NMI interrupts

   c Handle eight high priority interrupt lines

   d None of the above

11 The IRQ with the highest priority is

   a IRQ7

   b IRQ1

   c IRQ0

   d IRQ15

❏

▼▼▼▼ 3

PC I/O System Buses

What This Chapter Is About

System buses, also referred to as expansion buses and I/O channels, provide hardware attachment mechanisms that extend system capabilities beyond what system motherboards natively provide. Tightly coupling system buses to processor native *local buses* provides higher system performance. This chapter discusses how system buses work and how the contemporary VESA Local Bus and PCI mezzanine bus achieve their significant performance improvements over predecessor bus architectures.

PC Bus Origins

The original PC motherboard provided five motherboard connectors that permitted users to install five adapter cards in their system units. The PC-XT later appeared with eight connectors that were more closely spaced than the original PC. These connectors were connected to the motherboard's system bus—a signal highway that connected indirectly to the memory and processor through intervening logic called *buffers*. Among other things, buffers stage data to insure adequate signal levels between the processor and system bus. Paired buffers, referred to as *transceivers*, perform transmit and receive buffering within a single component.

Among other things, system buses generally provide their components the following facilities:

- Bus clock signals
- Adapter card power and ground

- DMA signals

- Address lines for selecting the target of a transfer

- Data lines for transferring data between the host and adapter card I/O ports, DRAM, or ROM

- Flow control mechanisms

- Interrupt lines for adapter card to signal interrupts to the interrupt controller

We now discuss how past and contemporary PC buses manifest these facilities.

The PC/PC-XT Bus—A Bus Design Primer

The original PC and PC-XT bus contains 62 signal lines that the 8088 processor and expansion cards use to communicate. Consequently, IBM selected a 62 pin connector that presented 31 signals on each side. The important bus lines for this discussion are:

- Reset line

- Five power and three ground lines

- Two clock signals

- Six interrupt lines

- An eight-bit bidirectional data bus

- 20 bidirectional address lines

- Two memory read/write lines

- I/O channel ready line

- Two I/O read/write lines

- Three DMA channel request lines, four DMA channel acknowledge lines, one DMA/CPU bus control line, and one DMA transfer-complete line

- Parity error indicator line

The reset line (RESET DRV) signals devices that system power-up or reboot is occurring. The five DC power lines provide one -5 volt, one -12 volt, one +12 volt, and two +5 volt power sources. The two clock lines provide 14.31818 MHz (OSC) and 4.77 MHz (CLK) signals. The six interrupt lines are IRQ2, IRQ3, IRQ4, IRQ5, IRQ6, and IRQ7—the motherboard reserves IRQ0 and IRQ1 use. The parity error indicator line (I/O CH CK) signals on-board expansion card parity errors (bus transfers are not parity checked). The remaining important signals control data transfer.

The eight-bit bidirectional data bus signals (D0–D7) transfer single data bytes to a memory address or I/O port. Since the PC and PC-XT accesses up to 1 MByte of memory, there are 20 bidirectional address lines (A0–A19) which are controlled by the processor or expansion cards. The address-latch-enable (ALE) line signals expansion cards that an address exists on the address lines that might pertain to them. The two memory read/write lines (MEMR and MEMW) distinguish whether a bus operation is a memory read where the expansion card should produce a byte or is a write where the expansion card should store a byte. The I/O channel ready line (IO CH RDY) allows expansion cards to pace read/write operations to suitable throughput rates by generating delays, a process called *inserting wait states*. The two I/O read/write lines (IOR and IOW) signal whether a read/write operation is an I/O port read or write operation.

Finally the three DMA channel request lines (DRQ1–DRQ3) and four DMA channel acknowledge lines (DACK0–DACK3) control DMA data transfer handshaking, the DMA/CPU line (AEN) signals bus control between the processor and an active DMA controller channel, and the DMA transfer complete line (T/C) signals DMA transfer completion.

In summary, the original PC bus allows users to connect relatively passive adapter cards to their processor-centric systems. In such environments, adapter cards require processor attention for proper operation and bus access.

The PC-AT Industry Standard Architecture (ISA) Bus

In 1984, IBM introduced the IBM-AT which used a 6 MHz Intel 80286 processor. The wider 80286 data bus allowed the PC-AT's system bus to use a 16-bit data bus which required 16 data lines (SD0–SD15) instead of the previous eight. In addition, the PC-AT addressed 16 MBytes of DRAM which required 24 address lines (SA0–SA19 and LA17–LA23) instead of the previous 20. It also provided more interrupt (IRQ9–IRQ12, IRQ 14 and IRQ15) and DMA lines (DRQ5–DRQ7 and DACK5–DACK7). Because processors only have one maskable interrupt line, the additional IRQ lines fed another interrupt controller whose output fed (*cascaded*) into the original interrupt controller. This preserved the original PC design but required cascaded interrupt processing for the additional interrupts.

Since IBM had already used all 62 PC and PC-XT connector signals, these additional system bus signals mandated a new connector configuration which was accomplished by adding a second in-line 36-pin supplemental connector to six of the eight available slot positions. This approach allowed many higher performance 8-bit PC and PC-XT expansion card designs to operate on the PC-AT's bus which used the same 6 MHz clock signal as the processor. The PC-AT distinguished between 8-bit and 16-bit operations via the *System Bus High Enable*, *Memory 16-bit Chip Select*, and *I/O 16-Bit Chip Select* AT bus signals that only PC-AT bus expansion cards provided. Finally, the PC-AT bus also provided a *Zero Wait State* signal that indicated whether an expansion card could process data transfers without inserting bus wait states.

Unfortunately, IBM never published precise PC-AT bus timing information, so expansion card design proceeded on a hit-or-miss basis. Eventually, the Institute of Electrical and Electronics Engineers (*IEEE*) formalized the bus timings in standard referred to as the *Industry Standard Architecture* or *ISA*. As higher performance Intel 80286, 80386, and 80486 systems appeared, the processors and motherboard memory subsystems operated significantly faster than their buses which stabilized at approximately 8.33 MHz after 12 MHz and 16 MHz designs appeared. Designers usually divided the processor clock to provide a bus frequency that equaled or was slightly under 8 MHz for compatibility.

The IBM Micro Channel™

In 1987, IBM introduced the Micro Channel Architecture (MCA) and implemented it in several new PS/2™ models. The 116 signal Micro Channel bus features included:

- Increased bus clock speeds for increased throughput

- Complete I/O address space access by requiring adapters to recognize all 16 I/O port address lines rather than the original PC's previous 10

- New miniaturized bus connectors with narrower connector pin spacing to house reduced size expansion boards utilizing surface-mount technology

- Improved bus power and grounding to reduce radio frequency emissions

- Hardware mediated, prioritized bus mastering and arbitration for 16 devices

- Selectable width bus data transfers

- New burst, streaming data, and matched memory data transfer modes for higher performance

- Programmable Option Select (POS) adapter autoconfiguration capability

- Shared level-sense hardware interrupts rather than the original PC's edge triggered interrupts that hindered hardware IRQ sharing

While the Micro Channel design met great technical acclaim, IBM required significant licensing fees which alienated the computing industry. In addition, it was not backwards compatible, making obsolete hundreds or thousands of board designs and millions of existing adapters, some still sitting on dealer shelves. Consequently, it enjoyed limited success, though some features merit comment.

Bus Mastering and Arbitration

The PS/2 Micro Channel allowed eight processors and eight devices, such as DMA controllers, to contend for complete bus ownership. In contrast to the PC's approach where the system processor had complete bus control, the system unit's processor was reduced to bus-contender status. Hardware bus arbitration circuits controlled bus access using hardware assigned priorities. The same notions were available three years earlier with SCSI and even earlier in some minicomputer and multiprocessor systems.

Selectable Width Bus Data Transfers

Micro Channel adapters could signal their bus transmit-width using the bus *Card Data Size* signal lines. Data source adapters enjoying wider bus transfer sizes could adapt their operation to accommodate less capable peers using the *Byte Enable Bits 0-3* bus lines. These signals allowed 8, 16, 24, and 32-bit-wide transfers. Wide SCSI also supports varying transfer widths depending on device capability—8-bits for narrow SCSI devices and 16-bits for wide SCSI devices.

New Data Transfer Modes and Speeds

The PC-AT moved data by presenting a memory destination address followed by a pair of data bytes for every pair of data bytes moved, requiring two bus cycles minimum. At 8 MHz, this allowed 4 million two-byte transfers per second for a total of 8 MBytes/sec maximum throughput. The Micro Channel initially operated at 10 MHz and introduced a new mode referred to as *burst mode* where a single memory destination address preceded multiple four-byte groups, each requiring two bus cycles. Combined with the 10 MHz bus speed, this provided 20 MBytes/sec throughput for sequential data transfers.

Streaming data mode later increased this to 40 MBytes/sec by transmitting one four-byte group every bus cycle. Using the unused 32-bit address lines during streaming data mode transfers further extended this to 80 MBytes/sec. Doubling the bus speed to 20 MHz eventually increased this to 160 MBytes/sec.

Programmable Option Select

The Micro Channel Architecture provided an environment that eliminated many adapter and device installation headaches, replacing them with the headache of keeping track of the reference configuration diskette. PS/2 systems remembered what card was present in what adapter connector, assigning I/O and memory address ranges as necessary based on identifier codes the Micro Channel architecture required. This eliminated jumper settings, DIP switches, DMA conflicts as well as IRQ conflicts.

However, in order to configure the system using this new method, users had to use the previously mentioned reference disk to install new adapters, rearrange adapters in slot-positions, reconfigure adapters, or remove adapters. This replaced one set of inconveniences with another.

Shared Level-Sense Hardware Interrupts

In the original PC, PC-XT, and PC-AT, devices signaled interrupts on the IRQ bus lines by producing a voltage level. The 8259 interrupt controller detected the voltage change and eventually scheduled the interrupt processing based on its priority. After raising the voltage and observing a minimum delay, the device could immediately lower and leave it down (or raise it again) waiting for service. This is referred to as *edge-sense* (or *edge-triggered*) interrupts—where interrupt controllers consider the rising edge of voltage increases as indicating an interrupt, based on interrupt controller initialization the processor performs during Power-On-Self-Test. If two devices simultaneously use the same IRQ line, the interrupt controller would likely not distinguish the one interrupt from the other.

In the Micro Channel's *level-sense* approach, devices produce voltages on an IRQ line and continue asserting them until the processor services them. If two devices share an IRQ line, processor software can quickly determine when more than one device needs servicing, by noting asserted voltage levels after servicing one device. Interrupt line sharing thereby reduces IRQ conflicts, although it requires interrupt service routines that permit multiple devices to share an interrupt line.

Enhanced ISA (EISA)

In response to IBM's Micro Channel Architecture, AST Research Corp., Compaq Computer Corp., Epson, Hewlett-Packard Corp., NEC, Olivetti, Tandy Corp., Wyse Corp., and Zenith Data Systems created the EISA standard. The EISA design incorporated numerous existing bus design features; such as bus mastering, interrupt sharing, and automatic configuration, as well as a software configuration feature that required using a reference diskette to reconfigure the system.

EISA added 55 new bus lines. Sixteen data lines were added to the existing ISA data bus to create a 32-bit bus and four new data transfer modes were defined. The most efficient mode allowed processors to present an address on a clock signal's rising edge and four data bytes on the same clock signal's falling edge. Since the EISA bus operated at 8.33 MHz for ISA compatibility reasons, this allowed a maximum 33 MBytes/sec data transfer rate.

While EISA uses the same physical size connector as the ISA bus, it stacks two signal tiers within each connector to support existing ISA cards on the upper tier. Connector design prevents ISA cards from reaching the lower, second level, though EISA cards do unfortunately partially fit into standard ISA connectors and can cause electrical damage when power is applied.

VESA Local Bus

While the ISA 8 MHz design was suitable for early text-based PC applications, Microsoft Windows applications quickly exceeded the ISA bus's capabilities to deliver massive amounts of data to display adapters. As Micro Channel and EISA support faded, efforts arose to connect display adapter memories directly to the processor's data and address lines, generically referred to as the processor's *local bus*.

These various proprietary approaches soon proved incompatible. In August 1992, the Video Electronics Standards Association (VESA) finalized and released its VESA Local Bus (VLB) standard for ISA, Micro Channel, and EISA system units. This document standardized the way vendors should electrically extend processor address, data, and control signals to a few high-performance devices—three slots for a 33 MHz bus which users often reserved for display, disk, and network adapters.

The VESA Local Bus was designed specifically for the Intel 80486 processor. New *bridge logic* circuits performed signal conversion to extend support for other processors. VLB maximum speed is 66 MHz, but that required read and write wait state insertions. Hence, most VLB transfers use a speed of 33 MHz which only requires wait state insertion for reads. Using Intel's 486 processor burst mode, VLB transmits four 4-byte data transfers following a single address transfer. This provides a maximum theoretical throughput of 105.6 MBytes/sec for 16 byte bursts. Non-burst transfers exhibit a maximum theoretical throughput of 66 MBytes/sec. In practice, the actual sustained transfer rates are significantly less.

Peripheral Component Interconnect (PCI)

In July 1993, the PCI Special Interest Group (PCI-SIG), with Intel support, released its Peripheral Component Interconnect Release 2.0 specification. This documented an open, high-speed interconnection strategy for processors and peripherals that minimizes intervening circuitry, referred to as *glue logic*, to decrease system cost while increasing system reliability. Rather than a traditional local bus, PCI embodies what the industry refers to as a *mezzanine* bus. PCI is the first PC I/O bus that is not tightly coupled to a specific processor like the VESA Local Bus is tied to the 486. Rather, it connects to the processor-memory subsystem through a *PCI-to-host bridge*. Consequently, PCI operates slower than a processor's local bus but significantly faster than popular traditional buses. This allows designers to use PCI with future Intel processor generations as well as non-Intel processors, such as the PowerPC processor used by IBM Corp. and Apple Corp.

PCI implementations conforming to PCI Release 2.0 support either a 32-bit wide data path or a 64-bit wide data path for increased Pentium compatibility. The specification contains provisions that allow designers to co-locate the self-sufficient PCI bus with ISA, Micro Channel, and EISA buses. Its flexibility, versatility, and performance are quickly making it the standard high-performance PC Bus.

Specification Overviews

In addition to traditional Intel memory and I/O spaces, PCI implementations contain configuration spaces that allow systems to identify installed components, referred to as *agents*. Each PCI agent contains a 256 byte configuration space. Among other things, the system processor uses configuration space information to set PCI agent memory and I/O space base address(es). This dynamic address assignment eliminates pesky address select jumpers present in older I/O interconnect bus designs, allowing fully automatic configuration by the system BIOS without user intervention.

To minimize costs, PCI electrical specifications allow large-scale Complementary Metal Oxide Semiconductor (CMOS) chips to drive the bus directly. The relatively low-drive current available from such chips and the high-speed operation of these parts combine to limit the length of the bus and the number of attached devices. The specification gives detailed rules for maximum round trip propagation delay and capacitance loading. Essentially, PCI buses can drive ten unit loads, where a unit load is a single PCI compliant chip or expansion slot connector. Since adapter cards contain a PCI compliant chip, each populated expansion slot consumes two unit loads. Thus, typical PCI configurations comprise three or four expansion slots with four or two motherboard PCI agents respectively. To provide additional slots requires separate, independent PCI buses or lower-level PCI buses that bridge to a higher-level bus using a *PCI-to-PCI bridge*. Bridge chips are PCI agents that consume one unit load and transfer I/O traffic between buses. Bridges can present performance bottlenecks in some circumstances, but actually improve performance in others because they allow multiple buses and traffic isolation.

Figure 3-1 illustrates a few possible bridge and bus combinations. All of the combinations increase expansion slot numbers, but some provide potentially better performance than others. Using two host-PCI bridges allows up to twice the I/O bandwidth of a single PCI bus, but processor-memory bus loading limits may preclude such implementations. Using a second level PCI bus through a PCI-to-PCI bridge does not increase I/O-to-memory bus bandwidth, but allows device-to-device transfers on second level PCI buses independent of other processing.

Most PCI equipped PCs also provide an ISA bus for legacy adapter support. Typically the ISA bus connects to the processor through a motherboard *ISA-to-PCI bridge*. This avoids the need for a special *ISA-to-Host bridge* for each new processor design and reduces loading on the high-speed processor-memory bus. However, there are some potential performance problems with this approach which will be discussed later.

To meet the twin goals of CMOS interfacing and high-performance requires strict motherboard and adapter card layout standards. To minimize bus length, PCI components attach to alternate sides of a motherboard's PCI bus at approximately one inch intervals. The stub length on an adapter card, including fingers, is limited to less

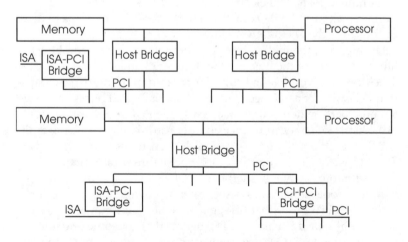

Figure 3-1. Possible Bridge and Bus Connections

than 2.5 inches. The PCI interface chips must reside as close to card connector edges as possible, centered with respect to the card fingers.

Anticipating future digital design directions, the PCI bus supports both 5 volt and 3.3 volt operation. Connector keys prevent accidentally inserting a 3.3 volt card in a 5 volt slot and vice versa.

The PCI specification defines 49 required signal pins and 51 optional signal pins for PCI devices. The optional pins include additional signaling, interrupts, and expansion to a 64-bit address/data bus. The principal signal groupings are:

Mandatory:

- 32-Bit Address and Data (includes 32 A/D signals, 4 Command/Bus-Enable signals and a Parity signal)

- Interface Control (6 signals)

- Error Reporting (2 signals)

- Arbitration (potential bus masters only, 2 signals)

- System (2 signals)

Optional:

- 64-Bit Address/Data Extension (includes 2 64-bit enables plus a second 32-bit A and D grouping)

- Interrupts (4 signals)

- Other Control (3 signals)

- JTAG (5 signals)

The basic PCI transfer mechanism is a *burst*, which consists of a single address phase and one or more subsequent data phases. *Bus Masters* initiate all PCI transfers after bus access arbitration, providing an advantage over PIO transfers. The PCI specification requires a central arbiter for each bus, but does not dictate arbitration algorithms.

Once a Bus Master gains access, it becomes the *Initiator* Agent, and uses the *Frame* signal to delineate transfers. *Initiator Ready* and *Target Ready*, signals provide transfer flow control. The *target* can force early termination with the *Stop* signal. The protocol inserts *Turn-around Cycles* whenever the driving PCI agent changes for one or more signals to avoid any overlap between the two devices. Thus four byte reads require a minimum of four clock cycles to complete, yielding 33 MBytes/sec at 33 MHz. However, long bursts approach 132 MBytes/sec on a 32-Bit wide bus and 264 MBytes/sec on a 64-Bit wide bus.

Because transfers hold the bus for their duration, the PCI protocol does not provide *split transaction* support. Split transaction support allows sending an address and a read command over the bus, the target to disconnect from the bus and then reconnect to the bus later for data transfer. Thus, peripherals connecting to low-speed buses bridging to a PCI bus require numerous PCI bus wait state insertions. This significantly reduces (squanders) available PCI bus bandwidth, requiring buffers that introduce other problems. Potential bridge deadlocks, another consequence of no split transactions, require forcing active transfers off the bus with the *Stop* signal. The terminated transfer must be retried later.

There are some concerns regarding the limited number of devices which can connect to individual PCI buses. In addition, potential extended bus-residency by single transactions can impact time critical applications such as multimedia (solved by a latency timer). Nonetheless, PCI's high peak performance and clean electrical design make PCI very popular in new PC and Apple Corp. systems. It also appears in workstation and mainframe designs, and may shortly become the dominant I/O bus.

Addressing / Plug and Play (PnP)

Basic Concepts

Many early minicomputers and mainframes used jumpers and switches to set memory bank and peripheral equipment addresses and options. When the PC arrived, it adopted similar techniques. Hence ISA bus add-in cards usually have dip switches or jumpers to configure address ranges, interrupts, and features. Obviously the success of the earlier minicomputers and the ISA bus based PCs attests to the general success of the jumper/switch strategy. But problems of conflicting card addresses or interrupt assignments have grown with the proliferation of desktop computer systems and their plethora of add-in cards. Because of this, and in keeping with the computer world's commitment to "user friendliness," automatic configuration has become a highly desirable feature.

In the 1980s many minicomputers and mainframes were introduced with auxiliary system console processors which automatically configured the host processors. *Plug and Play* is intended to provide the same automatic configuration for the PC market, without the expense of console processors, allowing backward compatibility with legacy host adapters, buses, and operating systems.

With Plug and Play, host adapter jumpers and dip-switches are absent. Instead, boot, BIOS and OS software automatically configures address and interrupt assignments of add-in cards when the machine first turns on. When devices are added after the machine is running (so called *hot plugging*), the goal is to reconfigure the operating system on-the-fly so that the devices can be used without rebooting the computer. But even without hot plugging, implementing plug-and-play requires substantial efforts by peripheral, system and system software vendors.

Many of the required enhancements are in the peripheral cards themselves. Information about the type and functionality of each card needs to be readable over the I/O bus. Similarly, address and interrupt assignments need to be settable from the host processor, through I/O bus writes.

To support Plug and Play across all platforms, auto-configuration features have been defined for all of the buses associated with the IBM PC: ISA, EISA, VL, PCI and SCSI. But how are individual cards addressed before the addresses have been set? How is the information obtained from the cards communicated to the operating system? And how do legacy expansion cards and existing boot code continue to function? Several different approaches exist to answer these questions and are described below.

ISA Plug and Play

The ISA bus existed well before auto-configuration became a desirable feature. Thus, ISA Plug and Play has, and requires, elaborate steps to function and maintain backwards compatibility. However, a scheme using long, unique IDs, now exists. As more ISA expansion cards conform to the Plug and Play standards, jumpers and switches will become a thing of the past.

The ISA Plug and Play specification calls for including a unique, 72 bit *serial identifier* on each expansion card. The number consists of a 32 bit vendor ID, a 32 bit serial number, and an 8 bit checksum. This number is used as part of an isolation protocol which allows selection of a single card without use of normal ISA bus addressing. During the protocol isolation phase, every participating card shifts its serial identifier onto the ISA bus one bit at a time. If the current bit of identifier for a given card is a 1, the card places a pattern of 1's and 0's on the bus. If the current bit is a 0, the card places its drivers in the high impedance state so as to not drive anything on the bus. Cards which are participating and not driving the bus check to see if any other cards are driving the bus. If so, they lose the isolation protocol round and remove themselves from participation. In this fashion, the isolation protocol eventually reduces the number of participating cards to one.

Once the isolation protocol is complete and a single card selected, it is assigned a *Card Select Number* (CSN) to allow easy access by configuration software. Once a card has had a CSN assigned it removes itself from subsequent isolation rounds. Eventually all cards are isolated and assigned CSNs. At this point the configuration software can enable the cards one-at-a-time using the CSNs and interrogate and set the card's configuration registers.

Because there is a long transition period where Plug and Play cards may be used in legacy systems, or legacy cards may operate next to Plug and Play cards in Plug and Play systems, the designers had to consider compatibility issues carefully. The Plug and Play configuration features are accessible through three port address, two fixed write addresses and a one read address that can be relocated. One of the write ports is used to set configuration register addresses for use by the other write and the read port. To initiate Plug and Play configuration, the host writes a 32 byte *initiation key* to the Plug and Play address port. Then the host initiates multiple isolation protocol rounds until all Plug and Play cards have been identified and assigned CSNs. This protocol is administered by the Plug and Play BIOS, which then attempts to crate a minimal configuration for booting. Determining the complete configuration, especially when legacy cards exist, can be very complicated and is left up to the Plug and Play operating system.

PCI Plug and Play

PCI was designed from the start with automatic configuration in mind. PCI devices have defined configuration spaces which can be addressed independently of the normal addressing mechanisms.

The configuration space for each device is 256 bytes in size, with the first 64 bytes standardized for all devices. The configuration space can be used to report device information, enable and disable features, set base memory and I/O addresses and assign interrupts.

Special PCI bus configuration cycles read and write configuration space registers. Each device has a *IDSEL* line which must be enabled for it respond to a configuration cycle. The system must ensure that only one IDSEL line is asserted at a time. This is done with a central hardware decoder which uses addressing information written to a special *CONFIG_ADDRESS* register in I/O space. The address consists of a bus number (for systems with multiple PCI buses), a device number (essentially a slot number) and the offset of the desired configuration register.

During configuration, the processor can cycle through the possible bus and device numbers to determine what devices are actually installed. If the processor tries to address a bus or device that doesn't exist, it is given an unambiguous indication that the bus or device is not present. Once it determines which buses exist and which device numbers on those buses correspond to actual devices, it can use the bus and device numbers to access each attached device's configuration space uniquely and configure it for proper operation.

This configuration mechanism is much simpler than the ones defined for ISA. It avoids world-wide unique ID numbers and no elaborate bit-by-bit isolation protocol. Instead, devices are simply addressed by location during configuration. Of course, the PCI bus is able to use this technique because auto-configuration was designed in from the beginning.

BIOS/Windows Plug and Play

While the ISA and PCI buses use hardware to assist with auto-configuration, most work is actually done through software. The task of configuring the system is split between the BIOS and Microsoft Windows. The BIOS does the minimum amount required to boot the system, then Windows or device drivers finish the job.

The BIOS, as part of its Power On Self Test must execute the basic auto-configuration protocol for any I/O buses attached to the system. If an ISA bus is present, then the ISA isolation is run and assigns a CSN to each Plug and Play ISA card. If a PCI bus is present, then its attached devices are identified and logged. In addition to all the attached buses, the BIOS should configure any motherboard resources. Once all devices and their resource requirements are known, the BIOS can begin system configuration.

The BIOS can optionally save information about previous configurations in non-volatile RAM to assist in the new configuration. This is the only way to configure legacy cards, whose resource requirements can not be directly determined. It can also assist the configuration of Plug and Play cards by allowing most, if not all of the cards to be configured the same way as on the previous boot. This ensures that repeated boots with the same devices will result in the same configuration.

Once all devices and their resource requirements have been identified, the Plug and Play BIOS must attempt to create a bootable configuration. Thus the BIOS' first priority is to configure the minimum boot requirements of a keyboard, display and IPL device in such a way that they do not conflict with each other or with any legacy devices. This may entail disabling some non-boot Plug and Play devices. There may also be non-boot Plug and Play devices which can only be configured by their device drivers. But at least the system will be able to boot to the point that those drivers can be loaded and used to configure their devices.

Ultimately, Plug and Play will have to support dynamically changing configurations due to "hot plugging" of devices. This requires both the BIOS and the operating system to change their device tables dynamically. The Plug and Play specifications include procedures for communicating run-time configuration changes between the BIOS and the operating system. If the OS can dynamically load device drivers and change its system resource tables, it will be possible for users to add new devices (or remove old ones) without having to reboot the computer.

Summary

Buses are shared system mechanisms that provide system data transfer facilities. Because processors use buses to access peripheral storage devices, graphics displays, and network adapters; transfer speeds should be several times as fast as maximum storage device transfer speeds.

PCI bus implementations provide a stable high-performance adapter card design that will soon provide 100 MByte/sec transfer speeds, sufficient for the near term. PCI's long-term prospect potential should admirably protect PCI peripheral investments. Some motherboards provide concurrent PCI, ISA, and VESA Local Bus implementations.

Chapter Questions

1 Paired buffers are called

   a Buffer pairs

   b Transceivers

   c Flip-Flops

   d Local bus Synchs

2 Buses usually provide

   a Address lines

   b Clock signals

   c Interrupt lines

   d Only a and c

   e a, b, and c

3 The ISA bus

   a Was developed by IBM

   b Was standardized later by the IEEE

   c Had 16 signals

   d a and b

4 Bus Mastering

   a Appeared with the IBM PC-XT

   b Uses specialized connectors

   c Requires edge-triggered interrupts

   d All of the above

   e None of the above

5   A local bus

   a   Is a side effect introduced with level sense interrupts

   b   Is something to take to work on spare-the-air days

   c   Is specific only to Intel 80486 processors

   d   Extends directly from processor data and address lines

6   Interrupts can be shared by

   a   Only having one edge-sense while the remainders are level-sense

   b   Using compatible software

   c   Using only level sense

   d   b and c

   e   None of the above

7   The VESA Local Bus can be used with the Intel

   a   80386 processor

   b   80486 processor

   c   Pentium processor

   d   All of the above

8   PCI bus is

   a   A local bus

   b   A mezzanine bus

   c   Standardized by Intel Corp.

   d   All of the above

9   The standard PCI bus is limited to how many unit loads?

   a   3

   b   4

   c   10

   d   20

10   The maximum data rate for the 32-bit PCI bus is

   a   33 MBytes/sec

   b   132 MBytes/sec

   c 200 MBytes/sec

   d 264 MBytes/sec

❐

4

Hard Disks

What This Chapter Is About

This chapter explores hard disk design and performance issues. It includes a review of magnetic recording, electronic and mechanical characteristics and components, servo systems, data encoding and recovery (reading) systems, formatting, and partitioning. This chapter is not a design guide but a high-level information source for disk drive internals.

Introduction

Magnetic disks are computing's non-volatile data storage work horses. Hard disks provide their system's essential storage capacity for:

- System and user data files

- System archival and backup activities

- Operating system paging and swapping areas

Available in various capacities, average user disk storage cost is plummeting through 20 cents per MByte with no near-term end in sight. For PC operating systems, the atomic read/write disk unit available is 512 bytes (which is called one sector), and the average delay time to retrieve it is typically about 10 ms (one hundredth of a second) for the first unit retrieved.

Magnetic Recording Overview

Magnetic disk data recording and recovery uses techniques similar to those used by audio and video tape machines. A permanently magnetizable (magnetically hard) material, called *media*, travels past a stationary transducer, called a *head*, at a constant rotational speed. The inductive head may be the conventional inductive type or the quite recently introduced Magneto-Resistive (*MR*) type. The head contains a ring shaped *core*, fabricated from magnetically conductive but not permanently magnetizable (magnetically soft) material with a very short open *gap* filled with a non-magnetic material. A low resistance metallic *coil* wraps around a portion of the core and carries electrical current when writing data that induces a magnetic field within the core, or produces a voltage when the head passes through small magnetic fields within the media (Figure 4-1).

The core's magnetic field *polarity* (north or south pole orientation) depends on the electrical current direction, reversing when the current reverses. The gap in the head flies very close to the media, forcing magnetic fields to leak through (or from) the media in order to complete the magnetic path. Several factors contribute to the leakage pattern's shape and magnetic intensity, including the core's shape and gap's size. During write operations, much of the core's magnetic field passes through the nearby media leaving an oriented magnetic pattern which slowly decays over many, many years.

Since changing the coil's current direction reverses the core's, and hence the media's, magnetic polarity, magnetic recording devices can construct periodic polarity reversals within the media with the

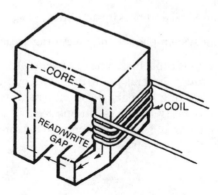

Figure 4-1. Magnetic Core (From *The Digital Large System Mass Storage Handbook*, Paul Massiglia, ed. Courtesy of Digital Equipment Corporation.)

assistance of accurate clock signals. The polarity reversal patterns signal digital data bit values. Subsequent read operations simply place the same head near previously magnetized media areas. As the media passes by at constant rotational speed, polarity reversals, called media *flux changes* or *transitions*, electromagnetically induce minute voltage fluctuations, or *pulses*, in the metallic coil (Figure 4-2).

An alternative *MR* sensor detects the presence of the transition by a resistance change due to presence of a magnetic field. The resistance change in conjunction with a sense current produces a voltage approximately proportional to the magnetic field. The MR sensor, if used, is located very close to the writing element, i.e., near or even within the gap in the writing core. (Since the same head structure that created the magnetic flux changes senses the patterns, all types of heads are usually referred to as read/write heads. The inductive head always writes, and reads if a MR sensor is not present.)

Bit-by-bit data recovery is a complex exercise. It requires sensing, amplifying, filtering, and interpreting the momentary electrical voltage fluctuations that the remnant polarity reversals induce. Peak detection and qualification circuitry isolates encoded transitions from unwanted noise. Signal interpretation includes both data and

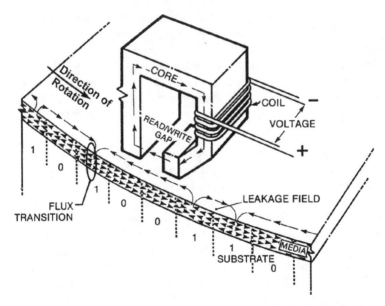

Figure 4-2. Flux Transitions (From *The Digital Large System Mass Storage Handbook*, Paul Massiglia, ed. Courtesy of Digital Equipment Corporation.)

clock extraction as well as head position information used for accurately positioning the head. In other words, there's a lot of tightly-designed hardware involved. Over time, it is becoming increasingly complex with the emergence of more sophisticated and powerful sequence detectors which replace the venerable peak detection and qualification circuitry.

Since maximum media linear recording density is inversely proportional to the length of magnetic transitions, it is important to create abrupt media polarity reversals. But sufficiently strong magnetic fields and abrupt polarity reversals can present conflicting goals that require practical trade-offs. And, there are even more conflicting goals than these.

Component Overview

A hard disk drive consists of one or more enclosed *disks* or *platters* that have both surfaces covered by media. The platters connect to a common *spindle* which a drive motor rotates at constant rotational speed. Typically, the motor is a *direct drive motor* where the motor's shaft is the spindle.

A read/write head attaches to an *air bearing slider* which attaches to a stainless steel gimbal. The gimbal permits limited slider height, pitch and roll movement while minimizing yaw, lateral, fore, and aft movements that alter head and media relationships. The gimbal suspends one read/write head near each platter surface from *access arms* and permits the slider to maintain *media compliance*—constant height, called *fly height*, over minor media surface irregularities. The collection of head/arm components are referred to as a *head stack* or *head stack assembly.*

The multiple access arms are *ganged* (rigidly connected) to a common *positioner* (servo motor) that is controlled by a *servo control system*. The servo control system precisely moves the access arms using *servo* position reference information recorded on the media to control positioning activities. This allows the selected read/write head to sweep the entire usable media's surface with great precision. All heads move in unison so that when one head is at a specific media position, all heads within the disk stack are essentially at the same approximate position with respect to their media's surface.

The *read/write channel* executes media read and write activities under control of the disk controller. When reading, a *preamplifier* receives minute read/write head analog signals and raises the signal levels to usable levels. The amplified analog signals typically are sent to each of two sections in the system depending on whether servo position and reference information is recorded or data is recorded. In each section, filtering is chosen and optimized to limit bandwidth (minimize noise) and to boost selected frequencies to minimize interference between recorded transitions.

If data is recorded in the area being read, filtered analog signals travel to clock and data separation circuitry, then to data detection circuitry which converts the bit-by-bit serial analog signals to encoded digital information. Finally, encoded data is decoded into user data.

If servo information is recorded in the area being read, filtered analog signals travel to either of two sets of circuitry depending on whether servo *position* information is present or servo *reference* information is present. For servo *position* information, a specialized servo position detector extracts head position off-track error to send to the servo control system. For servo *reference* information, a simple peak detector extracts digital servo reference information, e.g., start position of a servo field, index flag, low order bits of the track address, etc. Note that all servo information is written only at time of drive manufacture and never rewritten and is one good reason why drives should not be exposed to strong magnetic fields.

When writing data, user data is converted into encoded data and then circuits drive write heads with currents of alternating polarity. Polarity changes at the instant of each encoded "one" bit thus recording a magnetic polarity transition on the media. Media magnetic properties are optimized for maximum recording density of data at high reliability.

Near-permanent retention makes the "zeros" and "ones" essentially permanent until overwritten. This provides two of magnetic disk's most desirable characteristics:

- Unlimited usability
- Non-volatility

Clearly, hard disks require complex design and involve numerous chemical, physical, mechanical, electrical, mathematical, and system disciplines. These combined disciplines allow disk designers to develop:

- Stable mechanical mechanisms to rotate media under heads

- Inexpensive media that sustains repeated magnetization of adjacent areas with excellent signal-to-noise output

- Processes that consistently apply smooth, thin media layers on circular substrates such that defects are minimized, permitting incredibly low head fly heights

- Ever smaller, more sensitive head designs that write with acceptable magnetic field strength and that read the constantly decreasing magnetized areas with excellent signal-to-noise ratio

- Sliders and gimbals that allow heads to change position to precise locations within milliseconds when necessary while maintaining minute fly heights that conforms to microscopic media variations

- High-speed switching, amplification, filtering, and signal decoding electronics for servo position and reference detection and data detection and decoding

- Highly reliable host controller interfaces that compensate for hard disk delays and that help to provide excellent data integrity

Data Organization

A *track* is one fundamental hard disk organizational unit. A track is the circle described by a head on a media surface when the head remains in a single position for a complete platter rotation. For data writes and subsequent reads, it is the minimum position change increments since individual tracks are evenly separated by otherwise unused isolation zones, called *guard bands*, to avoid magnetic interference. Individual bit magnetic patterns, called *transitions*, lie along the track circumference and sequentially appear under the head. So, the recording process transforms parallel byte-wide information to encoded serial bit streams for writing and vice versa for reading.

Since heads move in unison over platters and assume a set number of positions, the collective tracks associated with any position comprises a *cylinder*. To read or write data, drive electronics *selects* the correct head, thereby selecting the correct cylinder track. To move to a new position, a positioner *seek* moves the selected head, hence all heads in the stack go to the correct cylinder. If other heads in the same cylinder are subsequently selected for reading or writing, only a minor position correction is required for precise positioning of the newly selected head.

User data is usually organized into fixed length *sectors*, 512 bytes or sometimes slightly larger. Sectors are the minimum read/write unit. A *header* frequently precedes the sector and Error Correction Code (ECC) symbols follow the 512 bytes of user data. The sector header, if it exists, identifies the correct sector address. The ECC information is used to both validate data and correct it if necessary. It follows that individual sectors are *addressed* using correct cylinder, head (track), and sector numbers—referred to as *CHS* addressing.

A frequently used additional data organization unit is, called a *zone*. In this scheme, several adjacent cylinders are grouped into a zone and a disk can have several zones. Different zones have a different number of sectors per track. But within each zone, each track has an equal number of sectors. Sectors are radially aligned in a physical sense though perhaps not in a logical sense. Zones increase a drive's usable storage capacity by allowing more sectors per track in zones further away from the disk spindle.

Sector Format

A sector is the smallest portion of a track that a drive can read or write. A sector must be read or written in its entirety. Each track is divided into sectors primarily for addressing, error detection and correction, and bad sector management. When a drive is manufactured, it is typically formatted by the drive's controller with dummy information and other associated formatting, ECC, etc., to establish sector boundaries and lock out media defects. Different drives, even from the same manufacturer, may use different formats, ECC, etc., so controllers are inexorably married to each drive. Since sector formats vary considerably, only a typical example is offered below with fields in sequential order.

* * Servo fields—See servo section
* ** ID Preamble—Used to establish clock and bit synchronization
* ** ID End-of-preamble word—Used to delimit start of the ID field

** ID field—Contains cylinder, head, sector addresses, bad sector offset information, etc.

** ID field CRC or ECC—Used to detect and/or correct ID field errors

** Read-to-write switch gap (*write splice*)

Data Preamble—Used to establish clock and bit synchronization

End-of-preamble word—Used to delimit start of the data field

Data field—Contains user data

Data field ECC—Used to detect and correct data errors

Write-to-read switch gap

In the above list, servo fields, labeled with * are not always positioned between data fields as indicated above. In zoned disk drives, they are frequently inserted between sections of the data field or between ID field and data preamble. When one bisects the data field, it is necessary to add an additional data preamble and end-of-preamble word to re-synchronize data read operations.

The fields labeled with ** associated with and including the ID field, are not always present. It is becoming increasingly popular to dispense with ID fields and rely on other methods to assure that correct address locations have been found and to manage bad sector offsets. This is referred to as *headerless recording*.

Bad Sector Management

Many ancient (in fact, some not so ancient) disk drives deallocated entire tracks even if just one small track area was bad. That inefficient practice has been abandoned in favor of de-allocating bad sectors as they are discovered. Two basic strategies have been used: 1) provide spare sectors at end of each track (or each cylinder) and 2) provide spare sectors at some convenient place within the drive, usually just beyond the nominal address space. Sometimes, both schemes are used together.

Method 1: If a bad sector is discovered, either at time of manufacture or later, the track (or the cylinder) is typically reformatted, moving all sector addresses from the bad sector onward down the track (or cylinder) by one sector. ID fields are rewritten with the new addresses and the bad sector ID field is made unreadable as a true ID field. This process may be repeated up to the limit of spares for each track (or cylinder) and is known as *sector slipping*.

Method 2: This scheme requires the disk controller to search a bad sector list, which may be initially stored on a private section of the disk or other memory, to find the alternate sector address. The alternate sector is accessed to perform the selected operation.

Method 1's advantage is that less time is required to arrive at the desired sector, since it is always adjacent to the nominal sector address. Its disadvantage is that more spare sector space is needed since defects are not always so kind as to distribute themselves evenly across a track or cylinder. Method 2 has exactly the reverse advantage and disadvantage. Most manufacturers today use Method 1 since storage space is inexpensive, and performance is slightly harder to achieve.

Density

Areal Density

As previously mentioned, bit transitions lie along track circumferences, so it is easy to calculate the number of bits per inch (BPI) for every track. Tracks at the inner radius of each zone have the smallest circumference for that zone, hence greatest bit density, so bits per inch are typically measured there. Likewise, it is easy to calculate the number of tracks per inch (TPI), referred to as *track density* or *radial density*, that occur between the innermost and outermost tracks. Tracks per inch are nominally constant from innermost to outermost tracks, regardless of zone. Multiplying maximum BPI and TPI provides the theoretical maximum bits per square inch, or *areal density*. The areal density multiplied by the total number of usable media surface square inches provides one possible measure of the drives *unformatted capacity*.

Maximizing areal density is essential since a drive's storage capacity is directly related to areal density. However, because servo fields, formatting losses of several kinds, sector headers, and ECC considerations consume media space, the storage capacity available to users, the drive's formatted capacity, is 10% to 20% less than a disk's theoretical unformatted capacity. Regardless, maximizing areal density is essential for drive designs because it enables:

- Disk drives with reduced size but equivalent capacity

- Disk drives with greater capacity at reduced cost per megabyte

- Disk drives with fewer expensive components such as heads but offering equivalent storage capacity at reduced costs

Moreover, reducing disk size reduces:

- Audio noise

- Required power and electrical costs

- Seek distances and associated delays

- Heat and the reliability problems it introduces

- Mechanical fragility

Clearly, higher areal densities enable improved capacities, performance, and reliability. Since, by many measures, smaller is better, it's no wonder areal density is the design-point battle ground and that areal densities have exponentially improved for decades. And the industry believes such improvement will continue for many years to come.

Bit Density

Bit density, or *linear density*, is a measure of the maximum user bits per inch which lie along the innermost track's circumference within each zone. As mentioned earlier, some area is reserved for servo fields, formatting losses of several kinds, sector headers, and ECC considerations. Servo fields may exist either between sectors or interspersed with data within a sector. Bit density improvements come from:

1 Media design improvements that provide improved signal to noise and permit lower fly heights:

   - Fewer defects

   - Thinner media

   - Smoother surfaces

- More consistent and finer crystalline properties

- Better magnetic properties such as higher coercivity and lower noise

2 Head design improvements that provide:

- Reduced magnetic transition lengths

- Stronger magnetic fields and focus for writing

- Smaller physical geometries such as narrower tracks

- More sensitive reading elements for better signal to noise ratios

3 Decreased flying heights that:

- Reduce magnetic transition lengths stored in the media

- Reduce unwanted stray magnetic fields at track edges to minimize width of guard bands

- Improve magnetic field coupling between head and media, for both writing and reading, improving signal to noise ratios

4 Improved data encoding and formatting methods that exploit media capacity more efficiently

5 Improved data detection methods that accept reduced signal to noise

At constant rotation rates, bit density increases naturally improve the *data transfer rate*, the rate the heads write or recover data from the media. Increasing the rotation rate using a constant bit density has the same effect as well as decreasing wait times for data to begin passing by the head (rotational latency). So, increasing both the rotation rate and bit density can provide a dramatic data transfer rate performance improvement that must be balanced against the cost of improved components that must handle the faster media transfer rates.

Track Density

Head recording width primarily determines track width which in turn primarily determines track density (assuming adequate positioning). Reducing core widths without compromising signal to noise ratios correspondingly reduces track widths, providing greater track density. However, increased track density places increased demands on positioning accuracy which must occur at high-speed. Track densities currently range form 2,000 TPI to 5,000 TPI. Since bit densities currently range from 100,000 BPI to 200,000 BPI, it follows that bits are nominally 50 times wider than long and that current areal densities are on the order of 1 GBit/in^2.

Performance

Performance is a measure of the time to service data requests by the host computer system, including both read and write requests. Ideally, data would be instantly transferred between host memory and disk without impacting host computational performance in any way. Data transfer is not ideal; in fact, it takes considerable time to service host requests, relative to the speed at which hosts can use or generate data. So, it is quite important to find methods for rapidly retrieving or storing data to disk drives.

Measuring or anticipating performance can be somewhat complex. It is highly dependent on issues such as:

- How much variability occurs in the above parameters

- Amount of data to be retrieved or stored at each request

- Whether data requests arrive in bursts or are spaced out in time

- Whether disk controller caching is present, and if so, what type caching

- Physical position of data for the current request relative to position of data at the previous request, called *locality*

Despite the difficulty in analyzing performance in light of the above variables, there are a few, well-understood disk performance measures which provide useful benchmarks. Depending on differences in requests, they more or less influence performance in meaningful ways.

Seek Performance

After a head is selected, the servo system, via the positioner, moves the selected head to the chosen track. Time to execute a move is approximately a square root function of number of tracks to be moved plus a constant which represents time for the head to finally settle into precise position on the chosen track. Since number of tracks is a variable, seek performance varies accordingly. So, a more comprehensive seek-time characterization is *velocity profiling* which designers use to fine tune servo systems for maximum seek performance using the fastest acceleration, maximum velocity, and appropriate deceleration that minimizes settling time over destination tracks.

But, there are various standard methods manufacturers and users accept for comparing seek performance. One measure is called *random average seek time*. It assumes all possible requested track addresses are equally likely. This applies to both starting and ending track addresses. So, random average seek time is the sum of all seek times from all possible tracks to all other possible tracks, divided by the total number of such seeks. Some manufacturers approximate this time by the time it takes to execute a seek length of 1/3 of total number of tracks (there is a small error in this over-stated estimate). This is known as 1/3rd seek time.

Another frequently referenced measurement is *single-track* (or *track-to-track*) *seek time*, which is the length of time for the actuator to move one cylinder and settle (without latency). This time can be especially important for transfers of large amounts of data.

A third measurement is so-called *typical seek time*. It is clearly a function of typical seek distance and dependent on seek locality, which is an application-dependent parameter. Typical seek time is always less than random average seek time since there is always some degree of locality. Frequently, typical seek time is about 40% of random average seek time.

For all of the above metrics, maximum positioner acceleration, mechanical stiffness and servo system performance determine how fast heads move from one position to the next and how fast the selected head settles into precise position for reading or writing.

Latency

After the head selected for I/O activity moves to a new position, the drive must wait for the desired sector to rotate into position under the head. This is called *rotational latency*. The average rotational latency is one revolution's time duration divided by two. In other words, the average delay after a seek is one half of the rotational rate, which is 8.33 ms for a 3600 RPM drive (one second divided by 60, all divided by 2) and 4.17 ms for a 7200 RPM drive. Increasing rotation speed reduces latency, but also increases heat and places additional demands on balancing and vibration elimination.

Data Transfer Rate

The selected track's radius, RPM and bit density determine the data transfer rate, which is essential to high-performance in many environments. Data transfer rate has a major impact on the drive's ability to sustain long transfers because it determines how fast data fills or drains a drive buffer or cache which may also affect bus interface performance. High data transfer rates usually accompany more expensive drive components found in high-end drives.

Other Performance Factors

In addition to the above factors, a few other drive-related factors of minor impact exist: Micro-processor service time, buffer overlap time (degree of overlap between disk-to-buffer and buffer-to-host transfers, or vice versa), and host interface bus performance. If the drive's controller contains a cache, it may or may not materially improve performance depending on locality, cache size and cache management policies. Summing the seek, latency, transfer time and the other various overheads provides a performance metric known as the *total service time* or just the *access time*.

Components

Disks (Media, Substrates, and Overcoats)

The structure of a disk today is a cylindrical aluminum, glass, or ceramic substrate (a thin platter) upon which all other layers are deposited on both sides. These additional layers include smoothing nickel phosphorus (NiP) layers (to overcoat blemishes or to provide a harder disk surface that is more resistant to damage than an aluminum substrate), magnetic media layers, very hard protective overcoats, and finally lubrication layers. The substrate occupies almost all of the total thickness with the smoothing layer most of the remaining thickness. Other layers are extremely thin. This type of thin film disk was first successfully introduced in the late 1980s.

The structure was different for earlier disks. The substrate was still present but it was over-coated with a painted on layer which contained a magnetic oxide pigment. Various methods were used to provide adequate durability of the surface. Each of the important features of disks are discussed in the sub-topics below.

Disk Diameter Evolution

Some early disk drives had disk diameters ranging from about 26 inches to 30 inches or more. Disk diameters quite quickly dropped to a standard 14 inches which was a convenient size for both floor-standing and rack-mounted disk drives. This standard was maintained for many years. Subsequently, diameters dropped to 10.8, 10.5, 9, and 8 inches; with 9 and 8 inches permitting multiple disk drives in a single 10 1/2 inch rack. Later, 5 1/4 inch disks displaced most larger sizes. For desktop systems, the initial standard was set at 5 1/4 inches but quite quickly dropped to 3 1/2 inches.

The primary reason for the transition to 3 1/2 inches was to reduce audio noise, power and space consumption. An important drawback to the reduction is lower signal-to-noise ratios. MR heads compensate for this by producing increased output at lower velocities. Arrays of 5 1/4 inch drives continued to be used in rack-mounted configurations for several more years—but finally are being abandoned because manufacturing volumes relative to 3 1/2 inch drives are insufficient to maintain competitive cost per megabyte.

While desktop systems continue to find 3 1/2 inch drives quite adequate up to this date, laptop and smaller systems demand considerably lower power consumption, particularly at startup. The 2 1/2 inch drives are the defacto standard for notebook systems and 1.8 inch drives are quickly appearing in emerging sub-notebook, pen computing and special-purpose portable computer and portable data acquisition markets. Drives as small as 1.3 inch diameter have been built but have not yet found applications with reasonable volumes.

Substrates

Substrates have been made almost exclusively from aluminum for the entire history of disk drives. For early disk designs, aluminum was used without any other overcoat for improving surface smoothness and consistency. This proved adequate while oxide media was applied as a relatively thick paint.

When metal media subsequently became viable, aluminum surface quality was not adequate by itself. Typically, nickel was electroless plated over the aluminum to seal its porosity, then polished until an extremely smooth surface was achieved. Note that substrate smoothness controls overall disk smoothness since metal media and other protective overcoats are extremely thin.

Only recently has there been significant progress in developing better substrates. Glass has also become an excellent substrate for very small diameter disks, 2 1/2 inches and below. It provides a smooth surface that is very tolerant of high shock environments—provided it has been processed correctly. It may eventually compete in the 3 1/2 inch market as well if costs become competitive. Aluminum with highly a polished nickel phosphorous overcoat is a strong alternative.

Media magnetic surfaces and flying heads prefer ultra-smooth surfaces with absolutely no blemishes. Alternatively, heads which are initially in contact with disks require a certain amount of roughness to reduce initial startup torque (stiction). For a number of years, these conflicting needs were met by compromising on substrate smoothness. More recently, they are being met by providing a roughened zone at the innermost head radius used exclusively for head take off and landing. The remaining flyable substrate surface is very smooth.

Magnetic Media

Prior to introduction of metal media, all media was *oxide* media. Magnetic material was almost exclusively gamma ferric oxide (Fe_2O_3), although other metal-based ferrites, such as barium ferrite, were also promoted from time to time. It was structured in tiny, acicular (pencil-shaped) crystalline particles, then mixed with a non-magnetizable phenoxy binder that comprised most of the total volume. Other plastic binders previously used met with limited success.

In later years, the mixture also contained additional aggregate, usually fine particles of aluminum oxide to provide considerably increased durability. A conflict always existed between maximum magnetic material content versus sufficient binder and aggregate to provide adequate strength and durability. The mixture was applied by spinning it on to the substrates, then baking it until it was dry and hard, then polishing it until it was very smooth and well controlled in thickness.

In the 1970s, *oriented media* was introduced. It was created by exposing the drying media to a strong magnetic field which oriented the thin, pencil-shaped particles in a generally circumferential direction to improve effective media coercivity. Eventually, oxide media gave way to metal media. Several reasons existed for this evolution:

- Ability to achieve much lower fly heights due to smoother surfaces and improved durability

- Physical ability to achieve very thin media

- Improved magnetic moment traits

- Higher coercivity which, when coupled with very thin media, permitted very short recording transition lengths

- Improved media noise

All of these factors provided a powerful influence on the recording density evolution. In fact, annually-compounded areal density growth rate had slowed from 30% to about 15% near the end-of-life of oxide media. Several abortive attempts had been made to introduce metal media while problems of achieving durability and manufacturability were being worked out. Finally they were all solved and metal media was permanently and safely introduced. Today, metal media is considerably more reliable and exhibits a competitive cost. The result has been a remarkable increase in areal density evolution rate to about 60% annually-compounded in recent years.

Metal media has been produced by *electroless plating, electroplating, sputtering,* and *ion beam deposition.* While problems of metal media were being worked out, all of these processes were tried by various laboratories and manufacturing operations. Eventually, all but sputtering were abandoned, primarily because of manufacturing cost, manufacturing consistency, flexibility of materials, and compatibility with overcoat deposition. Sputtering is a process where the substrate is placed in a vacuum chamber near a media material source that is bombarded by gas ions. The dislodged media ions uniformly deposit on the substrate.

Metallic magnetic media materials used are all cobalt based. Various alloys have been used by different manufacturers at different times including: cobalt-nickel, cobalt-chromium, and cobalt-platinum, sometimes with additional alloying elements such as tantalum. The intent of this succession of alloying options is to improve coercivities, reduce grain sizes and make them more uniform and better isolated from each other, improve surface smoothness, reduce defects, etc. The effect of this evolution is to reduce magnetic transition lengths and improve signal to noise ratios.

Protective Overcoats

Metal media by itself is not sufficiently durable to resist damage due to head landings and takeoffs and to resist occasional contact with heads via contaminants that can never be totally eliminated. So, a very hard protective overcoat is applied. Initially, various overcoats were tried, including many different metallic oxides and nitrides, and even lubricants without intermediate overcoats. Today, diamond-like carbon is most frequently used as a hard overcoat with an added mono-layer of lubricant that is actively bonded to the carbon. The result is a media which has incredible reliability, usually outlasting other drive components while providing upwards of 100,000 start-stop cycles of head take offs and landings. Some media even tolerates occasional head contact from so-called *pseudo-contact* heads.

Heads and Head Fly Heights

Head Structures

Head structures have exhibited dramatic changes over the approximately 35 years of disk drive evolution. At first, disk heads (minus head suspensions) were assembled structures, much as other disk electro-mechanics were assembled. Later, with the exception of coils, assemblies were bonded together using glass which fused at lower temperatures than other components within the assembly. Still later, heads were made using thin film techniques, much the same as integrated circuits, then machined to create the flying element called the *air bearing*. The working elements, write and read heads, are imbedded in or applied to one surface of the air bearing structure which flies over the disk surface at extremely low altitude (a few millionths of an inch).

Air Bearings/Fly Heights

The air bearing has changed in architecture over the years. Initially, it was a spherical or cylindrical shape created by lapping the head assembly. Later, the industry switched to so-called *taper-flat* air bearings. These could be gang-machined (several at a time) which reduced cost considerably over the cylindrical and conical air bearings. This architecture lasted for many years. More recently, air bearings of a variety of shapes have been used as fly heights have decreased almost to zero. These bearings have been used to permit very low fly heights, frequently less than 2 micro-inches, which vary little over the entire disk surface, even though head yaw angles and velocities change as the track radius changes. Some use a combination of positive and negative pressure air bearings so that effective preload increases to counteract increased opposing forces (lift). Others permit extremely light preloads for pseudo-contact, i.e., effective fly heights of about 1 micro-inch.

Sizes of air bearing surfaces have decreased dramatically as well, shrinking from about 1 inch square to less than 0.1 inch square. Sizes are now labeled full size, 70%, 50%, 35%, etc. Many drives today use 50% sliders which have dimensions of about 0.08" length by 0.062" width by 0.017" thickness, weighing less than .006 grams.

For ultra-low fly height heads, air bearing surfaces may be over-coated with a thin layer of diamond-like carbon to prevent excessive wear due to occasional head/disk/contaminant contact.

Read/Write Transducers

Over the entire disk drive history, write head elements or transducers were nominally ring heads, i.e., magnetically conductive ring cores, each with a short non-magnetic gap inserted in the core adjacent to the media. A coil of wire of good electrical conductivity is wrapped around the core. When current is applied to the coil, it induces a strong magnetic field in the core. Presence of the gap causes magnetic flux to fringe away from the core and pass through the media.

When the polarity of the current is reversed, the polarity of the magnetic flux likewise is reversed. As the media passes under the write head, each flux reversal creates a series of magnetized stripes of reversing polarity (like little bar magnets). Timing of the reversals is well controlled so that reversals occur at spacings which are equivalent to spacings of encoded "one" bits along the track. Write gap lengths have been reduced until today they are down to about 1/5 of a micron or about 8 micro-inches. Write track widths have been reduced down to about 3 or 4 microns or about 120 to 160 micro-inches.

For almost the entire disk drive history, read and write transducers were common, i.e., the same element. Magnetic cores, gaps and coils surrounding the cores were all common. So, size evolution affected both write and read elements. Read signals were created by induced voltages, i.e., magnetic fields creating voltages according to Lenz's law,

$$E = -N \, df/dt$$

where N is number of turns and f is magnetic flux. A change of magnetic flux direction and intensity along the track circumference created the voltage pulse. Read heads were thus called *inductive read heads*. Use of a common read/write transducer forced the need to compromise between optimal read vs. optimal write performance.

More recently, since 1991, MR heads have been used. MR heads sense flux rather than rate of change of flux. They do so by changing resistance as the magnetic flux in the read element changes its angular direction. The read element is magnetically biased such that voltage change is approximately linear with magnetic flux density changes driven by the presence of media. When a bias current is applied to the read element, the signal-induced resistance change is converted to a voltage change according to Ohm's law. The MR head has been one of the primary contributors to annual areal density growth rates changing from between 15% to 30% to its present 60% growth rate.

MR heads permit write and read elements to be separately optimized. And, MR read elements provide significantly higher signal to noise ratios than inductive read elements, particularly at high areal densities. They also create some problems. For example, separation of write and read elements creates the need for head position offsets (called micro-jogging) as yaw angle of the heads change over the range of track radii (Figure 4-1).

An additional problem is that servo position error signals are not nearly as linear for MR heads as they are for inductive read heads. (Recall that the same head reads user and servo data.) Positive and negative pulses are not of equal amplitude. Momentary contact between head and media (or contaminant) can thermally induce resistance changes, hence cause voltage spikes, i.e., noise. Despite these issues, MR heads support much higher areal densities than inductive heads. Even larger gains are in store for the industry when so-called Giant MR (GMR) heads materialize.

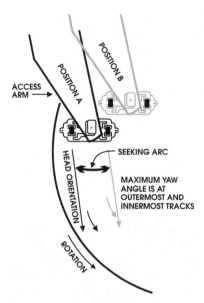

Figure 4-1. Microjogging (From *The Digital Large System Mass Storage Handbook*, Paul Massiglia, ed. Courtesy of Digital Equipment Corporation.)

Core materials have also evolved. Initially cores were made from permalloy, a nickel-iron alloy which exhibited good permeability, low coercivity and good magnetic saturation. These quickly gave way to magnetically soft ferrite cores (mounted on ferrite air bearings) which also exhibited good permeability and low coercivity but poorer magnetic saturation. However, they had somewhat better high frequency read response (little core loss) without the need for thin cores or laminated cores—and, perhaps more importantly, they were more reliable (less prone to head crash).

To significantly improve magnetic saturation for better write operation, metal-in-gap (MIG) cores were later produced. Then, cores reverted to permalloy at the onset of thin film processing—only this time, cores were very thin which permitted high frequency read operation with little core loss. Additionally, flying reliability was not impaired because the thin core was slightly recessed from the surface rarely, if ever, touching contaminants which might pass between head and media.

Even these thin cores are now starting to feel the pinch of core losses which are a bit high at today's high operating frequencies. So, laminated cores are now being proposed for inductive read heads. MR read heads escape this problem because their permalloy MR sense elements are even thinner and they do not use the thicker write core as part of their magnetic circuit. They sense flux directly from the media, usually with the aid of permalloy shields.

Overall, the evolution of read/write heads has helped to fuel the strong areal density evolution with little sacrifice in signal to noise ratio—even though track widths and magnetic transition lengths have both been dramatically reduced over time. However, the high frequencies of new and planned products place new demands on write head designs as well.

Head Suspensions

Head suspensions, sometimes called gimbals, permit limited motion of the head in vertical height, pitch and roll modes while retaining high stiffness in lateral, fore, aft and yaw modes (Figure 4-2). Permissible motions are necessary to accommodate manufacturing tolerance variations and head motions induced by disks which are never perfectly flat.

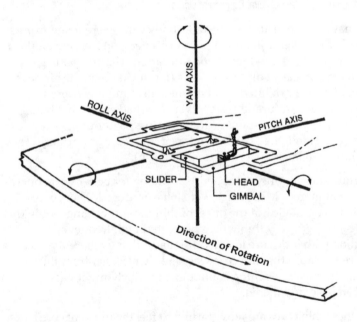

Figure 4-2. Head Suspension (From *The Digital Large System Mass Storage Handbook*, Paul Massiglia, ed. Courtesy of Digital Equipment Corporation.)

In the early days of disks, when heads were large and relatively heavy structures, suspensions included one or two axis pivots (much like universal joints) which accommodated pitch and roll modes and low spring-rate springs to accommodate vertical motion. When heads became smaller, pivots were replaced by well-designed springs which permitted needed motions but provided high stiffness in the modes demanding little motion. A fairly specialized mini-industry has grown up to supply suspensions to the disk industry.

Mechanics/Electro-mechanics

All mechanics/electro-mechanics plus disks, heads, and head preamplifiers are contained within a mechanical assembly usually called the *head/disk assembly* or *HDA*. The HDA housing encloses and also provides the mechanical structure for mounting other major mechanical/electro-mechanical elements. Each of the major sub-sections of the HDA will be treated below.

Positioners (Servo Motors) and Arm Assemblies

For many years, positioners were structured in two ways, either as linear positioners or as rotary positioners. Linear positioners (Figure 4-3) rolled along rails of various configurations and were powered by a linear motor. Rotary positioners rotated about a pivot and were powered by rotary motors of limited angular movement (Figure 4-4). Quite early in disk history, rotary positioners gave way to linear positioners, then reappeared in the 1970s in limited

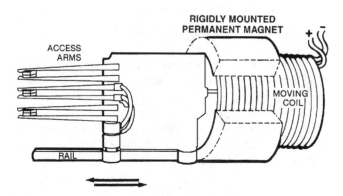

Figure 4-3. Linear Positioners (From *The Digital Large System Mass Storage Handbook*, Paul Massiglia, ed. Courtesy of Digital Equipment Corporation.)

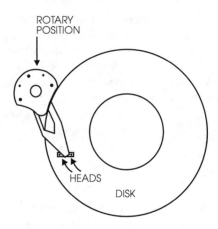

Figure 4-4. Rotary Positioner (From *The Digital Large System Mass Storage Handbook*, Paul Massiglia, ed. Courtesy of Digital Equipment Corporation.)

applications. Eventually, rotary positioners totally displaced linear positioners because of their lower cost and power consumption.

In the early days, servo motors were most often hydraulic. This required conversion of electrical power to hydraulic power to mechanical power. But, initially, hydraulics were easier to control in high-torque, fast acceleration applications. When control circuitry for high-torque electric motors improved, the costly hydraulic systems were abandoned. Also in the early days, many servo systems were quite crude—so they were supplemented with hydraulic, mechanical or magnetic (e.g., stepper motor) *detents* to perform moderately precise fine positioning. As servo technology improved, detents of all kinds were totally abandoned.

Modern disk drives utilize rotary positioners and servo motors built as one integral assembly, complete with the head arm stack upon which heads and head suspensions are directly mounted by swaging (a rivet-like process). The entire assembly is carefully designed as a unit to provide excellent dynamic mechanical stiffness with very low rotational inertia so that high-performance servos can achieve very fast seek times. The bearing system must also be precise and provide good stiffness with minimum run-out or else all other careful design effort is lost.

Spindle Drive Motors and Spindles

Rotational inertia is a function of disk diameter which dictates positioner arm length and number of disks, which dictates number of arms and heads. Disk drives prefer uniform rotation rates and can suffer from short-term (near instantaneous) and long-term variations. In early disk drives, spindle speed control was provided by the AC power system. Some very early drives used synchronous motors which phase-locked to 60 Hz AC lines for 1200, 1800, or 3600 RPM speed (for 50 Hz lines, 1000, 1500, and 3000 RPM). High-performance drives today usually rotate at 4500, 5400, and even 7200 RPM. Some rotate even faster.

Many early disk drives used a belt and inductive AC motor to power the spindle at approximately constant rotation rates. Either a synchronous or induction motor was used which ran at the exact (*synchronous*) or approximate (*induction*) rated speed. The motor may have been coupled to the spindle by direct drive or belt drive—both systems were used in different drives.

Good, low cost switching control circuitry for DC motors and small diameter disks eventually made the use of AC motors less desirable. So, DC direct-drive motors mounted directly onto spindles have become standard. These require motor driver switching circuits that handle modest current levels. Speed sensing is provided by position sensing of spindle angular position, usually an optical or hall-effect system. Later, back EMF was sensed in some systems to eliminate sensor cost. The system clock, derived from a crystal oscillator source, was used as a speed reference. To complete the system, a servo control system regulates speed.

For all of these systems, spindles must balance precisely and use high-quality bearings. Motors must have reasonable start-up torque to overcome the static friction between head and media surfaces and attain rotational speeds quickly. Without sufficient start-up torque, *stiction* (a natural, strong bonding between two extremely smooth surfaces) between the heads and media surface may prevent the platters from spinning. This is primarily an issue with laptop, notebook and sub-note book computer designs which demand ultra low-power consumption and minimum battery weight. Some drive systems provide a microprocessor-based speed sensor which the control system uses to maintain correct speed.

In modern drive designs, spindle drivers and speed control are provided by specially designed integrated circuitry that provides high torque at start up, yet reduces power while spinning at correct, servo-controlled rotational operating speeds. All needed circuitry is contained within a single chip or part of a chip.

As TPIs rise, spindle runout and noise become a large factor in the total servo error budget. In a few disk drives, spindle ball bearings have been replaced by hydro-dynamic fluid bearings. Hydro-dynamic ball bearings provide comparable bearing stiffness with very much lower spindle *runout* (wobble) and noise than ball bearings with a slightly higher power consumption penalty.

Air Filtering and Contamination

Air filtering and contamination are important considerations. The HDA is not hermetically sealed, in fact it frequently has some form of breather filter to maintain inside air pressure equivalency with external air pressure. As the disks spin, they provide a reasonably efficient air pump which is used to circulate internal air through simple but effective filters. These are used to maintain relatively clean air inside the HDA. The term "relatively" is used because no filter system can be made perfect—especially when there are dirt particle generators inherently built into the HDA (e.g., heads that taxi on the disks for takeoffs and landings which dislodge microscopic particles).

Materials inside the HDA are carefully selected and controlled such that they do not shed any more dirt than necessary and do not emit harmful chemical contaminants, including moisture. When materials have an inherent tendency to shed dirt, they may be coated with so-called conformal coatings to prevent the shedding process.

Small diameter drives generally do not generate much heat in the mechanical/electro-mechanical system. Small drives may consume up to several watts, depending on size and number of disks, spindle RPM, and positioner power, generating heat as RPM rates increase. Air, which is pumped by the disks, transfers heat via the outside HDA shell. Conduction through the shell disposes of remaining heat. There is always a temperature differential between internal and external air as a result.

While heat is generally viewed as harmful (to component reliability), it does have the benefit of minimizing relative humidity within the HDA. Humidity can become a monumental problem if left uncontrolled since it can corrode nickel-iron permalloy in heads, cause heads to stick to disks, corrode hardened steel ball bearings, contaminate lubricants, etc.

Overall, the apparently simple HDA, including its mechanical/electro-mechanical elements, is very carefully designed to provide good ruggedness, exceedingly high reliability, very low cost, and high-speed positioning with incredible accuracy in modest operating environments. It has taken an evolution of approximately 35 years to achieve this sophisticated status—plus, the beneficial effects of exponentially increasing areal density which permitted an evolution to small diameter disks.

Electronics

Read/Write Electronics

A drive's write electronics are fairly simple. The ENDEC (encoder/decoder, which sometimes resides within the controller) encodes user data into encoded data, dictated by choice of recording code. Encoded data is then used to toggle a current source with sufficient current to saturate the magnetic media. This toggling creates the media's transitions. In most modern systems, an additional feature is added to the write system, called *precompensation* or *precomp*. Early RLL use reduced the need for precomp.

Precomp is intentional time displacement (hence position displacement) of transitions such that less magnetic interaction is present between the most closely spaced transitions. This magnetic interaction is also called *non-linear ISI* (intersymbol interference). Precomp is applied in an optimized way to maximize overall reading performance. Non-linear ISI is reduced with minimal mis-positioning of the transitions.

Major components of the read system are:

- Preamplifier
- Amplifier/AGC (automatic gain control)
- Filters, including both low pass and equalizer (s)
- Data separator (clock extraction)
- Detector

- Data decode (ENDEC), sometimes in the controller

- Data synch detector, sometimes in the controller

- Error detection/correction, always in the controller (see Chapter 5)

Preamplifier

Signals at the head output are typically in the range of 200 to 1000 micro-volts peak-to-peak. They therefore require amplification before they are transmitted outside the HDA. The preamplifier chip is located inside the HDA, usually very close to the heads, for this purpose. Parasitic loading of the head with external impedances is thereby minimized and external noise pickup is reduced. The preamp chip also contains multiplex circuits for switching the head between read and write mode.

Amplifier/AGC

After preamp outputs are received by the electronics module, they are again amplified using a gain-controllable amplifier which is "servo-ed" via a feedback loop to maintain approximately constant peak-to-peak amplitude. This process is called AGC (automatic gain control).

Filters

Next, analog filtering takes place. One reasonably complex filter system (perhaps Butterworth or Equi-ripple with several poles) is used to roll off the frequency response to whatever bandwidth the detector requires and to boost high frequency response such that pulse shapes become more detectable. This may be the only filtering system or it may be followed by an analog or digital FIR (finite impulse response) filter for additional pulse shaping. If a digital FIR is used, an A/D (analog to digital) converter is also required.

Note that with zoned recording, bandwidths and frequency spectral responses of equalizers must be selected which are appropriate for the particular zone being read at the moment, since recording frequencies for each zone are different. So, appropriate filter parameters are selected on-the-fly and transmitted, via a serial port, to the read/write system by the drive's microprocessor before reading takes place.

Data Separator (Clock Extraction)

Data separation, or clock extraction, takes place using a *phase locked loop* or *PLL* in a feedback fashion. Depending on the equalizer / detector combination chosen for the design, a clock needs to be established which is nominally synchronized with the center of the peak or straddling the peak (clock ticks on opposite sides of each peak, equally spaced). To do so, frequent computations of clock phase error need to be made, as often as existence of peaks permit.

These phase error computations are used in a servo-like system to control clock phase and frequency such that the intended phasing with peaks is maintained. Obviously, individual peaks are rarely phased perfectly due to noisy distortions of individual peak positions and amplitudes. However, it is sufficient to maintain a minimum average mean squared phase error and let the detector sort out the local irregularities.

Detectors

Throughout most of disk drive history, signal detection has been done by so-called peak detector/qualifier systems of varying sophistication. Peak detectors usually operate by sensing change of slope of a signal from positive slope to negative slope or vice versa, although other forms of peak detectors have also been used (e.g., delay line detectors). Some form of amplitude qualification is usually present to assure that noise glitches which create slope changes are not falsely detected as peaks. In recent years, amplitude qualification, while simple in concept, has become much more sophisticated with amplitude reference levels being data-dependent.

Within the past few years, more elaborate and powerful detection systems have been used by some manufacturers based on Viterbi sequence detectors of various kinds. Sequence detectors examine sampled data from two or more bit locations in sequence in order to make improved decisions for each newly detected bit ("one" or "zero"). Sampled data is usually digitized, but it can also be analog. Other kinds of sequence detectors are possible, including some that rely on decision feedback equalizers as well as forward equalizers.

Sorting out the best system from among the many possible systems is currently an activity hot-bed. The problem is complex because it involves simultaneously evaluating a combination of equalizer system, detector, code, clock extraction and silicon used to implement all of the above in order to make a competent choice.

Codes and ENDEC

Recording codes have evolved over many years with significant efficiency improvements. For most of disk drive history, run length limited codes of various kinds have been used, also called d,k codes. Run length limiting implies that only a limited number of encoded "zeros" are interspersed between adjacent "one" bits, that number equal to the parameter k. The parameter d is the minimum number of "zeros" that must be inserted between adjacent "one" bits. The primary reason for the parameter k is to assure that phase error signals are frequently available to the data separator for reliable clock extraction. The reason for parameter d is to reduce the number of flux changes per inch relative to BPI (user bits per inch).

For peak detector/qualifier systems the most popular code was 2,7. To improve bits per flux reversal efficiency, most of the industry finally settled on the 1,7 code ($d = 1, k = 7$) as best for magnetic recording. This convergence of minds took many years to accomplish. For sequence detectors, the battle is still being waged. So far, the most popular d,k codes are 0,4 and 1,7. They both offer advantages and disadvantages making it difficult to correctly weight the overall net value of each code. Other proposed codes could well become dark horses in the race too. Location of the logic for converting user data into encoded data and back again (the ENDEC) is sometimes in the read/write system and sometimes in the disk controller.

Data Synch Detector

This read system element is also sometimes in the read/write system and sometimes in the controller. Its purpose in life is to determine where the start of user data begins. The read system is enabled by the controller when it is known that the read head is over a field of encoded bits called the *preamble*. The preamble contains a fixed, repeated sequence of "one" and "zero" bits which are used to initially establish clock (PLL) to bit synchronization. Choice of the sequence differs by manufacturer. It is usually … 0101010 …, or … 010010010 …, or even … 01000100010 … sometimes called 2T, 3T, or 4T respectively. Preambles are of sufficient length such that the clock is virtually always synchronized. Subsequently, an end of preamble or data synch pattern is recorded. This pattern may be chosen to either be unique, i.e., different from any possible data pattern, or be easily distinguishable even when detection errors occur. It is always distinctly different from the preamble pattern to insure it is known that the preamble has terminated and data is about to begin.

A detector senses when the correct pattern has appeared. Some detectors are capable of interpreting the correct pattern in the presence of a limited number of detection errors. Sometimes synch detection is done on encoded data and sometimes on decoded data. When it is done on encoded data, the ENDEC is turned on at the start of user data. Otherwise, it is turned on when the PLL has determined that clock synchronization has been established and synch detection must start.

Servo System

Servo systems have evolved from relatively slow, imprecise systems to extremely fast, very precise systems capable of accurately tracking to tolerances of several micro-inches. Today, average random seek times are frequently about 10 milliseconds or less. Servo systems are frequently controlled by time sharing the drive's micro-processor as a servo processor. Today's processors are fast enough to compute all needed information on the fly, as fast as the servo system needs it.

Servo position and velocity error is derived from factory-written servo information sensed by the selected read head. This information is usually in the form of bursts of magnetic transitions arrayed in a series of short, checkerboard patterns with some of the bursts on track centerlines and others which are 1/2 track off center. The read head senses amplitudes, or integrated amplitude, of whatever portions of the patterns happen to be under the head.

From the amplitude (or phase, in one system), it is known how much of the pattern is under the head and how much is not. The servo system can also determine by signal timing which pattern is being sensed. From this set of information, it is possible to determine how far off track the head happens to be at the time of sensing. By virtue of detecting position offsets at two consecutive servo patterns, it is also possible to compute average velocity between each pair of servo patterns. Resolution and accuracy of position sensing is very high so great servo precision is achievable.

Modern embedded servo systems intersperse these servo patterns at regular angular intervals, at least one every sector time and maybe two or more per sector thus providing reasonably prompt position and velocity updates. Therefore, good servo bandwidths and high-performance are possible.

In order to provide initial locations and references for the servo system, certain other encoded information is typically provided, for example the locations of index (a fixed angular reference point) and the low order bits of the track address, etc. A special set of servo fields is written to provide this information. It is typically preceded by a short erase field which is used to identify that a servo field will soon be arriving and another short field with a fixed pattern which is used to reset the automatic gain control. These servo information fields usually precede the position error patterns cited above.

In addition to the above, guard bands outside of the range of data tracks are often written with other special information so that the servo knows when it has passed the last data track.

Special servo detection and timing extraction circuitry is typically provided as an appendage to the read/write system to perform all needed types of detection, position error signal, track address bits, index, guard bands, etc.

Armed with the above information, the servo system can boot itself upon drive startup by finding guard bands and index, then first data cylinder and sector. Many drive designs use this time to adjust rotational velocity. From that point, it keeps a running track of its location, both radial and circumferential. As it seeks, velocity multiplied by time yields a coarse estimate of distance, even long distances over many tracks. The low order address bits provide the remaining precision needed so that an accurate cylinder address is always maintained. Servo pattern count from index is maintained by a counter or servo state machine to provide circumferential position.

When a seek of more than a few tracks is called for, and after selection of the desired head, the servo processor turns the servo motor full on in the desired direction until one of two conditions is met:

1   Maximum positioner velocity is reached, or

2   Velocity has reached an intersection with the deceleration velocity/cylinder profile the servo must follow when it is

braking to arrive at the target cylinder—in other words, the distance required to be sure of stopping in time

If condition 1, the servo coasts until it arrives at condition 2. Then, servo control follows the deceleration profile down until the head position is within a fraction of a track width from the final position. Then, it changes control to a tracking mode for settling and precise track following. It remains in this mode until another seek or head switch is requested. If a very short seek or head switch is called for, the servo system may use a less intense seek mode to avoid an unstable seek. See Figure 4-5.

When the servo is in settling and tracking mode, it sets goals for itself to assure that accurate tracking has been achieved. That is, one or more position error signals must show that the servo error is less than some small percentage of track pitch before write or read operations can begin. Write tolerances are more severe than read tolerances since excess error when writing can destroy adjacent track written data as well as cause unrecoverable reads.

Summary

Disk drive evolution has been phenomenal—from huge, refrigerator-sized (and larger) boxes storing a fraction of a megabyte, costing over $100,000, failing perhaps every few hundred hours—to boxes the size of a couple of bread slices, storing up to a few thousand MBytes, costing less than $500, and failing every half million hours!

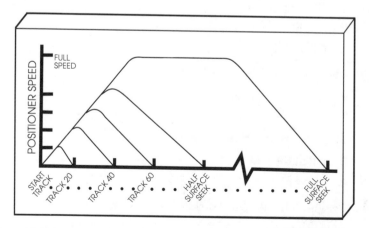

Figure 4-5. Velocity Profiles for Seeks (From *The Digital Large System Mass Storage Handbook*, Paul Massiglia, ed. Courtesy of Digital Equipment Corporation.)

Industry studies indicate that from 1976 to 1992, the physical space required for 100 MBytes of storage space dropped from 5400 in^3 to 8 in^3. Prices fell from \$560/MByte to \$5/MByte. Currently, the cost is less than \$0.20/MByte, areal densities are increasing 60% per year as costs decrease 12% per quarter.

Intense and persistent application of new technologies precipitated the evolution—plus an almost insatiable demand for on-line, permanent computer storage. These tiny little boxes contain a fascinating array of physics, chemistry, electronic, mechanical, electro-mechanical, control theory, information theory, communication theory, and systems technologies. There is truly a success story in the computer storage world though average profits have averaged a meager 1% from 1985 to 1995.

Chapter Questions

1 Magnetically hard materials

   a Are difficult to find

   b Are difficult to magnetize

   c Retain magnetization

   d Do not scratch

2 The collection of head/arm assemblies are referred to as the

   a Head stack

   b Ganged positioner

   c Gimble servos

   d Platter strobes

3 Servo information

   a Is written only at the time of manufacture

   b Gradually disappears over many, many years

   c Provides positioning information

   d All of the above

   e a and c only

4 The fundamental hard disk organization unit is

   a The track

   b The sector

c The cylinder

d The platter

5 Heat inside disk drives

a Causes uneven thermal component expansion

b Gently melts media surfaces for lubrication

c Keeps guard bands apart

d Keeps media non-volatile

6 Sector formats

a Are standardized

b Always have ECC

c Can be refreshed by disk drive maintenance programs

d All of the above

e None of the above

7 Maximizing Areal Density is important because

a It maximizes drive capacity

b It increases media transfer rates

c It eliminates guard bands

d a and b

e b and c

8 Disk drive performance elements are

a Seek, Media Transfer, Latency

b Seek, Media Transfer, Fly height

c Seek, Fly height, Latency

d Fly height, Media Transfer, Latency

9 Air bearings

a Eliminate head/disk/contaminant contact

b Are light weight

c Are sometimes coated with diamond-like carbon

d All of the above

e None of the above

10 Modern drives use

   a Integrated rotary positioners and servo motors

   b Integrated linear positioners and servo motors

   c Independent rotary positioners and servo motors

   d Independent linear positioners and servo motors

❐

5

Hard Disk Controllers

What This Chapter Is About

This chapter discusses hard disk controllers including their relationship to disk drives, system buses, BIOS, and system software. It provides an overview of what happens to requests that eventually result in disk I/O operations and explains how many current disk configuration problems arose from early PC designs. It also discusses how disk subsystem manufacturers bypass problems with varying approaches.

PC History

The original PC-XT contained a disk adapter that supported two ST506 fixed disks, each being one of four allowed types (5 MByte, 10 MByte, 15 MByte, or 25 MByte capacity). Users set disk controller DIP switches to specify what disk type each disk was so that BIOS could correctly identify and utilize them. During use, the controller resided in a system expansion bus slot and connected to one or two hard disks using two ribbon cables for each disk connection.

The IBM PC-AT allowed for two disks, each one being one of 14 allowed geometries. Users specified the disk types in a set-up program and subsequently stored the selection number in a NiCad battery-backed CMOS memory chip located on the motherboard. During the boot sequence, BIOS referenced the CMOS memory and built a BIOS Disk Parameter Table entry for each disk that completely specified the disk's geometry. Later PC-AT designs allowed for 30 disk types but soon even that flexibility fell far short of available options, giving rise to OEM utilities that provided support for additional drive types.

As PCs became more popular, disk drive products, variations, and incompatibilities increased. Eventually, disk subsystem developers over-ran the PC's design and abandoned the rigid controller/disk relationship dictated by early PC models that used the ST506/412 interfaces. SCSI and IDE/ATA disk drive manufacturers responded by migrating disk controller bus functions to the motherboard BIOS and disk controller electronics to disk drives, thereby blurring the previously clean distinction between disk controllers and disk drives. As an early example, Adaptec products such as its ACB-2070 (the first PC-XT RLL controller), avoided DIP switch limitations by developing an auto-configuration scheme.

Auto-configuration was enabled by embedding drive configuration information in spare header field bits on a drive's track zero. When power was applied to the system, the controller scanned the headers fields and later passed the information to BIOS during POST. Adaptec later enhanced the PC-AT market by having adapters temporarily store the disk parameter table in spare interrupt vectors before passing it to a null device driver during the boot sequence. This approach was critical for supporting ST412 interface drives using RLL encoding and ESDI drives.

Today, motherboard SCSI support is increasing, though SCSI disks still usually connect to SCSI bus adapters connected to expansion bus slots. In contrast, IDE/ATA disks completely eradicated the controller/drive distinction by allowing drives to connect to motherboard connectors that essentially are system bus extensions to a "ninth" ISA expansion slot (Figures 5-1, 5-2, and 5-3). BIOS producers

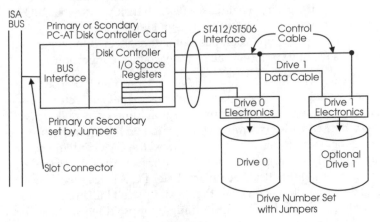

Figure 5-1.

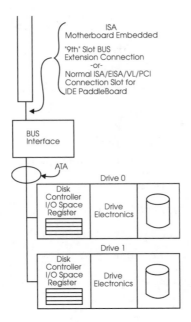

Figure 5-2.

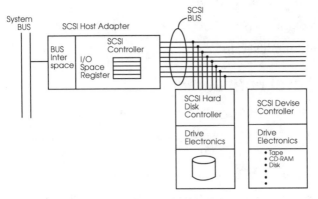

Figure 5-3.

responded to this hardware development and standardized I/O register specifications by integrating IDE fixed-disk BIOS functions into motherboard system BIOS. This increased disk drive intelligence, flexibility, and capabilities, allowing otherwise non-compliant disk drive subsystems to masquerade as "vanilla" disk subsystems. Nonetheless, the following discussion maintains the useful distinction between disk controllers and disk drives.

Disk Controller Functional Overview

Disk controllers sit between fixed disks and system buses and typically perform the following functions:

- Low-level formatting in expansion card BIOS
- In some systems, spindle rotation rate monitoring
- Actuator movement signaling (seek initiation)
- In some systems, servo read timing control
- Read/write selection and timing
- Encoding/decoding of serial (or parallel) digital data
- ID field verification (if the ID field exists)
- Error detection/correction/retry/recovery
- Data buffering between disk drive and host interface bus
- Mappings
- Caching
- DMA bus mastering
- Boot (int 19h)
- Int 13h BIOS calls

Low-Level Formatting

Low-level formatting is an operation that writes:

- Sector headers containing cylinder, head, sector, bad sector, and CRC or ECC information
- Dummy data and its ECC information

The format process writes the information using the disk drive's recording system (Chapter 4). Since formatting also writes the sectors, it can write track sectors in any order. However, for maximum performance sectors numbers should sequentially increase—called a *1:1 interleave.*

If a disk must have an interleave other than today's usual 1:1 interleave factor, the format step can also provide a designated interleave and separates sequential sectors with a fixed number of sectors, though programs can later perform interleaving at a different factor.

Note that it can be the case that a disk must be used only with the controller that formatted it—another good reason to combine disk controllers and disks. This is true for EIDE drives but notable exceptions are IDE and SCSI disk drives. Finally, some controllers will not allow programs to format their drives since the drives may contain critical geometry and otherwise proprietary information such as defect information and BIOS code. Storing BIOS code on a drive allows a controller to minimize its ROM by only placing boot code in it.

Spindle Rotation Monitoring

Some early non-PC disk drives used synchronous drive motors that locked their rotation rate to the 60 Hz AC frequency which resulted in 3600 RPM (or 1800 or 1200 RPM) spin rates. While synchronous drive motors were impractical for PC systems, early PC disks matched existing signal interfaces which meant they also exhibited 3600 RPM spin rates though they used servo controlled DC motors.

Some PC disk controllers contain spindle motor drive circuits that monitor the drive's spindle motor using a quartz crystal oscillator. Some of the more sophisticated ones monitor not only the rotational rate but how fast sectors appear under disk heads—an important consideration for multiple-zone recording disks. In other disk drives, spindle rate speed control is completely handled in drive electronics.

Actuator Movement Signaling (Seek Initiation)

All disk controllers, new and old, keep track of current cylinder position and initiate seeks via the drive's servo system. Disk controllers for old disk drives such as the ST412/ST506 (also known as ST412/506, ST506/412 or just the ST506), some of which used stepper motors, also sent the correct number of pulses to move the actuator the desired number of cylinders forward or backward. In contrast, modern servo drives only require a command to seek the desired number of cylinders forward or backward. In some disk drives, the servo control system microprocessor is also the controller microprocessor so a context switch to servo control mode is required. IDE/ATA drive controllers may accept cylinder seek commands. SCSI drive controllers accept LBA positioning requests; therefore, they must compute the correct cylinder to initiate a seek. Optional SCSI firmware can organize sector read/write operations in increasing or decreasing cylinder numbers for reduced seek latencies when multiple requests exist in the request queue, in a process known as elevator seeks.

Servo Read Timing Control

In some disk drives, one common state machine controls timing for both servo field sensing (a drive) and sector formatting (a controller function), further blurring controller/drive functions. In other disk drives, two state machines exist for timing control, one which controls servo read timing, another which controls sector timing.

Read/Write Selection and Timing

While read/write signal processing is imbedded in disk drive electronics, the controller plays the role of selecting the correct operation to be executed by the drive. It keeps track of head location within and between sectors and selects read and write operations when appropriate. When a read operation is selected, control passes to the read/write system in the drive to determine when bit timing has been achieved. After bit synchronization, control passes to synch detection circuitry to determine start of the data (or ID) field. This function may reside within the controller or within drive electronics, depending on the system. It sometimes precedes and sometimes follows the ENDEC (see below) depending on whether synchronization is executed on encoded or decoded data.

Encoding/Decoding of Serial (or Parallel) Digital Data

When it exists within the controller (sometimes it is included within the read/write system), the Encode/Decode function, sometimes called ENDEC, converts user data to encoded data. The encode process is based on the recording code in use by the drive's read/write system. All modern drives use run length limited (RLL) codes of one type or other and their discussion is beyond the scope of this book. The most widely used code as of this date is the so-called 2/3 rate 1,7 code using various encode tables, but other competitors exist and are also in use. One of the more recent is the 8/9 rate 0,4 or 0,4/4 code.

ID Field Verification (If ID Field Exists)

To locate the desired sector, the disk controller keeps a running track of sector addresses. When the selected sector appears under the head, the controller selects an ID field read operation to verify that the correct sector address has been reached. Cylinder and head addresses are also frequently verified. Possible sector substitution information is also read and interpreted. Similarly, if an ID field CRC exists, it is checked before verification information is accepted. If an ID field ECC exists, data is checked and perhaps corrected before verification information is accepted. Write operations use the same sector location process but the heads must switch from reading the sector ID field to writing data while the sector-header/data gap passes under the head.

A few of the more modern disk drives discard ID fields in favor of improved format efficiency, then rely on other methods to assure that the correct head, cylinder, and sector addresses have been reached and to discover replacement sectors when needed.

Error Detection/Correction/Retry/Recovery

After reading the sector data, the controller performs an ECC check on the data to verify data integrity. If the check fails, the controller attempts to correct the data using one of two approaches. Small errors are corrected on-the-fly within one sector time using hardware and the process is transparent tot the operating system. Larger errors still employ software algorithms using the ECC. After any correction attempt, the logic checks the result again. If the data is still corrupted, the controller may attempt to read the sector several times more until successful, perhaps with a head position offset in case the sector was written slightly off-track.

If the recovery operation is successful, the controller passes the data to the system along with a necessary ECC recovery indicator. Early MS-DOS versions would not accept data with correctable ECC errors, so retries were performed in an effort to retrieve error-free data. Later MS-DOS versions accepted sectors with correctable ECC errors, creating compatibility problems for many PC disk controller manufacturers. Certain controllers would stop sector data transfer following all ECC errors, even correctable ones. This was a problem when MS-DOS assumed that all correctable errors were repaired and that the entire data block was intact.

When a controller cannot recover the data, it reports a failure to the system. Note that the ECC information occupies additional bytes following each sector. The PC-XT used a four byte ECC strategy which could detect and repair single error bursts contained within 11 consecutive bits. The PC-AT used a seven byte ECC strategy which could detect and repair single error bursts contained within 17 consecutive bits. More modern drives can correct multiple error bursts of various lengths and number depending on the manufacturer's ECC system. When error bursts exceed the repairable length and/or number, the ECC can usually detect, but cannot repair them.

Data Buffering Between Disk Drive and Host Interface Bus

The ability of a disk drive to either store or deliver data cannot be synchronized with the ability of the host memory and interface bus to either send or receive data. Therefore, buffering is necessary. One of the principal functions of the controller is to provide data buffering using controller RAM memory. In some disk controllers, such memory is dual ported so drive data transfers to or from memory can proceed concurrently with bus/host memory data transfers and ECC corrections. In many other instances, less expensive DRAM or SRAM is used along with host and disk First-In-First-Out (FIFO) components which make the controller seem to behave like VRAM.

Mappings

As previously indicated, early PC designs specified a few allowable disk drive types that users could attach to their PC. These drive types had rigidly specified geometries which precluded zoned disk approaches. For multiple-zone recording disks to work, it was necessary for them to deceive system BIOS. These drives achieve this by masquerading as a rigid-geometry disk while possessing a flexible geometry. Besides boosting capacity, other type mappings boost disk performance.

Sector Mappings

To escape rigid-geometry requirements, drives resort to a technique variously named head translation, sector translation, head mapping, sector mapping, or translation mode—take your pick. Essentially, the controller represents its attached drives to the system as acceptable rigid-geometry drives but internally uses a completely different scheme. This allows it to translate system requests for its fictitious drives into genuine physical ones corresponding to genuine drive characteristics. It may determine the actual geometry by reading the drive's physical geometry specifications from a reserved drive track. Such controllers are referred to as auto-configuring.

In actuality, translation mode first appeared with early RLL disks that had 25 or more sectors per track. Various application programmers assumed all disk drives had 17 sectors per track like previous MFM drives. So their applications would not behave correctly with RLL drives. Today, MS-DOS can specify requests in one of two ways: by cylinder, head, and sector; or by logical block address.

As typically found in most computer systems, SCSI disk controllers and part of MS-DOS views any disk drive's sectors as a linear pool of logical sectors sequentially numbered from zero up to $2^{32} - 1$ (in MS-DOS versions 4.0 and later). So, abstraction translation has existed a long time since it is necessary to translate from logical blocks to geometrical physical addresses. Today's EIDE drives have abandoned CHS addressing for LBA (Logical Block Addressing) which references a sector's relative position on the drive rather than by its geometric CHS position.

Head and Cylinder Skewing

Head and cylinder skewing are low-level formatting approaches that improve head-switch and adjacent-cylinder seek response times. Essentially, the disk's low level formatting varies track start positions so that when a head-switch or adjacent-cylinder seek occurs, the switch duration matches the corresponding rotational delay, minimizing the apparent delay to the new track's first sector. Note that the head switch and adjacent-cylinder seek compensations are different since head switches take less time than track-to-track cylinder seeks in most drives.

Defect Mapping

Disk vendors extensively test disks during manufacturing and note defective sectors in a list written to the drive referred to as the P-list (on SCSI). Subsequently detected errors may be added to a grown list or G-list the drive controller manages. When the manufacturer formats a drive, it may create extra hidden sectors on each track or elsewhere that the controller substitutes for defective ones using one of two sector reallocation strategies.

In sector sparing, the controller marks the defective sectors header as defective and indicates the substitute sector's location. This creates an out-of-order sector and likely increased rotational delay—perhaps even additional seek time. In sector slipping, the controller marks the defective sector's header as bad. It then reads the entire track, reformats the track with new sector headers, eliminating defective sector(s), while leaving the remaining sectors in sequential order. This consumes a spare sector at the track's end, or perhaps cylinder's end, while minimizing rotational delay side effects since the sectors remain sequential. Finally, any controller that can perform such defect repair applies what is referred to as *hot fixes*.

Caching

With increased intelligence, drive controllers often try to capitalize on application disk reference locality by providing hardware caching exhibiting a variety of sophistication. Although the distinction is sometimes blurry, in increasing sophistication, they are:

Buffer: Buffers hold less than an entire track and potentially hold the next requested read sector or sectors. If not, the controller replaces the buffer's entire contents.

Track Buffer: Track buffers hold the entire track containing the last read sector which potentially holds the next requested sector. If not, the controller replaces the entire track buffer's contents. This may hold several sectors.

Read-Ahead Cache: Read-ahead caches hold the N sectors based on the last request.

Read Cache: Read caches potentially hold several tracks or track segments. The controller only replaces one segment of data at a time based on various strategies that are usually more sophisticated than track buffer approaches. The caches are also larger than track buffers.

Write-Through Cache: Write-through caches immediately write sectors to disk and then notify the system it has written the data. It holds a copy in the cache in case the system needs to read the data again.

Write-Back Cache: Write-back caches receive system write requests and data, then immediately signal write completion if the cache can hold the received sector data before the data is actually written to disk. The controller subsequently writes the sectors to disk, usually during the first available idle time. While the system processor still experiences command-building, data transfer, and command complete processing delays, it avoids experiencing seek and rotational delays. There is a limit to the number of requests this strategy queues before the space recovery process may delay the processor if write requests arrive too rapidly. It also puts the system in danger of losing data due to power failures. (If the cache is volatile (the usual case) losing power before writing the data to disk can cause data loss.)

For all of the last three true caches, some form of data replacement policy is chosen, e.g., LRU (least recently used), LFU (least frequently used), or perhaps other policy chosen by the manufacturer. Any of the above caches may be:

- Fully associative
- Direct mapped
- Set associative

as defined in Chapter 11.

Summary

Disk controllers provide the translation between detected, digitized data (either encoded or decoded) and user data which is transmittable to the host's memory. Today's IDE controllers reside on their respective disk units to provide intelligent media exploitation such as geometry translation that neutralize most BIOS and MS-DOS restrictions.

SCSI adapters such as the Adaptec AHA-1542® provide head translation BIOS functions which software references. Other SCSI controller functions typically reside on their respective disk units as they do for IDE controllers. High-end disk controllers often have hardware caches which can substantially enhance performance if their operation is compatible with their request characteristics. Regardless of cache size, poorly conceived caching strategies may negate performance advantages and may introduce performance penalties due to their overhead.

Chapter Questions

1 Disk controllers control

   a Seek initiation

   b Encoding/Decoding

   c Read/Write selection and timing

   d All of the above

2 Controllers may not allow surface reformatting because

   a Zone information is lost

   b It wears out guard bands

   c Caches cannot handle the traffic

   d None of the above

3 The servo system

   a Provides electrical inductance

   b Monitors data transfer timings

   c Keeps track of current cylinder position

   d All of the above

4 Synch detection circuits

   a Synchronize cache flushes and rotational positioning

   b Determine the start of the data or ID field

   c Monitor servo information during seeks

   d Minimize read delays during ECC error correction

5 Head and cylinder skewing

   a Improve head-switch and adjacent-cylinder seek response times

   b Offsets uneven thermal component expansions

   c Minimize zone guard-band inefficiencies

6   A cache that immediately writes sectors to cache and then notifies the system it has written the data is a

   a   Write-back cache

   b   Write-through cache

   c   Write-over cache

   d   Write-under cache

7   Defective sectors are listed in the

   a   Disk directory

   b   Disk partition list

   c   The G-list

   d   The R-list

8   Disk caches may be

   a   Set associative

   b   Direct mapped

   c   Fully associative

   d   a and b

   e   All of the above

9   ENDECs

   a   Are incompatible with MFM encoding

   b   Signal End-of-ECC

   c   Are no longer popular

   d   Convert user data to encoded data

10   IDE disk drives

   a   Can connect to a bus extension connector

   b   Integrate disk controllers and disks

   c   Allow close capability matching of controllers and disk
drives

   d   All of the above

   e   Only a and b

❑

6

Other Rotating Storage

What This Chapter Is About

This chapter provides a brief overview of the following rotating media storage devices:

- Floppy disk drives

- Bernoulli drives

- Floptical drives

- Write-Once Read-Many (WORM) drives

- Magneto Optical drives

- Phase Change Optical drives

- CD-ROM drives (in depth)

Floppy Disk Drives

Floppy disk drives are read/write devices that utilize removable, flexible magnetic media called *floppy disks*. Floppy disk drives provide from 125 KBytes to 250 KBytes/sec throughput. Diskette storage capacities range from 160 KBytes to several MBytes and future technology continually pushes capacities higher.

Like hard disks, floppy disk drives use sectors and tracks to store data as well as CRCs to detect sector errors. When most floppy disk drives are idle, they stop rotating to conserve power and minimize head/media contact. Subsequent accesses must wait for the media to achieve correct rotation speed. Because of their average 200 ms access rates, slow rotational speed and low densities, floppy disks are significantly slower than today's hard disks—though the drives and media are very inexpensive. Their capacity is typically less than one percent of a CD-ROM disk.

Actual diskette capacity can sometimes vary since some diskette drives are *soft sectored* (allow varying number of sectors on a track). Diskette drives usually use an index hole in the diskette media to determine track starts. Some old diskette drives require an index hole for each sector start which fixes the number of sectors per track and is referred to as *hard-sectoring*.

Bernoulli Drives

Bernoulli drives use removable 5 1/4 inch diameter, 44 to 150 MByte, flexible disks housed in a plastic cartridge. As the disks rotate the read/write heads float close to the flexible media on a filtered-air cushion—making it a floppy disk and hard disk hybrid. Filtering the air is important because it keeps most particles outside the cartridge. When a disk is inserted, the drive spins faster than in normal operation to clean the media surface. Because the media is flexible, it can flex when unwanted particles get between it and the read/write heads. This prevents head crashes and makes the devices very shock-resistant.

Current Bernoulli drives offer 18 ms access times, 2.67 MByte/sec maximum transfer rates, and 1.92 MByte/sec sustained transfer rates. The drives stop spinning after a user-selectable inactivity period. The spin-down requires three seconds and a subsequent spin-up requires five seconds. Bernoulli drives are available from Iomega Corporation (800-777-6654).

Floptical® Drives

Floptical drives combine optical and magnetic technology. They have been commercially available for some time but have achieved limited success because of their high media cost. Optics precisely detect permanent track servo information on 3.5 inch cartridges, allowing track densities to jump from 135 TPI densities to approximately 1,000 TPI. This provides over 20 MByte capacities. Floptical drives have 135 ms seek times and can also read/write standard 3.5 inch magnetic diskettes using a second read/write head set.

Write-Once Read-Many (WORM) Drives

WORM drive read write heads use lasers to create dark spots (phase changes) on 800 MByte capacity metallic platters which the same read/write head lasers detect. While magnetic encodings are usually only good for about 10 years, WORM data is good for decades. Typically WORM drives are SCSI devices and media is not interchangeable across vendors.

Magneto Optical (Erasable Optical) Drives

Magneto Optical drives read, write, and modify 3 1/2 and 5 1/4 inch cartridges with as much as one GByte capacity. Powerful lasers heat a media track to approximately 300 degrees Fahrenheit (above the media's Curie temperature) on one revolution as a magnetic head sets all magnetic domains to the same polarity. During the next revolution the magnetic head writes an opposite polarity only on areas reheated by the laser. Focusing the light heats a tiny area, providing improved recording densities and emerging drives do not require the pre-write operation.

A second lower power read-laser reflects light off the media. The light rotates clockwise or counter-clockwise depending on the media's polarity and sensors decode the light polarity. It is believed the media wears out after approximately 1,000,000 writes but products have not existed long enough to know for sure. Finally, unlike phase change optical drives, magneto optical drives usually observe either the ISO A or ISO B international standard (which are themselves incompatible).

Phase Change Optical Drives

Phase change drives use media that changes from an amorphous state to a crystalline state and back depending on laser energy strength. High laser temperatures result in amorphous states while lower temperatures result in crystalline states. The different media states produce different reflectivity for lower-power laser read operations. Because encoding occurs on a single pass, phase change optical drives have inherently higher write speeds than magneto optical drives. However, phase change optical media eventually wears out after about 100,000 uses (one tenth as many as with magneto optical media) and there is no phase change optical ISO standard.

CD-ROM Drives

CD-ROM Hardware

Phillips and Sony developed the first Compact Disk, Read Only Memory (CD-ROM) products in 1980 as audio stereo components. Adapted to computer use, these devices now provide 680 MByte removable media and most likely will be the preferred distribution media for entertainment, publishing and software products. Single speed CD-ROM drives provide approximately 150 KBytes/sec data rates with seek times taking over a second in some cases. Double (2X), triple (3X), quadruple (4X), and 6X speed drives provide 300, 450, 600, and 900 KByte/sec data rates respectively. Many installed CD-ROM drives use SCSI interfaces, though many others are available with non-standard interfaces and custom device drivers. Most are now appearing with the ATAPI interfaces.

Unlike hard drives, CD-ROM drives use lasers to generate surface reflections off mirrored CD-ROM platter surfaces. This allows CD-ROM designers to place *photo detectors* (media decoders analogous to disk read/write heads) far from media platters—versus hard disks that require tight proximity of heads to hard disk media to detect faint magnetic variations. In addition, rather than use concentric tracks, CD-ROMs use one long spiraling track that begins near the center spindle slowly and winds its way towards the outer edge. Finally, most CD-ROM disks are created in their entirety during a single molding process. Newer CD-ROM discs allow adding data at a later date. These newer CD-ROMs are referred to as *multisession CD-ROMs*.

CD-ROM Media

CD-ROM discs appear in various forms but share common properties. While most hard disks utilize *Constant Angular Velocity (CAV)*, rotating their media at constant RPM, CD-ROMs utilize *Constant Linear Velocity (CLV)*. Here media rotation speeds depend on radial head position which experiences different media path circumferences at different head positions. CD-ROM media's constant linear velocity for head operations produces input data at a constant rate, so each media revolution presents maximum data which simultaneously maximizes storage utilization. This is equivalent to a huge number of zones. CLV's disadvantage is long access time experienced during media acceleration and deceleration phases.

On CD-ROMs, data records exist on one continuously spiraling track (as opposed to numerous hard drive concentric tracks) with data addressing expressed in sectors and angular minutes and seconds. To retrieve data, CDs approximately position their heads, adjust motor speed, read a sector address, and make positioning refinements until locating the desired address. In contrast, since hard drives use CAV, they simply position their heads over the requested track and wait for the desired sector to rotate to the head.

Standard size CDs share a common physical format:

- A 120 mm diameter disc

- A 15 mm center hole

- A 1.2 mm thickness

CD-ROM media is typically a mass-produced polycarbonate disc, covered with an extremely thin reflective aluminum layer, and protective plastic labeling film. The innermost 6 mm surrounding the center hole is the *clamping area*. The next approximately 4 mm wide *lead-in area* contains the disc's *volume table of contents* (*VTOC*). The next 33 mm contains program data on a single long spiral comprising approximately 20,000 revolutions. Tracks progress from the disc's inner portion toward the edge. A 1 mm *lead-out area* signifies the disc end. A 3 mm area around the edge is reserved for handling and contains no data.

Although a CD's program area only contains one long physical track, software logically organizes it as one to 99 tracks. A given track only contains one type of information, such as digital audio or computer data, but different tracks can contain other data types.

CD surfaces consist of pits and lands (the normal surface level between pits). Pits and lands do not represent actual on/off bit binary data as one might expect. Pit and land transitions and their associated timings represent *channel bits*. Fourteen channel bits comprise a *data symbol* that translates to traditional 8-bit data values. This data redundancy provides improved accuracy. The 8-bit data to 14-bit channel encoding process, called *eight-to-fourteen modulation* (*EFM*), results in *pits* and *lands* during the *mastering process*. Each CD-ROM player ROM contains a ROM lookup table that reverses the process to decode modulated data.

The channel bits organize into groups called *frames* with 588 channel bits per frame. Of the 588, 200 represent data, and the remaining 388 are for control and error correction. The 200 bits can contain either 24 bytes of computer data or twelve 16-bit audio samples (six stereo samples). In addition to 14 channel bits for each data byte, frames also contain:

- 24 synchronization channel bits

- 14 channel bits for each of eight 8-bit error correction parity words

- 14 channel bits of an 8-bit control and display word

- 3 merge bits separating each data symbol

Groups of 98 frames comprise:

- *Blocks* in CD audio

- *Sectors* in CD-ROM and CD-I (CD-Interactive systems)

Blocks or sectors are the smallest addressable CD technology unit. Every second, single speed CD rotations produce 75 blocks or sectors, yielding 7,350 frames per second. *Cross Interleaved Reed-Solomon Code (CIRC)* provides error correction.

CIRC combines three error correction methods:

- During encoding, *cross-coding* shuffles bits out of sequence using a key. During playback, the key helps arrange bits in their original order. Shuffling disperses long error effects throughout the data, allowing error correction during decoding.

- *Interleaving* helps minimize large errors by delaying data encoding for fixed time periods before combining it with the input data stream.

- *Reed-Solomon coding* corrects small anomalies commonly resulting from disc surface scratches or dirt.

1980 Red Book

The compact disc industry started in 1980 when Philips and Sony introduced the *Compact Disc Digital Audio Standard*, an international standard (ISO 10149) published with a red cover, commonly known as the *Red Book*. Because all audio discs conform to the Red Book Standard, all audio compact discs play in all audio compact disc players. This interchangeability is a major factor in CD music industry growth, with hundreds of companies marketing players worldwide.

The Red Book defines the *CD Digital Audio* (*CD-DA*) music track format which stores audio information only. Here, CDs may contain one or more music tracks which conform to the CD-DA (Audio) standard. These tracks are further subdivided into blocks (sectors) that are 1/75th of a second in duration containing 2352 audio data bytes. In addition to the 2352 audio data bytes, the Red Book specifies two error detection and error correction code layers, referred to as EDC/ECC). If CD player heads cannot read a damaged disc, the CD player uses the EDC/ECC to recreate the music. Within each sector are 98 control bytes, referred to as subchannel information, which contain timing information indicating song playing time.

Red Book CD+Graphics

Original Red Book specifications did not utilize subcode channels R through W and set their data values to zero. This wasted more than 24 MByte of audio CD space. Several specification addenda defined subcode channels R through W for CD+Graphics use. The intended CD Graphics application displayed still images while music played and required separate CD player subcode output for graphic output. Suggested uses ranged from multilingual text and electronic sheet music, to album graphics on separate channels. Japanese karaoke sing-along devices used the capacity for lyrics. Unfortunately, the feature's maximum image resolution was 288 x 192 in 16 colors and images required an unacceptable 7 seconds to load. Manufacturers eventually dropped the subcode jacks on U.S. products, effectively dooming CD+Graphics.

1984 Yellow Book

Seeing Red Book specifications restrain CD-ROM's tremendous digital storage potential, Sony and Phillips introduced the CD-ROM Yellow Book in 1984, which superseded the Red Book. Significant extensions exploited information data areas for uses other than digital audio and introduced more stringent error correction routines required for data storage applications.

Although new CD-DA disc bit error rates are one per 10^{-12} bits, scratched or dirty disc bit error rates could present error rates worse than one per 10^{-9} bits. Such error rates are tolerable for audio data where occasional annoying clicks are acceptable but they are categorically unacceptable in computer applications where single bit errors could spell disaster.

To decrease bit error rates, Sony and Philips provided an additional error correction layer by adding Error Detection Code (EDC) and Error Correction Code (ECC) bytes in each sector.

Yellow Book Mode 1

Yellow Book Mode 1 utilizes 2,048 byte data fields with 288 bytes for additional error correction. A method called EDC/ECC (Error Detection Coding/Error Correction Coding) supplements the standard CIRC method which is sufficient for audio, but insufficient to insure computer data integrity. Nominal Mode 1 disc capacity with all 270,000 sectors containing 2,048 bytes of data exceeds 527 MByte.

Yellow Book Mode 2

Yellow Book Mode 2 does not add any error correction above standard CICR error correction, and thus provides a full 2,336 user bytes per sector. Mode 2 applications often do not require high data integrity such as audio and still or moving images. As a rule, most CD-ROMs use Mode 1.

Mode 2 differs from Mode 1 in effective storage capacity and data retrieval speed. While CD-DA CD-ROMs hold 74 minutes of audio, manufacturers often have trouble accurately recording more than 60 minutes. Yellow Book Mode 1, at 2048 user bytes per sector, stores 552,960,000 bytes (527 MByte) and reads data at 153,600 bytes (150 KByte) per second (at standard spindle speed). Yellow Book Mode 2 provides 630,720,00 bytes (601 MByte) storage with 175,200 (171 KByte) per second data rates. A disc may have both modes on it, but can only use one mode for any given track.

Various vendor marketing departments exploit this mode capacity difference by claiming 175 KByte/sec transfer rates—implying their products are faster than others only claiming 150 KByte/sec. While product performance differences could exist, beware that CD-ROM product throughput measurements may use different modes. This warning also applies to drives operating at higher (2X, 3X, 4X and 6X) spindle speeds, with analogous claims. Since standardized rotation rates constrain sustained transfer rates, there is little differentiation between drives of the same speed.

High Sierra and ISO 9660

While the Yellow Book ensured data encoding/decoding, frame, and sector architecture uniformity, operating system data access remained undefined, generating cross-platform compatibility problems. Consequently, shortly after the Yellow Book's 1984 announcement, representatives from a few key manufacturers including Apple, DEC, Hitachi, Microsoft, 3M, and Philips gathered near Lake Tahoe at a Sierra Nevada mountain resort to develop a standard file organization and indexing method enabling cross-platform access. This successful effort was named *High Sierra* and standardizes a universal Volume Table Of Contents (*VTOC*) organization and positioning, as well as logical sectors, logical blocks, fixed-length records, variable-length records, and character encoding schemes. An amended version became the ISO 9660 standard.

A VTOC holds information representing each file's direct path, avoiding painfully slow CD-ROM speed searches through directory layers. High Sierra also provides a mechanism for multiple CD-ROMs to act as multiple volume sets, thereby extending application data access. Host systems with drivers that can translate between native operating system and the High Sierra standard can locate and access any High Sierra CD-ROM file, though the data file itself must still be compatible with applications for meaningful utilization.

As an example, ASCII text files pose no cross-platform problems, but PCs must grapple with Macintosh PICT files, taking care to reverse numeric byte values as appropriate. For this reason, many High Sierra CD-ROMs contain redundant image libraries in a variety of popular formats. As an additional example, a potential MS-DOS compatibility problem comes from allowed filename characters. The High Sierra spec recognizes a subset of valid MS-DOS file name characters, prohibiting characters such as !, @, and $.

Red Book and Yellow Book—Mixed-Mode

When CDs have both data and audio tracks, they are *mixed-mode* discs. The most common mixed-mode disc has a Yellow Book CD-ROM *Mode 1 Track* as the first track with the remaining disc tracks being normal Red Book audio tracks.

A normal audio CD player can play this type of mixed-mode. However, playing a CD-ROM Mode 1 track produces static noise at full volume, possibly damaging speakers and eardrums. Some of the newer players mute the CD-ROM track.

The following table shows a sample mixed-mode disc track layout:

Track #	Track Type	Contents
1	Mode 1	Computer Data
2	Audio	Song 1
3	Audio	Song 2
4	Audio	Song 3

1986 Green Book and CD-I

In 1986 Philips and Sony again met to address incompatibilities with:

- Operating systems
- File formats
- Hardware such as display adapters and audio cards

This produced the CD-I (Compact Disc Interactive) Green Book which is an extension of the Yellow Book CD-ROM Mode 2. The difference here is that the CD-I spec encompasses system hardware as well as the CD-I media. To standardize on the single media format and the programs in it, the designers chose to specify a complete processing environment based on the Motorola 68000 microprocessor family.

According to this specification, CD-I players must have the following:

- OS9 RTOS operating system
- 16-bit 68000-based microprocessor
- CD-ROM drive with PCM decoder and DAC capable of handling CD-DA audio.
- 1 MByte RAM minimum, with expansion capabilities
- Video processor for decoding and displaying various format graphics
- Audio processor for decoding various audio formats
- User input device

Here, the CD-I mode track does not appear in the disc's table of contents, preventing audio players from inadvertently playing the CD-I track. A CD-I system consists of a stand-alone player connected to a TV. The standard also allows interleaving computer data and compressed audio on the same track, greatly improving the ability to synchronize them. With sufficient available memory, both audio and images appear simultaneously to users, significantly enhancing their experience.

Standardizing the operating system ensures all CD-I players can access all CD-I discs. All CD-I files must be created in or converted to RTOS-accessible files. RTOS real-time aspects handle synchronizing and prioritizing multimedia graphics, text, audio, video, and associated data. Like all CD devices, CD-I plays standard audio CD-DAs without any problems.

CD-I supports six digital audio format types—three quality levels in either mono or stereo. These quality levels allow audiovisual producers to trade sound quality for data storage and throughput. All use Adaptive Delta Pulse Code Modulation (ADPCM)—a technique that encodes audio according to changes between amplitude values rather than the absolute values. Consequently, fewer bits convey audio data at a given quality:

- *Level A* audio offers approximate LP quality, requiring about half the data as Red Book audio (CD-DA).

- *Level B* audio is equivalent to the best FM broadcasts.

- *Level C* audio offers quality similar to average portable cassette decks.

A total of 16 channels, each providing 72 minutes of audio, are available —though this consumes full disc capacity. The channels collectively provide from 2 hours of Level A stereo audio, to 19 hours of relatively continuous Level C audio. Alternately, tracks can provide narration tracks in 16 different languages. The higher quality levels employ several channels simultaneously.

CD-I Audio Formats					
Audio Level	Resolution	Sampling Rate	Bandwidth	Concurrent Channels	Storage for One Minute Stereo
CD-DA	16-bit	44.1 KHz	20 KHz	2 Stereo pair	10.09 MB
CD-I Level A	8-bit	37.8 KHz	17 KHz	2 Stereo pair or 4 mono	4.33 MB
CD-I Level B	4-bit	37.8 KHz	17 KHz	4 Stereo pair or 8 mono	2.16 MB
CD-I Level C	4-bit	18.9 KHz	8.5 KHz	8 Stereo pair or 6 mono	1.08 MB

This chart refers to sampling rates in KHz. Audio format requires:

- Every audio second requires 75 data blocks.

- Every block has 98 frames.

- Every frame has 24 8-bit monaural samples.

- Four symbols provide four monaural samples or one 16-bit stereo sample—one left and one right.

- Every frame therefore provides six stereo channel samples.

- Every block therefore provides 588 (6 x 98) stereo channel samples.

- Every frame therefore provides 44,100 (6x98x75) stereo channel samples at a 44.1 KHz sampling rate.

Several image resolutions are available and offer reduced quality video and storage requirements:

CD-I Video Formats		
Video Standard	Normal Resolution	High Resolution
NTSC	360 x 240	720 x 480
PAL	384 x 280	768 x 460
Compatible	384 x 280	768 x 460

CD-I players provide three composite video outputs—NTSC, PAL, and a compatible format NTSC and PAL both translate to their format. Unfortunately, the compatible image output's aspect ratio does not match either NTSC or PAL aspect ratios. So, displayed compatible format images appear slightly stretched vertically on NTSC systems, or slightly squashed on PAL systems. Thus, the compatible format is best in international productions requiring both NTSC and PAL viewing.

CD-I's heavy integrated-media emphasis facilitates interleaving data such as error-sensitive text and less sensitive audio on the same track—though it allows only one mode per track. This motivated developing CD-I Mode 2's Form 1 and Form 2:

- *Form 1* provides the same 2,048 byes of user data per sector as CD-ROM Yellow Book Mode 2 complete with the same EDC/ECC error correction. The 1986 Green Book added a new 8-byte sector subheader right behind the header. This subheader is where most of the additional data types are described and the interleave information is defined.

- *Form 2* offers no error correction and is similar to CD-ROM Yellow Book Mode 2 except that headers consume eight bytes, allowing 2328 user data byes per sector.

CD-I discs have only one Mode 2 data track—track 0. This track potentially spans the entire disc. Different tracks can have various data types, some of which can be designated as normal (sent to RAM) and some of which can be designated as real-time (prioritized and interleaved). A CD-I disc can also incorporate CD-DA tracks beginning with Track 0.

1989 CD-ROM XA

One computer multimedia problem is that multimedia content often demands simultaneous sound and video, though computers typically only access one type of data at a time. Consequently, applications separately load graphics and audio into DRAM and display graphics as audio plays. Sony and Microsoft addressed this clumsy problem in 1989 when they introduced a Yellow Book extension referred to as CD-ROM Extended Architecture (CD-ROM XA). Naturally, this specification did not require Motorola 68000 processors or the OS/9 RTOS operating system.

Microsoft realized some Green Book CD-I specified formats might be useful, particularly the ability to retrieve 2,048 bytes of Form 1 error-corrected data as specified via the High Sierra System file format. Microsoft was also interested in interleaving the new audio formats with other material and the resulting increased disc audio capacity. Philips now refers to the XA format as a *bridge disc*, because consumers and computer users can both use it. Kodak subsequently chose the XA format for its Photo CD® system.

Yellow Book Mode 1 specifies computer data formats. Yellow Book Mode 2 specifies compressed audio and video/picture data. The XA extension defined the *XA Mode 2 Format* and applied to computer data, compressed audio, and video/picture data. All XA tracks are Yellow Book Mode 2. Similar to the Green Book Mode 2 Form 1 and Form 2, XA Mode 2 Form 1 has the 3rd layer of EDC/ECC for computer data. XA Mode 2 Form 2 does not, and is used for compressed audio, video and pictures. Normal uncompressed CD-DA Red Book audio cannot reside on an XA track.

XA allows computer data and audio data to reside on the same track. Computer data can reside on the track as Form 1, and audio and/or video/picture data can reside on the same track as Form 2 data. Because both Form 1 and Form 2 are XA Mode 2 Format, they can exist on the same track. With the proper Form 1 and Form 2 interleaving, tracks can gracefully blend audio, video, and computer data—important to sophisticated multimedia applications.

In contrast, mixed-mode discs have computer and audio data on different tracks. CD-ROM drives reading a mixed-mode disc cannot read computer data while playing audio. The XA disc has compressed audio and computer data interleaved on the same track, so it read, the computer data and plays the audio at the same time. This is the advantage of the XA standard.

1989 Photo CD and CD-ROM/XA

In 1989, Eastman Kodak Co. and Philips developed a still-image storage system known as Photo CD. Photo CD Systems electronically scan photograph negatives and store digitized images on CDs at various resolutions. Kodak's Photo CD players, Philips's CD-I players or CD-ROM/XA drives display the digital images.

Each CD-ROM-XA scanned negative is in a Kodak-proprietary compressed image file format known as *Image Pac*. These become ISO 9660 files with CD-ROM/XA Mode 2, Form 1 sectors. The disc is an Orange Book Part 2 Hybrid Disc, enabling photographs to be written in several passes, called sessions, as photos are subsequently added. Additionally, the disc uses the CD-Bridge disc format, allowing both CD-I and CD-ROM/XA players to read it.

Orange Book CD-R

All previously discussed CD-ROM standards are for Read-Only discs. Disc users cannot add, delete, or otherwise modify disc data content. The Orange Book defines a CD type that allows users to add audio and/or data to the disc. Part 1 of the Orange Book describes a CD-MO (Compact Disc-Magneto Optical) disc where the data can be written, erased, and re-written. Part 2 of the Orange Book describes a CD-WO (Compact Disc-Write Once) disc where the data can be written but not erased or re-written.

Chapter Questions

1 CD-ROM drives
   a Use CAV
   b May contain over 1024 tracks
   c Use high temperature lasers to melt the media surface
   d a and b
   e None of the above

2 The 1980 Red Book
   a Has been superseded by the Green Book
   b Was abandoned
   c Is for music CDs
   d Defines image formats for color video

3 The High Sierra format
   a Was defined near Lake Tahoe USA
   b Defines variable length records
   c Provides cross-system data compatibility
   d Standardizes VTOC formats
   e a, b, and d

4 CD-I

a Stands for Compact Disk Interactive

b Uses the OS9 operating system

c Requires a CD-ROM drive

d All of the above

5 CD-I audio supports

a Three quality levels

b Mono and stereo

c Absolute value encoding

d a and b

6 CD-ROM XA

a Requires Motorola 68000 processors

b Requires the OS9 operating system

c Allows computer data and audio data on the same disk

d a and c

❑

7

SCSI Primer

What This Chapter Is About

SCSI is an acronym for the *Small Computer System Interface*. The 1986 ANSI X3.131 standard defines this technology's first variation, referred to as SCSI-1. Though implementations had existed for years, in 1994, the ANSI X3.131 committee finished a 462 page specification defining the second variant, referred to as SCSI-2. Others exist (Table 7-1) and as of this writing, the committee is currently developing the SCSI-3 specification. Since these specifications share many designs, this chapter focuses on SCSI-2 and its variations that include *Fast-SCSI*, *Wide-SCSI*, and *Fast-and-Wide SCSI*. Therefore *SCSI* means *SCSI-2* in the following text unless otherwise qualified.

Table 7-1: SCSI Flavors

SCSI Flavor	Data Bus Width	Bus MHz	Max Speed MBytes/sec
SCSI-1	8	-	3
SCSI-2	8	5	5
Fast SCSI-2	8	10	10
Fast and Wide SCSI-2	16	10	20
Ultra SCSI	8 or 16	20	20 or 40

SCSI Background

Chapter 2's PC motherboard and BIOS discussion illustrated that early PCs could natively work with few disk types. For example, the PC-XT could only natively work with the following BIOS-defined disk types:

Table 7-2: PC-XT Disk Models

Disk Type	Cylinders	Heads	Sectors/Track	Capacity
0	306	2	17	5 MBytes
1	375	8	17	25 MBytes
2	306	6	17	15 MBytes
3	306	4	17	10 MBytes

For years, PC BIOS disk logic rejected disk access requests for cylinders beyond cylinder 1023. Consequently, machine BIOS routines were tightly coupled to attached disk characteristics, exhibiting *device dependencies*. As disk technology rapidly evolved and disk capacities dramatically increased, this approach became increasingly untenable.

For example, early low-end PC disks used MFM recording technology and were (incorrectly) referred to as MFM disks. As technology progressed, RLL eventually replaced MFM and was subsequently superseded by ESDI technology which gave way to IDE technology. Each disk technology required new disk adapter cards. Meanwhile, bus technology moved from 8-bit PC buses, to 16-bit PC AT ISA buses, to Micro Channel buses, to EISA buses, to VESA Local Buses, and to today's PCI buses.

Clearly, both PC disk and bus designs were very turbulent. Disk technology advances often meant disk or disk adapter obsolescence or both, presenting users with chronic migration problems to new technologies. While disk and other peripheral designers could do little to effect bus designs, they could cooperate on a peripheral subsystem interface definition that partially insulated users from bus design technology impacts by decoupling peripheral designs from bus designs. This would provide unrivaled peripheral attachment flexibility, allowing users to capitalize on technology advancements while preserving existing peripheral investments. And, this is precisely what SCSI accomplishes.

SCSI Overview

SCSI provides a well-defined bus that is independent of computer system buses. This bus is a shared, contention-based resource. Unlike system buses, a SCSI bus contains no clock signal, allowing data transfers to accommodate different speed devices with no impact on devices with faster transfer rates.

The SCSI definition allows up to eight SCSI *device* bus connections or up to 16 connections for the Wide SCSI variation. A SCSI device connects to a SCSI bus via its *controller* and may be either a peripheral device or a host computer. Thus, eight hosts can connect to a single bus that provides communication with one another. More typically, one or more hosts connect to a SCSI bus with one or more connecting peripheral devices. This allows connecting host computers to access peripherals and users to upgrade or supplement the device-pool with minimum disruption to already connected SCSI devices.

SCSI devices are either *initiators*, *targets*, or both. Initiators are devices which initiate and deliver requests to targets for fulfillment. If a device can be both an initiator and target, it may only behave on the bus as one at any instant. Target controllers have from one to eight *logical units* numbered zero through seven. The SCSI standard requires targets contain logical unit zero. Other logical units are optional and may be present in any combination. In the case of tape drive subsystems, a tape drive controller may control several tape drives that each have their own logical unit number ranging from zero to seven. Some RAID designs utilize logical units as well.

SCSI devices communicate with one another using a well defined protocol involving sequential states called *phases*. SCSI buses can only be in one phase at a time and buses enter most phases only after exiting previous specific states. Initiators communicate with targets to deliver requests called *commands*. Thereafter, the targets control request resolution. After receiving a command, but before fulfilling it, a target may disconnect from the bus. This allows initiating devices to perform other work (such as issuing or responding to previous commands to/from other targets) as the target performs request fulfillment internal processing for requests.

SCSI Buses

The SCSI standard defines two electrical bus variations: a *single ended* bus and a *differential* bus. The 8-bit version of each use 50 wire cables and connectors. Each SCSI signal is paired with a second wire which is grounded for single ended buses and is the opposite signal level for differential buses.

The differential bus type uses 41 of the 50 wires. With differential SCSI buses, devices detect signal voltage levels by comparing matched wire-pairs. While this provides longer cable lengths (up to 25 meters or over 80 feet total) and increased noise immunity, using differential SCSI buses increases costs. So, differential buses are not typically found in desktop systems or to connect disks within an enclosure, though they are used for external device connections.

Single ended Fast SCSI buses use 18 of the 50 cable wires and can be up to 3 meters (about 9 feet) long. Of the remaining 32 wires, 26 wires are grounded to help abate signal interference, four are reserved, one is open, and one provides power from initiators to required terminators. Terminators at each cable end mitigate unwanted signal reflections through electrical impedance matching and are essential for proper signaling. Their absence usually results in improper bus operation and phantom symptoms that appear and disappear over time.

On single ended buses, SCSI devices communicate with each other by *asserting* or *deasserting* voltage levels on the 18 wires. An asserted voltage level between zero and .8 volts indicates a *true* or binary 1 (one) bit value. Deasserted voltage levels between 2.0 and 5.25 volts indicates a *false* or binary 0 (zero) value. When no device asserts a wire's voltage level, the terminators insure the voltage level indicates a *false* or binary 0 (zero) signal value. In summary, the two essential elements in setting up a SCSI bus are

1   Exactly two devices, each located at a bus end, have terminators.

2   Each device has a unique bus ID.

Table 7-3 illustrates the 18 signal pin numbers, their signal abbreviation, name, use, and whether initiators and targets can assert the signals. The minus sign preceding the signal abbreviation indicates the value is a binary 1 or *true* when it is close to zero volts. This approach increases bus performance. Some signals are *OR-tied* meaning that when a signal is Or-tied one or more devices can simultaneously assert the signal. Other signals are *non-OR-tied* meaning only one device can assert it simultaneously.

Data Bus Parity

Initiators and targets use the SCSI data bus as a 9-bit wide bidirectional bus to exchange data. Eight bits provide a parallel data path for single data-bytes. A ninth data bus signal provides parity checks that helps detect transmission errors during the selection, reselection, and information transfer phases optional in SCSI-1 but mandatory in SCSI-2. The SCSI parity signal insures that the number of

Table 7-3: SCSI Bus Signal Assignments

Pin Number	Abbr.	Name	Use	Initiator Asserted?	Target Asserted?	OR Tied?
2	-DB(0)	Data Bus Bit Zero	Data Bus Transfer	Y	Y	N
4	-DB(1)	Data Bus Bit One	Data Bus Transfer	Y	Y	N
6	-DB(2)	Data Bus Bit Two	Data Bus Transfer	Y	Y	N
8	-DB(3)	Data Bus Bit Three	Data Bus Transfer	Y	Y	N
10	-DB(4)	Data Bus Bit Four	Data Bus Transfer	Y	Y	N
12	-DB(5)	Data Bus Bit Five	Data Bus Transfer	Y	Y	N
14	-DB(6)	Data Bus Bit Six	Data Bus Transfer	Y	Y	N
16	-DB(7)	Data Bus Bit Seven	Data Bus Transfer	Y	Y	N
18	-DB(P)	Data Bus Parity Bit	Data Bus Transfer Parity	Y	Y	N
32	-ATN	Attention	Requests Msg Out Phase	Y	N	N
36	-BSY	Busy	Bus Busy Indicator	Y	Y	Y
38	-ACK	Acknowledge	Byte Transfer Acknowledge	Y	N	N
40	-RST	Reset	Resets Bus	Y	Y	Y
42	-MSG	Message	Information Transfer Phase	N	Y	N
44	-SEL	Select	Select or Reselect Phase	Y	Y	Y
46	-C/D	Control/Data	Information Transfer Phase	N	Y	N
48	-REQ	Request	Byte Transfer	N	Y	N
50	-I/O	Input/Output	Information Transfer Phase	N	Y	N

binary one signals on the data bus is an odd number. That is, SCSI specifies *odd* parity.

For example, if -DB(0) and -DB(7) both signal binary one while the remaining signals transmit binary zero bits, the number of data-bit signals transmitting a binary one is two—an even number. Therefore, if used, the parity signal DB(P) transmits a binary one making the number of binary one signals on the data bus three—an *odd* number. Alternately, if -DB(2), DB(6), and DB(7) each signal a binary one and all other signals transmit binary zero values, DB(P) transmits a binary zero value keeping the number of binary ones on the bus an odd value—three.

If an initiator detects a parity error on data it receives, it can signal the target by asserting the -ATN line which causes the target to switch phases. This allows the initiator to indicate a parity error occurred that the target should handle.

Bus Resets

Any SCSI device can issue a bus reset by asserting the -RST signal for 25 microseconds. SCSI devices sensing the reset signal either perform a *hard* or *soft* reset, usually depending on jumper settings.

Hard resets are draconian responses. Devices release all SCSI signals, clear incomplete requests, release reserved devices, and reset operational parameters to their power-on values. Soft resets are more moderated responses. Devices release all SCSI signals, attempt to complete outstanding commands, and do not reset their operational parameters.

Hard resets are more common than soft resets and all devices on a single bus must perform the same type reset. Initiators can determine what type reset a target performs by inquiring.

Arbitration Phase

The SCSI architecture allows two, and only two, devices to communicate over its 18 wire bus simultaneously. A single device cannot broadcast signals to two or more devices simultaneously, and no conference calls are permitted. Though the 18 wire bus is a shared medium, access to and control of it is not democratic. Each SCSI device has a unique bus ID which users set using switches, jumpers, or set-up routines (see SCAM discussion). SCSI IDs range from zero (lowest priority device ID) to seven (highest priority device ID) for regular SCSI, up to 15 for the Wide SCSI variation. With wide SCSI, the highest priority from seven to zero followed by 15 to eight as lowest priority (7, 6,..., 0, 15, 14,...8). Hosts typically have the highest SCSI bus ID, allowing them to initiate requests with minimum peripheral device interference.

To obtain bus control, devices must wait for the bus to achieve a *bus free* phase which indicates the bus is idle. This phase occurs when both the -BSY and -SEL lines signal *not active* for at least 400 nanoseconds. Usually, devices must then *arbitrate* for bus control, though SCSI allows configurations with single initiators that do not require arbitration.

To begin the arbitration phase, each interested device detects a bus free phase. It then asserts -BSY and places its bus ID on the bus by asserting its associated data bus signal (i.e., device seven drops the voltage on -DB(7) while device two drops the voltage on signal -DB(2)). After a brief 2.4 microsecond delay, the device with the highest bus ID value, signals its victory and directs lower priority devices to back off the bus by asserting -SEL. The entire process from bus phase to the winner obtaining control consumes from 4.8 to 5.8 microseconds depending on bus device speed. From the description, it is clearly essential that devices have unique bus IDs to prevent arbitration collisions.

Selection Phase

Assume an initiator with bus ID seven controls a SCSI bus and needs to contact another bus device with bus ID five to give it a command such as "read." It does this in the *selection phase*. In the selection phase, the initiator asserts -ATN and continues to assert -SEL (which it first asserted during the arbitration phase). It also simultaneously asserts its bus ID and the target's bus ID on the data bus but deasserts -BSY (which it asserted during the arbitration phase).

Normally, the target detects that both -SEL and its bus ID are asserted, and responds by asserting -BSY and remembering the initiator's bus ID in case it disconnects from the bus during processing. The initiator detects that the target has asserted -BSY and the selection phase is complete when the initiator deasserts the -SEL and data bus signals.

If the target does not exist or is inoperative, the initiator times out after 200 microseconds and the operation fails. The initiator may assert -RST and reset the bus. In any event, the bus eventually enters a bus free phase. At this point, the target now has bus control. These bus free, arbitration, and selection phases are referred to as a *connect*. Alternately, the initiator *connects* to the target.

Message Out Phase

Continuing our assumption that an initiator with bus ID seven is delivering a "read" request to a bus ID five device, the target now must establish what target logical unit (or device routine depending on a message bit setting) to address the command to. This is facilitated by the initiator asserting -ATN during the selection phase, indicating it wishes to send a message to the target. The target therefore continues to assert -BSY, additionally asserts both -C/D and -MSG, and deasserts -I/O. This signals the initiator to enter the *message out* phase and transmit a message *out* of it, into the target. Note the implied directionality:

> *Out* and *In* are always initiator perspectives. Thus, *message in* phases allow initiators to receive *in*-bound messages while *message out* phases allow initiators to transmit *out*-bound messages.

The initiator responds by transmitting an *identify* message—a one byte message that identifies the target logical unit (or device routine) and whether the initiator can allow the target to temporarily *disconnect* while handling the impending request.

Command Phase

To obtain the initiator's impending request command, the target asserts -C/D and deasserts -I/O and -MSG. This places the bus in the *command phase*, allowing the initiator to transmit the command on the data bus. Commands assume the form of *command descriptor blocks* (*CDBs*) which can be ANSI or vendor defined. The ANSI standard defined CDBs can be six, ten, twelve, or sixteen bytes long. Each CDB type has a field to specify the target's logical unit in case the target does not recognize the identify message. If the target did accept the identify message, then the target ignores the CDBs logical unit field.

The target now asserts -REQ, in effect saying "ready." In response, the initiator places the first CDB byte on the data bus and asserts -ACK, in effect saying "it's on the data bus." This first CDB byte contains the command code "read" and an indicator of how long the CDB is, allowing the target to calculate the number of, and prepare for, the remaining bytes. The target now deasserts -REQ in effect saying "got it." Subsequently, the initiator deasserts -ACK. The other CDB bytes contain other pertinent details such as where to begin reading and how many sectors to read. The CDB transmission process continues similarly for each byte:

- The target asserts -REQ: "ready"
- The initiator places the next CDB data byte on the bus and asserts -ACK: "it's on the data bus"
- The target reads the data byte and then deasserts -REQ: "got it"
- The initiator deasserts -ACK: "you're welcome"

This *REQ/ACK* lock-step handshaking continues until the initiator transmits the entire request's CDB.

In SCSI, this type of transmission is referred to as *asynchronous* SCSI. SCSI devices use asynchronous transmission to transmit all command CDBs, status information, and messages. SCSI devices optionally use asynchronous transmission to transfer data as well, and that asynchronous transmission availability allows automatic speed matching between targets and initiators exhibiting different performance characteristics and obviates the need for a bus clock signal.

Target Disconnect and the Reselect Phase

At this point, the target can determine from the CDB's operation code field that it has received a "read" request that specifies a starting sector address and the number of contiguous sectors to read. Assume the target can also determine that request fulfillment will be a time-consuming operation, perhaps requiring a long seek. The target, if permitted by the identify message, can instruct the initiator to disconnect from the bus, allowing other devices to use the SCSI bus and the processor to continue with other activities while the target processes the request. Alternately, the initiator can assert -ATN and transmit a disconnect message to the target during the subsequent message out phase which the target may optionally accept.

To instruct the initiator to disconnect, the target asserts -C/D, -I/O, and -MSG, forcing the bus into a *message in* phase. The initiator senses the phase change and prepares to read the target's message from the data bus. In contrast to the CDB transfer, for *message in* transfers the asynchronous transfer sequence is:

- The target places a data byte on the bus and asserts -REQ: "it's on the data bus"

- The initiator reads the data byte and asserts -ACK: "got it"

- The target then deasserts -REQ: "thanks"

- The initiator deasserts -ACK: "you're welcome"

In this case, the disconnect message is a single-byte message so the target transmits a single byte. The initiator inspects the message's hexadecimal 04 single-byte value and notes that its value is less than hexadecimal 20, concluding the message is a single byte message. To comply with the message, both the target and initiator allow the bus to assume a bus free phase by deasserting all bus signals.

Sometime later, the target assembles the fetched data in preparation for transferring it to the initiator that requested it. To do this, the target waits for a bus free phase and arbitrates for bus control. Once in control, the target asserts -BSY and -SEL and enters the *reselection phase* by asserting -I/O, signaling that the arbitrating device was a target. The target then places the target's and initiator's bus IDs on the bus, and deasserts -BSY. The initiator must verify that its ID bit and only one other is on the bus before asserting -BSY to signal the *reconnect* awareness.

The target asserts -BSY and then deasserts both -SEL and -I/O. When the initiator detects that -SEL is deasserted, it deasserts -BSY, leaving the target to assert -BSY until relinquishing bus control. The target next forces a *message in* phase and uses it to transfer an *identify* message, allowing the initiator to associate the reconnect with a previous target's logical unit request.

The Data In Phase

The initiator is now reconnected to the target from which it optionally disconnected. To transfer the requested data to the initiator, the target enters the *data in* phase by asserting -I/O and deasserting -C/D and -MSG. Data transfer then occurs using the previously described REQ/ACK asynchronous transfer process used during *message in* phases. Alternately, the transfer could use synchronous data transfer where the REQ/ACK handshake is altered (discussed below).

The initiator maintains the *pointers* it uses to place the arriving data bytes in the proper buffer locations. When parity errors occur, these pointers are modified to retry data transfer operations. In addition, the initiator keeps track of the number of bytes it requested from the target to insure the received count matches the requested count.

Status Phase

When the data transfer is complete, the target deasserts -MSG and asserts both -C/D and -I/O, signaling a *status phase*. This allows the target to use a one-byte asynchronous transfer to report the operation's final status that should be passed to the operating system.

If no errors occurred, the target transfers a one byte hexadecimal zero value signifying a *good* status. Otherwise, it transfers a non-zero value. If it transfers a hexadecimal 02 (check condition), this indicates the initiator should check the target's condition using another I/O process starting from bus free, etc. The target then forces another *message in* phase in order to transmit a *command complete* message to the initiator. The target and initiator then deassert all signals, allowing a bus free phase.

Command and Command Descriptor Block (CDB) Format Summary

Initiators communicate one or more commands to targets by transferring Command Descriptor Blocks (CDBs) during a single command phase. CDBs can be six, ten, or twelve bytes long. The first CDB byte contains an *operation code*. The operation code's high-order three bits specify the CDB's *group code*, which implies a CDB length.

Group Code Bits	Group Code Value	Comment
000	0	Six-byte CDB
001	1	Ten-byte CDB
010	2	Ten-byte CDB
011	3	Reserved
100	4	Reserved
101	5	Twelve-byte CDB
110	6	Vendor Unique
111	7	Vendor Unique

The five remaining low-order operation code bits specify the *command code*. Since there are 5 command code bits, each CDB form can have 32 command codes. Because ten-byte CDBs were the most popular CDB format and needed more than 32 command codes, two group codes were defined to provide a total of 64 ten-byte CDB command codes.

Note that a given command code value can have different meanings for different devices. Therefore SCSI specifies command meanings within the following device class contexts and discusses them in the specified ANSI SCSI-2 standard chapters:

Device Type	SCSI-2 Standard Chapter
All Device Types - Applicable to Most SCSI Devices	Chapter 8
Direct Access Devices - Disks and Diskettes	Chapter 9
Sequential Access Devices - Tapes	Chapter 10
Printer Devices - Printer Controllers	Chapter 11
Processor Devices - Computer	Chapter 12
Write-Once Devices - WORM Drives	Chapter 13
CD-ROM Devices - CD-ROM Drives	Chapter 14
Scanner Devices - Scanners	Chapter 15
Optical Memory Devices - Optical Media Devices	Chapter 16
Medium-Changer Devices - Tape Juke Boxes	Chapter 17
Communication Devices - Network Devices	Chapter 18

Finally, to appreciate the flexibility variable-sized CDBs afford, consider that direct access devices have both a six-byte and ten byte *read* command referred to as read(6) and read(10) respectively.

- With the six-byte CDB format, the starting relative sector number (the *Logical Block Address* or *LBA*) is a 21-bit field and the *Number Of Blocks* field is an eight bit field. Since PC disk sectors are typically 512 bytes, *this allows initiators to read from 512 bytes up to 128 KBytes (2^8 or 256 sectors) from a one Gigabyte drive (2^{21} sectors) with a single command.*

- The ten-byte CDB format contains caching considerations absent in the six-byte CDB format. The starting relative sector number LBA is a 32-bit field and the *Number Of Blocks* field is an sixteen bit field. *This allows PC initiators to read from 512 bytes up to 32 MBytes (2^{16} or 64K sectors) from a two terabyte caching drive (2^{32} sectors) with a single command.*

And, if more performance is required, SCSI CDBs accommodate command chaining. This allows a single command phase to transmit multiple read commands in a linked form for sequential execution.

Establishing and Using Synchronous Data Transfer

The command, message out/in, and status phases use the asynchronous transfer REQ/ACK handshake method for data bus transmission. SCSI-2's 5 MHz, 8-bit bus asynchronous data transfers typically provide a maximum *3 to 4 MBytes per second* throughput. The data in and data out phases can also use the default asynchronous transfer to transmit data but the optional higher performance *5 MByte per second* synchronous transfer approach may be available. Ten MHz and 20 MHz options provide 10 and 20 MByte transfer rates respectively and wide versions provide 20 and 40 MByte transfer speeds respectively.

To determine if synchronous transfer is available requires an initiator to conduct *synchronous negotiation* with its targets, agreeing on a rate and maximum time delay (*offset*) to acknowledge individual byte (or individual word for wide SCSI) transfers. If both an initiator and target supports synchronous transfers, then all subsequent data in/out phases between the pair use synchronous data transfers until the next power-on or bus reset. Otherwise, the given pair use the default asynchronous transfer. The SCSI bus can alternate between which transfer type it uses depending on whether targets support it.

For example, either targets or initiators can initiate synchronous negotiation. For simplicity, assume that the initiator does so by connecting to a target and keeping -ATN asserted after transmitting an *identify* message. This allows the initiator to transmit a *synchronous negotiation* message. The target may not recognize the message and reply with a *message reject* message. At that point, the pair continues with their various activity phases and will use asynchronous transfers for data in/out phases. Alternately, the target might respond with a synchronous negotiation message. From this, both initiators and targets can determine if synchronous transfers are possible and under what constraints.

Asynchronous transfers require a tightly coupled REQ/ACK sequence for each transferred data byte which inhibits performance. Synchronous transfer allows a relaxed, coupled REQ/ACK sequence for each individual byte transfer (word transfer for wide SCSI) but requires a minimum 200 ns for each transmitted byte, yielding a theoretical 5 MBytes/sec throughput. While each byte results in a REQ/ACK sequence pair, the relaxed coupling significantly outperforms asynchronous tight coupling—particularly with longer cables.

SCSI Plug and Play (PnP) or SCSI Configured Automatically (SCAM)

The SCSI bus accommodates multiple SCSI devices and needs a mechanism to assign device addresses without resorting to jumpers or switches. Since the SCSI bus was developed before the need for automatic configuration was realized, there is no designed-in support for it. However, a mechanism that extend the SCSI protocol for Plug and Play has been developed which facilitates automatic address assignment and is backward compatible with many legacy devices. The protocol is called SCAM, for "SCSI configured automatically."

SCAM is an optional distributed algorithm which a group of participating SCSI devices collectively executes to dynamically assign SCSI bus IDs. SCSI SCAM initiators initiate SCAM protocol by first winning bus arbitration and then performing SCAM selection. Not all existing SCSI devices are SCAM tolerant (can tolerate the SCAM protocol). Intolerant devices, such as some legacy devices, are incompatible with SCAM and cannot reside on a SCSI bus where SCAM protocols execute.

As with the other buses, the first problem is isolating specific devices for configuration without using the normal addressing mechanisms. The isolation protocol relies on a device-unique identification string and a bit serial, distributed arbitration protocol to select the device with the largest identification string. At the end of the isolation protocol, a single device is selected, and a unique SCSI ID is assigned to it. The device receiving the SCSI ID then drops out of the next isolation protocol round. Repeated isolation protocol rounds result in all SCSI bus devices having unique SCSI IDs.

The serial isolation protocol transmits a thirty-one byte identifier one bit at a time from most significant to least bit. The identifier is principally composed of an eight byte vender ID and a twenty-one byte vendor specific code, which may be the device's serial number. As each bit appears on the bus, each device participating in the current isolation round compares the observed value with the value it is driving on the bus. Because of the SCSI bus's wired-or nature, if any device places a "1" on the bus, all devices will observe a "1." Any device placing a"0" on the bus recognizes that a device with a larger valued identifier string exists on the bus and drops out of the isolation protocol round. Because each identification string is unique, at the end of an isolation round only one device is left.

The SCAM protocol and SCSI ID assignment is controlled by a SCSI initiator. If there is more than one initiator, one is selected as dominant by a preliminary arbitration protocol. The wining initiator must first check for legacy SCSI devices by cycling through all SCSI IDs, then use the isolation protocol to assign unused IDs to the SCAM devices. At the end of the protocol, all SCAM devices have unique SCSI Ids, and hopefully so do legacy devices (through, of course, the SCAM protocol cannot guarantee that two or more legacy devices won't be in conflict).

There are two SCAM levels. SCAM Level 1 is a subset of SCAM Level 2 and is aimed at typical end users. Its relative simplicity reduces hardware and software requirements over Level 2 requirements. SCAM Level 2 supports advanced features such as SCSI device hot plugging and multiple initiators. While only one SCAM Level 1 initiator can be on the bus, there can be more than one SCAM Level 2 initiator on the bus and provisions exist to mediate SCAM protocol initiation in such instances. A variety of other SCAM considerations and requirements exist which are beyond the scope of this book. SCAM's net result is that after initiators win initial arbitration, the SCAM protocol isolates individual devices and assigns device IDs, relieving users from having to set jumpers or switches.

An additional aspect of SCSI Plug and Play is proper termination of the SCSI bus. In the past, SCSI devices have often included terminators, which must be physically removed or disabled if the device is not at the end of the bus. The Plug and Play specification generally calls for separate terminators which are plugged into the ends of the SCSI bus. Where an internal SCSI cable exits the host computer's cabinet, an active terminator which is disabled by plugging in an eternal cable is allowed. The goal is to make SCSI termination as fool-proof as possible.

Advanced SCSI Programming Interface (ASPI)

SCSI buses support a variety of devices such as scanners, printers, disks, etc. Individual devices have unique programming considerations which are usually intricate and complex. Beyond that, programs must also interface with SCSI host adapters to pass commands to target devices. Since different adapters have different programming interfaces, it is useful for a single standard programming interface that passes commands to devices uniformly, without regard to specific SCSI host adapter designs. This is what ASPI does.

ASPI originally stood for Adaptec SCSI Programming Interface but was changed to Advanced SCSI Programming Interface to facilitate standard acceptance. ASPI provides a SCSI host interface that is available with most SCSI adapters, regardless of manufacturer. The *ASPI Manager* software accepts SCSI commands from ASPI modules, such as device drivers, and performs the adapter-specific activities necessary to have the adapter deliver SCSI commands to devices.

ASPI therefore provides an abstraction layer service that greatly simplifies software development efforts. In addition, it also provides application programs the capability of passing SCSI commands to devices without directly involving device drivers. Finally, it also provides I/O concurrency, giving applications the ability to continue executing after requesting an ASPI Manager to queue SCSI commands for it. When such commands eventually complete, the ASPI manager sets an indicator or executes a specified routine to signal completion. Such facilities allow limited multi-threading in MS-DOS, similar to the way Local Area Network NetBIOS implementations provide limited multitasking.

Finally, because different operating systems provide different services, ASPI interface implementations necessarily vary from operating system to operating system. While this complicates portability, ASPI still delivers significant software porting advantages since most ASPI implementations are similar though no ASPI UNIX implementation exists.

ANSI CAM

As an alternative to ASPI, ANSI developed the *Common Access Method* (*CAM*). CAM is significantly more elaborate, hence complex, than ASPI but provides a common SCSI programming interface for many operating systems including UNIX variations. CAM provides target mode operation as well as improved error handling and bus control. Though most vendors find ASPI's capabilities completely adequate, Digital Equipment Corporation and Future Domain (an Adaptec company), adopted CAM. The CAM specification is ANSI X3T10/792D, available from http://www.symbios.com/x3t10.

Summary

SCSI allows users to access different type peripherals using a well-defined, industry standard connection. I/O operations are independent of the host computer system buses allowing users to upgrade peripherals and host computers as necessary. It also decreases peripheral design costs by allowing peripherals to connect to numerous computer bus designs. SCSI throughput speeds range from 2 MBytes/sec up to 40 MBytes/sec. SCSI device disconnect/reconnect and queuing ability provide additional attached host computer performance potentials.

Chapter Questions

1 SCSI disks

    a Are only for small systems

    b Are limited by the 528 MByte barrier

    c Require ASPI for multitasking support

    d None of the above

2 CDBs may be

    a Six bytes long

    b Ten bytes long

    c Twelve bytes long

    d a and b

    e All of the above except d

3 SCSI devices are

    a Initiators

    b Targets

    c Targets and Initiators but not both simultaneously

    d Single ended or differential

    e All but d

    f All but e

4 SCSI devices communicate with each other by

    a Selectively terminating the bus

    b Passing messages and then staying on the bus until complete

    c Comparing voltage levels on wires to a programmed constant

    d None of the above

5 Terminators on SCSI buses

    a Are optional

    b Receive power from initiators

    c Minimize electrical reflections

    d b and c

    e None of the above

6 The SCSI data bus

    a Cannot be longer that 18 inches

    b Only determines whether the bus is allocated

    c Is controlled by initiator

    d Is a 9-bit wide bidirectional data bus

7 The highest SCSI priority is

    a Determined democratically at power-on reset

    b Zero

    c Seven

    d None of the above

8 The SCSI Selection Phase

    a Determines the arbitration winner

    b Uses all SCSI signals before it completes

    c Can use any size CDB

    d Releases control to the target for further phases

9 Message In refers to a message

   a From the system unit to the SCSI adapter

   b From the SCSI adapter to the system unit

   c From the target to the initiator

   d From the initiator to the target

10 ASPI

   a Provides insulation from SCSI hardware adapter specifics

   b Allows programs to bypass device drivers and pass CDBs directly to SCSI adapters

   c Replaces multitasking services when possible

   d Is incompatible with synchronous data transfers

❏

▼▼▼▼ 8

IDE, EIDE, and ATAPI Device Interfaces

What This Chapter Is About

This chapter discusses IDE evolution and the legacy challenges it leaves for extensions commonly referred to as *Enhanced IDE* or *EIDE*. These extensions include:

- **Large Drive Support:** Where IDE and previous BIOSs together only accommodate hard drives up to 528 MBytes, EIDE allows the use of larger drives with changed BIOS.

- **Improved Data Transfer Rates:** Depending on the hard drive, EIDE can yield a maximum burst transfer rate of up to 16.7 MByte/sec using multiword DMA mode 2 and PIO Mode 4. In actual practice, transfer rates are significantly less and provide modest performance improvements over IDE.

- **Dual-channel Support:** IDE used a single data channel which supported up to two hard drives. With two channels, EIDE supports up to four internal hard devices, two per channel.

- **Internal CD-ROM Support:** While IDE only supports hard drives, EIDE offers low-cost CD-ROM drive connections.

Historical Perspective

IBM selected a Xebec controller for its PC-XT hard disk adapter which combined features from two existing Seagate Technology Company interfaces referred to as the ST412 and ST506 interfaces. Subsequently, the interface became known as the ST412/ST506 interface. This interface initially connected 625 KByte/sec MFM technology drives, but later supported 780 and 937 KByte/sec RLL technology drives.

Because of the 8-bit bus and 4.77 MHz clock rate, the PC-XT controller had a maximum transfer rate of 2 MByte/sec to and from the motherboard using the motherboard's DMA controller. When the PC-AT arrived with a faster clock rate and a 16-bit bus, it used PIO rather than the PC-AT's motherboard DMA since the DMA controller still only provided 2 MByte/sec transfer rates while PIO provided 3.3 MBytes/sec.

The PC-AT disk drive adapter used a WD1003 disk controller chip and the IBM's original PC-AT architecture reserved separate hardware I/O addresses and interrupt levels for two disk drive adapters —referred to as primary and secondary adapters or channels. However, the original PC-AT system BIOS only supported the primary adapter, which consequently limited standard PC system units to two disk drives.

During the 1986–1988 period, the industry migrated to IDE drives which integrated primary adapter functions into disk drives. While IDE for the PC/XT fell into disuse and IDE for the IBM Micro Channel Architecture achieved limited success, the IDE/ATA interface for the ISA bus achieved major success. Prior to IDE, ISA adapters supported up to two disks connected to the same primary disk adapter. For operations, the BIOS differentiated between the two disks by setting a *Drive Select Bit* in commands issued to the I/O registers. This allowed the individual drives to differentiate between themselves.

As IDE drives incorporate both controller and drive electronics, it was imperative for systems with two installed IDE drives to act collectively as if a single controller was present to minimize both driver and BIOS impacts. This requirement led to the existing *master/slave* configurations IDE drives use. Subsequent BIOS revisions and ISA IDE adapters eventually supported secondary adapters, permitting up to four ATA/IDE disk drives in a system unit. Eventually IDE/ATA reached the limits in 1993 summarized in Table 8-1.

Table 8-1

Feature	AT-IDE (ATA/IDE)	SCSI
Supporting Systems	PC Only	PC, Macintosh, Sun, Silicon Graphics, Hewlett Packard, etc.
Device Connectivity	Internal Only	Internal and External
Supported Peripherals	Disks Only	Disks, Tapes, CD-ROM, Printers, Scanners, etc.
Number of Drives	2/Channel	7–15
Error Checking	N	Y
Multitasking Support	N	Overlapped Commands, Queuing
PC Drive Capacity	<528 MBytes	Unconstrained
Transfer Rates	PIO Only 2–3 MByte/sec ISA Bus 5.5 MByte Local Bus	DMA or PIO 5–20 MBytes/sec
Cable Length	18 Inches	3 Meters (Single Ended) 25 Meters (Differential)

Alphabet Soup

Before proceeding, it is useful to review a few acronyms and standards setting groups.

- **ATA** or **ATA-1** (AT Attachment Disk Drive Interface): The term AT stands for Advanced Technology and refers to work first developed by the Small Form Factor Committee (*SFF*). SFF is a fast-response, ad hoc industry-consensus group that, among other things, defined the PCMCIA connector. SFF passed its ATA work to ANSI to become a standard (X3.221-1994) developed by Accredited Standards Committee Task Group X3T9.2. This standard defines a 16-bit disk drive interface based on the WD1003 controller register set referred to as the *Task File Register Interface*.

Table 8-2 summarizes ATA PIO and DMA transfer rates, which the ISA bus further constrained.

Table 8-2: ATA/IDE PIO and DMA Burst Rates in MBytes/sec

Mode	PIO	Single Word DMA	Multi-Word DMA
0	3.33	2.08	4.17
1	5.22	4.17	N/A
2	8.33	8.33	N/A

- **IDE/ATA:** A term describing an IDE drive providing an ATA interface.

- **FAST ATA:** Fast ATA is for local-bus ATA connections. It is defined by ad hoc SFF work supported by, but outside of, ANSI X3T9.2. It provides support for drives with more than 528 MBytes and defines which provides two new data transfer modes which yield 11.1 (Mode 3 PIO) and 13.3 (Mode 1 DMA) MBytes/sec.

Table 8-3: Fast ATA PIO and DMA Burst Rates in MBytes/sec

Mode	PIO	Single Word DMA	Multi-Word DMA
0	3.33	2.08	4.17
1	5.22	4.17	13.3
2	8.33	8.33	N/A
3	11.1	N/A	N/A

- **ATA-2** (AT Attachment-2): Refers to second-generation ATA that defines hard drive *multiple block read* and *write commands* that perform efficient I/O by transferring multiple data blocks with only one CPU interruption. Without this feature, interrupts occur for each sector transfer, requiring CPU processing that flushes caches, lowering overall throughput. ATA-2 has completed its public review. ATA-2 is intended to replace ATA as a standard. ATA-2 was developed by Accredited Standards Committee Technical Committee X3T10. It provides 11.1 and 16.6 MByte/sec transfer rates using PIO Mode 3 and 4 respectively. DMA was considered obsolete and Multiword DMA provides 13.3 and 16.6 MBytes/sec transfer rates for Modes 1 and 2 respectively.

Table 8-4: ATA-2 PIO and DMA Burst Rates in MBytes/sec

Mode	PIO	Single Word DMA	Multi-Word DMA
0	3.33	2.08	4.17
1	5.22	4.17	13.3
2	8.33	8.33	16.7
3	11.1	N/A	N/A
4	16.7	N/A	N/A

- **ATA-3** and **ATA-4:** ATA-2 follow-on proposals dealing with data integrity issues, speed enhancements, overlapped I/O, command queuing, and numerous other items. ATA-3 may attempt limited queued simultaneous device-I/O and ATAPI, (discussed below). ATA-4 may provide CRC, 3.3 volt support, and faster transfer rates while requiring a different cable design—perhaps requiring terminators.

- **ATAPI:** AT Attachment Packet Interface for non-disk devices. This proprietary interface passes packetized messages similar to SCSI CDBs through the Task File interface to CD-ROM drives. ATAPI consolidates numerous proprietary CD-ROM drive interfaces into one low-cost specification. Advocates are proposing ATAPI tape devices.

- **EIDE:** Enhanced IDE. A term Western Digital Corporation uses for IDE/ATA interface extensions. EIDE is not a formal standard, though Western Digital Corporation publishes documents that define various EIDE aspects. Unfortunately the EIDE definition is still evolving (the 1993 and 1995 definitions are different) though implementations marketed as EIDE curiously already exist.

- **IDE Bus Mastering:** A proposal by SFF and Intel to provide on-board DMA controllers for ATA drives.

Growth Pain RX

Simply put, EIDE is a collection of IDE extensions and any single EIDE definition remains elusive. For low-cost hard drive connections, manufacturer-installed CD-ROM drives and single-tasking operating systems, EIDE provides practical solutions. EIDE's most

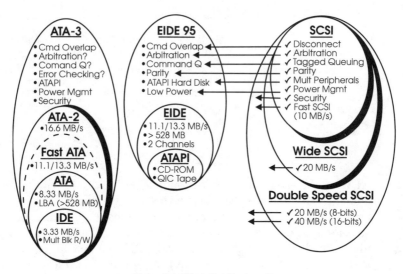

Figure 8-1. Who's Not Confused?

attractive advantage is low cost so most computers now arrive with EIDE-compatible BIOS and hardware on the motherboard.

Evolving IDE/ATA beyond its historic limitations to provide increased storage capacity that accommodates emerging requirements threatens to introduce creeping featurism that complicates the interface, increases its cost, and will likely prove incompatible. This may generate numerous problems for users and their suppliers. A quick examination of proposed IDE/ATA ad hoc extensions illuminates the problems.

The 528 MByte Barrier

The infamous 528 MByte barrier arose from a maximum allowed-value collision between IDE architecture and PC BIOS calling conventions. EIDE can remove the barrier in either of two ways that both typically require *CMOS setup and BIOS changes*:

1 Have BIOS perform automatic CHS (Cylinder, Head, Sector) translations that conform to conventional BIOS int 13h register calling conventions. This supports disk drives with the maximum BIOS capacity (up to 8.4 GBytes) and requires BIOS to create modified Enhanced Drive Parameter Tables (EDPTs) during power-on-self-test (POST) initialization.

However, there are two different approaches to perform this translation that are incompatible. This can prevent using drives formatted as boot drives under one with a BIOS in another machine that uses the competing approach. This is a consequence of the MS-DOS format command using the EDPT information within the boot record without checking an EDPT translation indicator to see if the CHS information is intended for translation into actual CHS values by the BIOS before presenting them to the IDE task file. Note that Microsoft® Windows® NT™ device drivers completely bypasses BIOS with but still uses CHS addressing.

2 Providing logical block address (LBA) support via a Microsoft/IBM int 13h extension. This allows drives with a maximum 16 TeraBytes (2^{64} bytes). When BIOS loads the task file registers to execute read/write operations, it sets a bit indicating whether the value is an LBA or a CHS value.

Currently UNIX, Novell NetWare, and Microsoft Windows 95 use LBA support which requires the operating system to sense to extended services and to pass data requests to BIOS in a *disk address packet* residing in memory. This avoids the CHS constraints imposed by conventional int 13h register calls. After receiving the disk address packet, the BIOS can pass it to an IDE disk that supports LBA requests as an LBA request by setting an LBA bit in a task file register. Otherwise the BIOS converts the request to a CHS request using the CHS information extracted from the drive during POST. If a CHS request format is used, the drive is limited to 136.9 Gbytes maximum.

Slow Transfer Speeds

Traditional ISA bus transfer rates severely constrain modern disk drives. Because of sluggish bus transfer rates, it is possible that disks with faster media transfer rates will fill drive caches before the bus empties them. This can cause fast disks to perform more poorly in a system than drives with slower media transfer rates which enable systems to transfer entire tracks in one operation, with slower media transfer rates into the buffer.

Regardless, any deviation from the original PIO operations requires either (or both) software changes and new hardware. As a software change example, consider the PC's evolution from lower-performance *single sector reads* and *multi-sector reads,* to high-performance *read-multiple* reads, and still higher-performance DMA read operations.

All disk read operations require the processor to wait for the IDE controller on the correct channel to signal it is not busy so the host can access the controller registers. The controller does this by setting its status register *busy* indicator bit to a zero value ($BSY == 0$) and the *device ready* indicator bit to a value of one ($DRDY == 1$). (Actually there may be two controllers on the channel but the two controllers appear as only one controller.)

The processor then programs the IDE controller with how many sectors to read, whether to read from the master or slave drive, and whether the request is specified as a cylinder-head-sector (CHS) request or as a logical block address (LBA) request. Lastly, the processor initiates the read operation by writing a specific *read command* to the IDE command register.

Whenever an IDE controller receives a command in its command register, it immediately ceases any activity, resets its internal state, sets the busy indicator (BSY), and checks the master/slave bit to see if the command applies to it (or to another controller possibly on the channel). All in-processing activity is immediately halted and the controller's behavior can be unpredictable if an operation was actually underway. This is why conventional IDE channels cannot perform overlapped I/O operations—**any attempt to write a command to one IDE controller interferes with ongoing operations in another controller on the same channel.**

With a *single sector* read, the processor specifies to read one sector and presents a read command with a value of hexadecimal 20. When the drive transfers the requested data to the drive buffer, the controller sets the DRQ (*data request*) indicator, clears the BSY indicator, and presents an interrupt. The interrupt routine, checks the IDE controller's status register which notifies the controller to clear the interrupt signal. If the status is OK, the processor transfers the single 512 byte sector to memory using Intel InstringW (*in word*) instructions with a repeat count of 256. When the drive transfers the last word, it clears the DRQ indicator and the operation is complete when the processor checks the status register after all transfer operations are complete.

With *multi-sector* reads, the processor specifies to read more than one sector before presenting the read command with the value of hexadecimal 20. The process to transfer the first sector is identical to a single sector read and the entire process repeats for each sector *with an interrupt preceding each sector transfer.*

With *read multiple* read operations, the processor requests more than one sector before presenting the read command with a value of hexadecimal C4. When the drive transfers the requested data to the drive buffer, the controller sets the *DRQ (data request)* indicator, clears the BSY indicator, and presents an interrupt. The interrupt routine checks the IDE controller's status register which notifies the controller to clear the interrupt signal. If the status is OK, the processor transfers more than one sector to memory.

After transferring an intermediate sector, the IDE controller may clear the DRQ indicator and set the BSY indicator. This allows it to retrieve more disk data and stage it into the drive buffer. When the controller is ready to resume data transfer, the controller sets the *DRQ (data request)* indicator, clears the BSY indicator, and presents another interrupt. The processor responds as before and transfers the data. The controller repeats this process until he read is complete. and the transfer is completed when the processor checks the status register after all transfer operations are complete.

Clearly, these various PIO read procedures require different supporting software. DMA transfers require yet another software routine since it uses a command with the value of hexadecimal C8. *DMA read data transfers use one interrupt at the end of the entire data transfer operation.* Of course, new DMA transfer speeds also require new hardware, not to mention original IDE controllers only supported PIO transfers.

PIO Transfer Considerations

All PIO transfers are blind transfers for the host. For host data input (reads), after initiating the read operation, the host waits for an interrupt indicating the IDE controller is ready to transfer the disk data. The host then selects the IDE data register by placing the IDE data register address on the address line, then asserts the IOCS16- signal to signal a 16-bit operation, then asserts the bus DIOR- signal indicating a read operation, and then waits for a brief period. To obtain the desired information, the host samples the 16 bus data signals when it finally deasserts the DIOR- signal. An analogous operation occurs for data writes using the DIOW- bus signal.

This process occurs at regular intervals for every 2-word transfer and is called a *cycle time*. If the intervals occur every 600 ns, the transfers provide 3.33 MByte/sec throughput and the PIO transfer is Mode 0. Shorter intervals provide faster transfer rates. For example, PIO Mode 2 has a 240 ns cycle time and an 8.33 MByte/sec transfer rate.

Essentially, when a drive indicates it can support PIO Mode 2 during BIOS POST processing, it guarantees that if the host is operating with a 240 ns cycle time, it can keep up—though nothing forces the host to actually operate at that speed. Unfortunately, many IDE drives report they can support faster transfer rates and often cause no problem because the system never actually operates at the maximum allowed speed. However, the disks fail when installed in faster machines which actually do operate at the rated speed. Theoretically, a device can temporarily delay a host transfer by asserting the IORDY bus signal. However, this bus signal is optional and rarely works as desired if available. The end result is data corruption and hung systems.

Finally, with local bus PIO implementations, sector data to or from fixed disk controllers passes through intervening components that connect to the local bus and coordinate the data transfers with the processor. These components allow drives to operate at maximum rated transfer speed across the ATA bus and speed-match transfers across the local bus by halting the processor when necessary—usually impossible on ISA buses. For read operations, some implementations allow processors to use the Intel *InstringD* (*in double word*) instruction to receive 4 bytes per executed I/O operation rather than the normal 2 using the Intel InstringW instruction.

While the IDE and EIDE controllers still only perform single word transfers to the intervening circuitry, the intervening circuitry collects and presents two words (four bytes) to the processor when they are available. The performance advantage occurs when the processor writes the four data bytes to DRAM with a single bus transfer as part of the InstringD instruction versus the two transfers using InstringW requires, which only transfers two bytes per bus transfer. While advanced SCSI controllers have successfully exploited this technique for years, various IDE and EIDE implementations have unfortunately exhibited compatibility problems attempting to match SCSI's success, resulting in data corruption.

DMA Transfer Considerations

EIDE systems now provide faster DMA transfers which are supported by system motherboards. The original PC-AT included an Intel 8237 DMA *slave processor* for *third party* DMA transfers. The term *third party* refers to a third component, the DMA processor, which the host programmed for the transfers between source and destination (the first and second parties). When EISA appeared it abandoned the PC-AT 2 MByte/sec, also called *compatible DMA*, approach and used a new DMA facility, called *Type B* DMA. Type B DMA increased DMA transfer rates to 4.1 MByte/sec.

Current PCI motherboard peripheral chip sets now offer *Type F DMA*. This is a *bus master* DMA architecture which is defined by SFF-8038i, titled *SFF Committee Information Specification for Bus Master Programming Interface for IDE ATA Controllers*. Bus master DMA provides significantly faster DAM transfers by seizing the system bus from the processor where slave processors only seize alternating cycles. Usually, bus master DMA processors are incorporated in controller interfaces but in this instance, they exist on the motherboard. Regardless, increased bus rates and better bus control allows bus master DMA engines to provide significantly improved transfer rates with minimum IDE cable noise. Consequently, increased EIDE transfer rates will use DMA since PIO is inherently more noisy.

IDE Cable

Single ended SCSI cables are carefully designed cables that provide 26 ground signals to absorb signal interference and cross talk. SCSI differential cables are even more immune to noise. However, the IDE cable is an inexpensive, unterminated, and unshielded cable that uses inexpensive connectors. During PIO transfers, the I/O system must assert and deassert the IOCS16- bus signal every time a data transfer occurs, indicating 16-bit data transfers are occurring. However, disk drive manufacturers traditionally use high current drivers for this signal to insure signal timing requirements are met. With low PIO Mode 0 transfer rates, this causes no problem.

However, at higher transfer rates, the high-current IOCS16- signal generates ringing and signal cross-talk inside the IDE cable—sometimes generating spurious IDE interrupt signals. Consequently, the maximum PIO transfer rate is relatively constrained and special cable provisions are recommended for local bus implementations to terminate this cable wire, minimizing this signal's severe noise. Since all DMA transfers are 16 bits minimum and do not use the IOCS16- signal, this is not a DMA problem. Future EIDE transfer rate improvements will require DMA.

Dual Channels

EIDE supports four devices by providing the equivalent of two IDE channels within one subsystem component. However, IDE designs historically assume that a device owns the cable from the moment a command is received to the moment it is completed and commands for devices sharing the same cable execute serially, without overlap. The industry now recognizes that various EIDE implementations share individual circuits and cables which prevents independent operation of connected devices even when connected to different channels. While not critical to MS-DOS and MS Windows performance, performance suffers when using a true multitasking operating system under heavy I/O loads.

Considering just cable sharing issues, it is possible that cable length and electrical loading specifications are exceeded. Even with correct cable configurations, removing the assumption that devices own the cable exclusively during operations requires new controllers, hence new disk drives. And, if a new device shares a cable with an older device, then overlapped I/O can only occur by issuing a command to the new device, disconnecting, issuing a command to an older device and waiting for completion, and then reconnecting to the new device to complete its command. This approach is referred to as *weak overlapped I/O* because the mechanism lacks an arbitration scheme. These severe constraints result from EIDE's IDE serial device legacy and EIDE's ad hoc nature. It follows that EIDE is the low-cost, widely available defacto standard for single tasking operating system storage subsystems.

Non Disk Peripherals

IDE originally only supported disk drives. Now, CD-ROM and tape units are rapidly becoming a desktop requirement for product installation and hard disk drive backup respectively. However, non SCSI devices historically required a dedicated controller card that could not be shared. Thus non-SCSI implementations were historically fragmentary, not to mention costly. ATAPI attempts to address this problem.

ATAPI is an approach that passes packetized messages similar to SCSI CDBs through the EIDE program register set to a non-SCSI CD-ROM. However, because a CD-ROM may share the same channel with a hard disk and because EIDE does not have SCSI's overlapped I/O capability, sharing an EIDE channel may often reduce hard disk performance, possibly to that of a CD-ROM. Worse, some hardware implementations, called *multi channel IDE bridge controllers*, share cache and control signals which reduces performance on both EIDE channels. Here, high disk drive performance may be reduced to CD-ROM performance. Caveat emptor.

EIDE Limitations

Despite initial attractive costs, EIDE exhibits a variety of limitations. Though integrated on motherboards, EIDE may not be the right choice for a particular system. Consider the following:

- **Software and hardware incompatibilities:** Older IDE systems offer some degree of software and hardware compatibility because EIDE drives resemble IDE drives. However, EIDE requires new BIOS and device drivers. Attempting to upgrade computers purchased prior to 1994 may prove costly and require enhanced BIOS upgrades.

- **CPU-based I/O processing limits multitasking performance:** EIDE now predominantly uses CPU controlled PIO functions. In multitasking environments, PIO activity may waste the CPU power, resulting in an overall system performance loss. EIDE does not provide the overlapped I/O support true multitasking operating systems such as Novell NetWare, UNIX, Windows 95, OS/2 Warp, or Windows NT require. Finally, many BIOS systems configure the transfer rates on a per-channel basis. This forces faster components on a channel to operate at the slower component's speed.

- **Connectivity:** EIDE only provides internal device connectivity and is designed for low-cost hard disk or ATAPI CD-ROM drives. EIDE does not provide necessary connectivity for external devices such as scanners, tape drives, DAT, MO and other peripheral devices common to many desktop and server applications.

- **No standard implementation:** Not surprisingly, EIDE continues to emerge with numerous different implementations and a general lack of industry-wide standards despite an active standards group. These variations lead to incompatibilities with various BIOS systems, other host adapters, and over-promised data transfer rates.

- **No parity checking:** As desktop system speed increases, it becomes increasingly important to ensure data integrity. EIDE does not provide device parity checking, which is strongly recommended in the PCI specifications. This prevents EIDE from detecting data transfer errors.

These limitations were usually not obvious to MS-DOS users because MS-DOS performs no multitasking, overlapped I/O, channel release/reconnect, queuing, etc. In summary then, IDE was well matched to MS-DOS's modest demands and capabilities. But, advanced operating systems such as Microsoft Windows NT and Windows 95 significantly reshape the landscape and present IDE with challenges that may well doom mixing new IDE devices with newer, more powerful EIDE devices on the same cable.

At the minimum, it's a good bet that future EIDE devices will eventually use well designed cables. In the absence of legacy devices, they may even reconfigure themselves into devices with significantly increased capabilities. In the process, they may even abandon the IDE programming model for superior operating mode capabilities which make future EIDE devices further resemble SCSI.

SCSI Advantages

SCSI is entering its second decade as the PC I/O performance choice. Future peripheral development is focused on SCSI-based devices in order to achieve the highest possible performance. SCSI provides the following advantages:

- **Reduced CPU demand for increased system performance:** SCSI is capable of independently processing I/O with minimal impact to the computer's CPU. It frees the CPU to work on other tasks for improved system throughput. Until EIDE DMA transfers come into wide use, EIDE will continue to use CPU-consuming PIO for data transfers.

- **Multiple device support:** A narrow SCSI bus controller card supports up to seven peripheral bus IDs (15 for wide SCSI) from one expansion slot—each bus ID can have as many as eight peripheral LUNs. Increasing disk storage simply requires adding drives to existing systems.

- **Support for external devices:** SCSI is not limited to devices within the computer's enclosure. Portable devices can connect externally, giving tremendous flexibility for exchanging data among computers and users.

- **Expanded peripheral support:** Where EIDE only supports hard disk and CD-ROM drives, SCSI opens computers to the widest range of peripherals, including scanners, DAT, removable media drives and other devices.

- **Hardware and software compatibility:** As an established international standard, SCSI is compatible with all current application software and operating systems running on many hardware platforms. SCSI drivers are typically available for MS-DOS/Windows, Windows 95, Windows NT, UNIX, OS/2, Novell NetWare, and other operating systems.

- **Multitasking capability:** Unlike EIDE, SCSI simultaneously processes multiple I/O requests which increases overall system performance. Multitasking at this I/O processing level is increasingly important as operating systems such as Windows NT and Windows 95 exploit this.

- **Easy upgrades:** With SCSI, adding peripherals is quick and relatively easy by plugging in peripherals and installing related software drivers.

SCSI reflects a proven technology that continues to pace increasing processing power and the demands of today's applications, while maintaining compatibility with industry standard specifications. Finally SCSI can co-exist within a systems unit with IDE and EIDE devices. Of course, SCSI only works with SCSI peripherals.

SCSI Flavors

You may encounter the following terms used to describe SCSI and SCSI-based peripherals:

- **Fast SCSI-II:** Provides performance up to 10 MByte/sec, based on an 8-bit data bus. Fast SCSI devices are completely compatible with all other forms of SCSI.

- **Fast and Wide SCSI-II:** Provides performance up to 20 MByte/sec, based on a 16-bit data bus. Wide SCSI was developed to accommodate the enhanced performance of high speed hard disk drives. Thirty-two bit implementations are possible though products are rare.

- **Ultra SCSI:** Provides performance up to 20 MByte/sec, based on an 8-bit data bus. Designed to accommodate high-performance SCSI devices with an 8-bit data bus. Ultra SCSI was previously called *Double Speed SCSI* or *Fast-20 SCSI*.

- **Wide Ultra SCSI:** Provides performance up to 40 MByte/sec, based on a 16-bit data bus. Wide Ultra SCSI was previously called *Wide Double Speed SCSI* or *Wide Fast-20 SCSI*.

Conclusion

As the Western Digital Enhanced IDE Implementation Guide Revision 5.0, November 10, 1993 document states:

> The historical success of AT-IDE within the PC market resulted from a perfect match between its offerings and the requirements of the market it served. Specifically its low cost of connection, compatibility, and ease of use were advantages in the single user, single tasking world. These markets present some challenges, however as newer markets demand greater flexibility. In today's market, the Small Computer System Interface (SCSI) has provided this flexibility to the higher performing workstation and commercial markets.

How perfect a match IDE was for personal computers is certainly open to discussion since many IDE disk drive combinations cannot coexist within a single system. But it is unquestionably true that Microsoft Windows NT multitasking and high performance Intel Pentium Pro symmetric multiprocessor systems are moving personal systems into industrial strength arenas previously enjoyed by workstation and commercial markets

It is therefore no surprise that any IDE follow-on strategy would attempt as the *Western Digital Enhanced IDE Implementation Guide* states "to remove the limitations and disadvantages that relegated IDE to a personal computer only interface and thereby allow it to be a successful interface in the workstation and commercial markets." However like many undertakings, the journey from desire to fulfillment is proving daunting.

EIDE is presently an incompletely defined entity. It represents an incremental move from IDE's simplicity and tight PC-AT bus coupling into a more complex environment. Since users must still carefully select compatible IDE drive models for successful installation, EIDE will inevitably introduce many new user problems. Current proposals suggest that EIDE's weak overlap will certainly be subordinate to SCSI capability.

Ad hoc development processes are best suited to low-cost, proprietary products. However, the approach fails for open, industry standard products that require multiple supply sources, field upgrades, and evolution. The IDE family resulted in incompatible implementations that endure to this day while SCSI is the result of a long, strenuous standards process. The difference is predictable.

For example, on August 15, 1995, the San Jose Mercury News printed an article titled "Intel leads move to discover bug impact" on its business section's first page. It states:

> ...The problem is in early PCI motherboards that use an RZ-1000 EIDE controller chip made by PC Tech in Lake City, Minn. This controller chip serves as a traffic cop for the hard disk drive by governing access to permanent memory.

> The chip, when used in combination with certain PC operating systems that can handle more than one task at a time and use a "fast mode" feature to access a hard drive, causes problems such as lost or altered data.

> ...it's important to remember that many kinds of motherboards, chips, disk drives and other devices go into a computer. On top of that are several operating systems and the huge array of software applications.

> All this software and hardware is interconnected. Because of the many combinations, "there's all sorts of things that can happen," says Fred Zieber, president of the market research firm Pathfinder Research...

The problem reportedly is a result of the "RZ-1000's inability to fully compensate for all the implications of running IDE hard disk as an extension of the PCI bus, instead of running as an extension of the AT bus which it was originally designed to do." It's small wonder many folks sense that extending IDE with creeping SCSI features is all pain, no gain. Many designers express the sentiment *why retrofit IDE with extensions when SCSI already has them working.*

Chapter Questions

1 IDE legacy problems include

   a Drive capacity limitations

   b No tape or CD-ROM support

   c Single Channel support

   d Slow data transfer rates

   e All of the above

2 How many hard disk adapters did the original PC-AT support?

   a Two in hardware but only one in BIOS

   b One in hardware and one in BIOS

   c One in hardware but two in BIOS

   d Two in hardware and two in BIOS

3 SFF stands for

   a Single Failure Factors

   b Single Form Factor

   c Small Form Factor

   d Single Form Features

4 EIDE

   a Is an ISO standard

   b Is an IEEE standard

   c Is an ANSI standard

   d Is an evolving defacto agreement

5 The 528 MByte barrier was solved partly by

   a Using LBA addressing instead of CCHHSS addressing

   b Using dual channels

   c Installing an enhanced Drive Parameter Table

   d a and c

6 Using a pair of 18" cables for shared dual channel cables

a Violates electrical loading specifications

b May cause serious problems

c Is cause for industry and user concern

d All of the above

7 EIDE provides overlapped I/O support through

a Single threading at the device driver level

b Queued requests and using drive selection bits in command registers

c Weak overlapped I/O

d Compatibility with IDE

8 ATAPI

a Provides a SCSI-like command interface for CD-ROM drives

b Stands for ATA Packet Interface

c May be used for Tape devices

d All of the above

9 ATA-2

a Introduced two new PIO Modes

b Introduces two new multiword DMA Modes

c Will replace ATA as a standard

d All of the above

10 Task File Registers

a Accumulate file information for CPU registers

b Are one task in multitasking operating systems

c Are where task files are registered

d None of the above

❒

Serial SCSI Protocols

What This Chapter Is About

SCSI actually consists of two layered protocols. An upper-level protocol defines SCSI commands and the logical handshaking between
initiators and targets. The separate lower-level *transmission* protocol
defines electrical characteristics, coding schemes, and parallel transmission procedures. Consequently, with minimal device driver and
firmware rewriting, device or subsystem implementations currently
using SCSI-2 can replace its lower-level parallel transmission protocol with a serial transmission protocol. This explains why SCSI's
command sets continually appear in international standard proposals.
The following material discusses two popular serial protocols—
Serial Storage Architecture (*SSA*), IEEE 1394 (*1394*), and Fibre Channel
Arbitrated Loop (*FC-AL*).

Background

IDE and SCSI currently dominate PC I/O markets. While their parallel cable technologies presently perform well within their designs,
increasing application demands may warrant technology evolution.
Some of these emerging requirements include:

- **Ease of use demands:** Plug and Play, endorsed by industry
  leaders including Adaptec, Intel, and Microsoft, simplifies PC bus
  configuration. SCSI Configured Automatically (SCAM), SCSI's
  Plug and Play equivalent, simplifies SCSI bus configuration.

- **Increased peripheral bandwidth:** Future applications demand
  increased media bandwidth. In response, high-end disk drive

media transfer rates are projected to exceed 200 MBits/sec by 1998.

■ **Smaller cables and connectors:** Integrating more parallel cables and device connectors is difficult in some system units since connectors may require unavailable space and cables may be inflexible or interfere with internal airflow.

■ **New device types:** New applications often require new devices. As an example, emerging multimedia applications require video cameras which currently have no standard digital interface.

■ **Rate based throughput:** Future multimedia applications demand guaranteed deterministic data delivery to preclude lost video frames and audio degradation.

■ **Increased peripheral connectivity:** IDE controllers have a two-drive, 18 inch cable length limit. SCSI connects up to seven targets (15 for Wide SCSI), each with as many as eight LUN peripherals. Future applications, including disk arrays and file servers, may mandate substantially increased connectivity.

■ **Standardized commodity parts:** SCSI supports numerous devices and device types including hard disk, CD-ROM, magneto optical drives, tape drives, scanners, and printers with a few standardized connector designs.

Serial Benefits

Since physical parallel cable widths present one emerging parallel bus problem, potential solutions *reduce* cable size by transmitting data serially rather than serially. Such implementations are referred to as *serial links* or *buses*. Given a wide bus's potential bandwidth, this may seem regressive. However, serial I/O connections exhibit several innate advantages:

■ Popular transmission media such as ATM and fiber optic are already serial, simplifying connections to other serial I/O connections.

■ When numerous signals simultaneously change state, as wide data buses require, severe signal *cross-talk* interference is possible. Serial technologies avoid this problem.

- Signal skew becomes a problem with long cables and higher data rates.

- In most technologies, pin counts, rather than logic cell counts, dictate computer chip (*ASIC*) cost. Serial bus ASICs have fewer connection pins, hence reduced costs.

A serial interface:

- Has fewer electrical connections, hence less signal driver and receiver circuitry to consume power and generate unwanted heat. So, more integrated circuit area is available for the remaining driver gates. With CMOS circuits, larger gates handle the increased power necessary for higher data rates.

- Uses less cable wire. Beyond cost and bulk advantage, this allows substantially improved shielding at less total cost than with multi-signal cables.

- Avoids clock skew as data rates and cable lengths increase.

In numerous environments, these advantages compensate for reduced data path widths, ultimately increasing the transfer frequency by 10 to 50 times and the net throughput by 200 times over parallel approaches.

All For One

It is simplistic to believe serial connections comprise single wires. Unfortunately, media characteristics, data speeds, and connection protocols make one wire connections endangered species. To wit, the ubiquitous RS232 serial link typically uses between four and nine wires.

Buses frequently require multiple electrical connections because:

- Transmission protocols often use simultaneous two-way (*full-duplex*) communication for reliability and performance. Secondary (reverse) communication paths usually provide simple acknowledgments, concurrent bidirectional data transfer, or both. When loops provide second paths, media bandwidth doubles or provides alternative routes, gracefully compensating for failed connections.

- As with SCSI differential connections, copper wire most reliably transmits high frequency (data rate) signals using differential pairs where paired wires transmit signals using opposite polarity on matching wires. The two signals experience similar noise and signal corruption during transmissions but interference cancels, recovering high quality signals.

High Performance PC Bus I/O Candidates

Five new high performance PC I/O bus candidates exist—two parallel and three serial. They are:

- Parallel:
  - Fast-20 SCSI providing 20 to 40 MBytes/sec
  - ATA-2 providing up to 16.6 MBytes/sec
- Serial:
  - Fibre Channel Arbitrated Loop
  - Serial Storage Architecture (SSA) IEEE 1394

The following material discusses SSA and IEEE 1394, leaving Fibre Channel for a future edition of this book.

The IEEE 1394 Serial Bus

The IEEE 1394 proposal is a serial point-to-point digital bus which provides 100, 200, or 400 MBit/sec transfers. The proposed standard includes:

- A physically thin, powered cable specification
- An asynchronous and isochronous packet transmission protocol

1394 Bus Topology

A 1394 *bus segment* uses a daisy chaining or branching-tree topology where a bus trunk emanating from a *root node* optionally splits into limbs, which optionally split into branches, which further optionally subdivide into twigs etc. The 1394 bus segments connect a maximum of 63 devices, referred to as *nodes*, without requiring bus terminators or user-selected node IDs. Bridges may connect over 1000 bus segments, each with their own unique *bus ID*, to support thousands of devices.

Node Ports

Each 1394 node has from one to 27 ports, each allowing one point-to-point cable connection to another node's port. Three connection restrictions exist:

1 Individual point-to point node cable connections must not exceed 4.5 meters (approximately 15 feet).

2 Unique connection paths must exist between any two nodes (no loops).

3 Less than 16 intervening nodes can exist on a maximum 72 meter path between any bus node pair.

Single 1394 bus configurations can interconnect multiple users to one or more servers, allowing access to all interconnected peripherals.

1394 Data Transmission

The 1394 nodes transfer data using source and destination addressed packets. There are two 1394 packet transfer modes:

- **Asynchronous:** Normal data transfers providing acknowledgments and data integrity support

- **Isochronous:** Time dependent data transfers guaranteeing just-in-time, metered delivery but not acknowledgments or data integrity

Traditional storage devices, such as disks, tapes, and CD-ROMs, will likely use asynchronous data transfer. Digital consumer electronics devices, such as cameras and VCRs will likely use isochronous transfer to obtain just-in-time data deliveries without expensive memory buffering.

Bus Initialization and Native Hot Plugging

Bus resets re-initialize 1394 buses and typically occur following:

- Applying bus power
- Node addition or removal

Because device addition or removal forces bus initialization, the 1394 bus inherently supports hot plugging and dynamic bus reconfiguration.

Node Assignments

Segment bus initialization superimposes segment topology and assigns node IDs. To determine the bus topology, the initialization process first determines the root node.

- If the bus does not support *isochronous* data transfers (below), any node is a root node candidate.

- If the bus does support isochronous transfers, the *isochronous cycle master* (below) must be the root.

Selecting the root node determines a segment's topology and physical node IDs. The root node assigns physical IDs in a *post order* fashion:

- The current node's ID is assigned after all node ID's below it are assigned.

- The assignment starts with the root node's Port 1 nodes, Port 2 nodes, etc., progressing through remaining ports in ascending numeric order.

1394 Data Integrity

For data security, all asynchronous packet receivers immediately acknowledge all non-broadcast packets. But asynchronous broadcast packets are not acknowledged. Nodes cannot transmit another packet to a destination until the prior one is acknowledged. Typically, acknowledging nodes only wait the brief acknowledgment gap before arbitrating and sending the acknowledge packet. If the longer subaction gap is sensed before receiving an acknowledgment packet, the node that sent the original unacknowledged packet must assume the packet was lost. Acknowledge packets all one byte long: four bits provide acknowledgment and the remaining four bits provide data integrity checking.

1394 Node Addressing

The 1394 nodes use 64-bit addresses to specify both data transfer sources and destinations. The high-order 16 bits specify root-assigned node IDs and the low-order 48 bits specify a target node starting memory location. Node IDs have two subfields:

- The first 10-bit subfield specifies the node's bus. A binary 11.1111.1111 value specifies the local bus. Other values specify another bus reached through bus bridges.

- The next six-bit subfield specifies the node's ID. A binary 11.1111 value specifies an all-node bus broadcast. Any of the 63 remaining values specifies a node ID.

1394 Packet Formats

Packet formats and transmission protocols vary depending on the transfer mode. The 1394 asynchronous packets contain headers with a cyclical redundancy check (CRC) and an optional data block with a separate CRC. The two CRCs independently detect transmission errors on their respective packet areas.

Packet headers also include sending and receiving node bus IDs, as well as 6-bit transaction labels. This allows receiving nodes to respond to specific packets by using the same transaction label in response headers. The transmitter subsequently associates responses with requests. This is analogous to how parallel SCSI uniquely identifies specific I/O processes

Finally, when packets contain a data block, packet headers include a block length. The data rate determines the maximum data block length which varies from 512 bytes at 100 Mbit/sec, to 1024 bytes at 200 MBit/sec, and 2048 bytes at 400 MBits/sec. When the message sizes exceed allowable block lengths, messages must be divided into multiple data payloads.

SCSI-3 1394 Serial Bus Protocol (SBP)

The 1394 packet protocol makes no assumptions regarding packet data field contents. Higher protocols effortlessly map data into 1394 packet data fields as appropriate. For example, the SCSI-3 committee is defining the Serial Bus Protocol (SBP) that maps SCSI protocol onto 1394. Here, the 1394 data fields include four information types:

1 Command data structure:

- SCSI Command Descriptor Block

- Data pointers

- Status

- Sense areas

- Control information

2 Data

3   Status

4   Sense Information when errors occur

SBP fully supports the SCSI-3 Architecture Model (SAM), including queuing and automatic contingent allegiance provisions. Finally, SBP extends SAM with isochronous data transfer support.

Half Duplex Transmission

The 1394 bus segments are *half duplex*—point-to point connections only supporting data transmission in one direction at a time. To send packets, nodes first arbitrate for the bus. This establishes the winning node and points all point-to-point connections away from the winner. Transmitting the winner's packet across all point-to-point connections allows all bus nodes to inspect the packet. For broadcast packets, all nodes receive the packet, thereby eliminating segmentation bandwidth gains. Otherwise, only the destination node receives the packet even though all nodes see it.

Transmission Overview

If more than one node simultaneously arbitrates, the node closest to the root wins. Once a node wins, it cannot arbitrate again until all other nodes have had an opportunity to arbitrate and send a packet. Defined time intervals which nodes must wait for before they arbitrate again are referred to as *gap times*. These gaps, similar to SCSI bus free phases, represent bus inactivity periods when no node arbitrates or sends a packet and ensures all nodes have equal bus access.

When nodes initially arbitrate or have not transmitted for a relatively long period, they only need delay a *subaction gap*. The 1394 standard specifies approximately 10 μsec as the default subaction gap time. This time accommodates worst-case 72 meter bus lengths between the most distant node pairs. The Serial Bus Manager can optionally reduce this interval if it detects the configuration is not worst-case. Among other duties, the Serial Bus Manager manages system resources: isochronous bandwidth allocation, power distribution throughout the bus, topological optimization. The serial bus manager is chosen according to who is willing to be the manager.

When nodes send packets, an internal flag prohibits the nodes from sending another packet until an arbitration reset gap delay interval passes. After an *arbitration reset gap*, the internal flag resets and the node can subsequently arbitrate. The 1394 standard specifies that arbitration reset gap values are approximately twice subaction gap values. Having arbitration reset gaps longer than subaction gaps guarantees all nodes have the opportunity to send packets before any one node sends subsequent packets. This democratically divides bus bandwidth among all nodes transmitting asynchronous packets.

After receiving non-broadcast packets, receiving nodes must acknowledge packets to their sender, requiring receivers request the bus. The 1394 standard defines an *acknowledge gap* delay interval that is much shorter than the subaction gap (approximately 0.04 µsec). Since acknowledging nodes delay shorter intervals than other nodes before arbitrating, they are guaranteed to be the only requesting node and, therefore, win. This prevents other packets from getting between a packet and its acknowledgment.

The 1394 protocol does not require a special disconnect feature. Fair bus access is inherent, requiring no special node decisions. When nodes send multiple packets, 1394 protocol guarantees all other nodes have opportunity to interleave one packet between each of the other node's packets. This prevents, for example, tape drives from monopolizing the bus.

Asynchronous Data Transfer

Asynchronous packet headers include transaction codes that specify requested operations. The 1394 protocol supports three different transaction types:

1 **Read:** *Requesting* nodes transfer read requests to *responding* nodes. Responding nodes transfer the data to requesters.

2 **Write:** Requesting nodes transfer the write request and data to responders. Write transactions also support broadcast, allowing all bus nodes to receive the data.

3 **Lock:** Requesting nodes transfer data to responders, which return a result to the requester after processing the original data via some method. Lock transactions allow nodes to modify the responder's memory space and receive updated values without intervening transaction interference.

1394 Isochronous Data Transfer

Isochronous data transfers support time dependent data and guaranteed delivery rates. The 1394 buses supporting isochronous data select a *cycle master* which becomes the bus topology root node during initialization. This guarantees the cycle master always wins arbitrations when it's time to broadcast its clock to commence isochronous transfers. The master is chosen according to who has the best local clock. If a bus is to support isochronous transfers, it must have a cycle master, and the master must be the root.

Cycle masters maintain a bus reference clock. Every 125 μsec, cycle masters wait for the next subaction gap and request the bus when they sense it. After winning, cycle masters send an asynchronous broadcast packet containing its current clock value that all bus nodes then write into their clock register. Since asynchronous clock broadcasts are not acknowledged, all isochronous senders only wait the acknowledgment gap before arbitrating. The difference, of course, between asynchronous acknowledgments and isochronous transfer is that the former guarantees only one node attempts to acquire the bus, while the latter may have zero, one, or more arbitrating nodes.

All nodes having data to transmit, and previously granted isochronous transfers bandwidth, enter bus arbitration when they next sense an acknowledge gap. One by one, each isochronous sender wins and transmits an isochronous packet. If a node has multiple channels to service, it does not arbitrate for each channel—it simply sends each channel's data contiguously. When the last sender sends its final isochronous frame, nothing happens until a subaction gap occurs, at which time the bus returns to asynchronous transfer mode until the next 125 μsec cycle time and awaiting asynchronous transfer nodes start arbitration.

Isochronous packets use *channel numbers* instead of transaction labels, source IDs, and destination IDs. The cycle bus manager assigns the nodes channel numbers upon request. Isochronous packet headers include channel numbers and the data field byte-count. Nodes awaiting isochronous data interrogate isochronous packet headers for appropriate channel numbers. When they see their channel(s), they consume the packets without acknowledgment. Isochronous transfers therefore provide no data integrity.

Serial Storage Architecture

Serial Storage Architecture (SSA) initially appeared as a low-cost high-performance disk drive serial connection though it seems likely it will emerge in other arenas. Its two signal connection provides *full duplex* communication (simultaneous transmit and receive). It uses *self-clocking codes*, meaning SSA recovers clock signaling from the data signal rather than from separate transmitted signals. SSA links can use a maximum 2400 meter long fiber optic cable or a maximum 25 meter copper four wire cable, where it uses two differential pairs similar to differential SCSI cabling technology. All links support 20 MBytes/sec in each direction for a total link bandwidth of 40 MBytes/sec, referred to as the *link speed*. Nodes typically have two links for a total node throughput of 80 MBytes/sec. Technology permitting, the protocol gracefully accommodates speed increases with existing plans to extend transmission speeds to 40 and 100 MBytes/sec in each direction, for a total node throughput of 160 MBytes/sec and 400 MBytes/sec, respectively.

Serial Storage Architecture currently comprises two components:

- **SSA-PH:** This is the serial link's physical and electrical specification.

- **SSA-SCSI:** Since SCSI-2 provides excellent protocols and serially attached peripheral addressing, international standards organizations are mapping these to SSA's physical interface. This provides SCSI to SSA transition with minimal re-engineering.

SSA-PH Overview

SSA-PH serial links exhibit the following characteristics:

- **Topology:** Supports strings, loops, and switched loops.

- **Distance:** Wire cable supports point-to-point connections up to 25 meters. Fiber-optic connection distances between two nodes on a loop can be up to 680 meters.

- **Bandwidth:** Full duplex communication providing 20 MBytes/sec (200 MBits/sec) in each direction.

- **Format:** Frames are the atomic transmission unit and can be up to 136 bytes long. The minimum frame overhead is 8 bytes, or a minimum 6 percent depending on frame size.

- **Reliability:** The highly reliable link provides considerable error detection, significant transparent error recovery, and node hot-swapping.

- **Physical:** The cables and connectors have small form-factors. Each external SSA connection uses compact shielded four-wire cables with overall diameter less than 6 millimeters. External connectors are nine pin micro-miniature D-shell connectors. Enclosed connections can use lower-cost connectors and cables, such as back planes, twisted pair, and flex cables. There is also a unitized connector for power.

- **Heartbeats:** Otherwise idle links continuously transmit synchronization characters to facilitate failed link detection.

Link Topology

SSA allows extremely flexible connectivity, providing support for simple strings, or loops, complex switched strings, and cyclic paths. This flexibility allows cost, performance and availability trade-offs. Three different SSA node types provide this flexibility:

- **Single Port:** Provides connection to one and only one node.

- **Dual Port:** Provides connection to two nodes (typical for peripherals)

- **Switch:** Provides connections for up to 126 other nodes including switches

Strings

Strings comprise simple linear networks with two or more nodes. Referencing Figure 9-1, ports at either string end are optionally single-port nodes, while the others must be dual-port nodes. *Dedicated connections* are special string cases where two single-port nodes connect to each other using one link. Strings are not popular since link failures present single points of failure, breaking string networks into two networks.

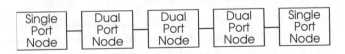

Figure 9-1. SSA String Topology

Loops

Loops are the prevalent connection topology. Referencing Figure 9-2, loops are cyclic networks containing only dual-port nodes. Since two data paths exist between any two nodes, loops have higher bandwidth than strings. Also, since single nodes can fail without prohibiting communication between other nodes, loops have higher reliability than strings. Finally, inserting nodes into operating loops does not terminate node communication. Loops can have a maximum of 127 nodes but no switches.

Switches

Figure 9-3 depicts a complex network that uses a switch. Switches can have up to 126 ports and facilitate interconnecting large numbers of nodes while providing alternate fault tolerant paths. Note that switched networks can also include other *cyclic* paths such as meshes which, by definition, are not loops since they contain switches, not just dual-port nodes.

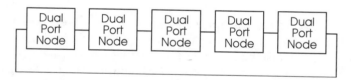

Figure 9-2. SSA Loop Topology

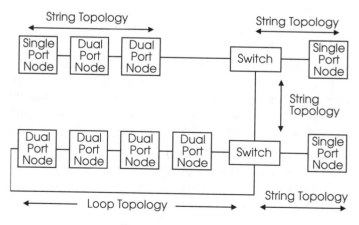

Figure 9-3. SSA Switches

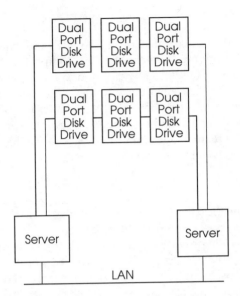

Figure 9-4. High Availability Server Configuration Using SSA Disk Subsystem

Figure 9-4 depicts an example of a high availability file server using SSA that tolerates single network faults by identifying failing links with some potential bandwidth loss, otherwise leaving network operations unimpaired. This network contains two loops. An outer loop connects servers and array controllers. The inner loop connects controllers and devices. Each path provides up to 4 times a single link's bandwidth as a consequence of SSA's *Spatial reuse* capability (discussed below).

8B/10B Encoding

SSA uses a form of coding called 8B/10B encoding The name reflects that 8 data bits become 10 encoded signal bits. This immediately introduces 20% signal overhead. In 8B/10B, ten-bit combinations assume one of 1024 combinations. However, 8B/10B discards many of the values according to the following rules:

1   Within transmissions, there are no more than 5 consecutive bits of the same value (within bytes as well as spanning adjacent bytes). This run length limit ensures constant success-ful clock recovery.

2 The maximum *Digital Sum Variation* (*DSV*) is 6 (+3 to -3). The DSV is as follows: Maintain a running count during encoding with binary ones counting as +1 and binary zeros as -1. The DSV is this count's maximum value minus its minimum value. Constraining this value effectively forces transmitted signal DC components to zero since, overall, there are as many 1's as 0's in the stream.

To observe the second rule, selecting transmission codes depends on previous codes, as well as current data values. Thus each byte can map onto more than one transmitted encoding, accounting for most of the coding method's redundancy.

In practice, 8-bit source data bytes map onto one or two encodings. Bytes split into two parts, a 5-bit string and a 3-bit string. A 5B/6B code encodes the first substring and a 3B/4B code encodes the second. Each substring has an equal number of 1's and 0's, or the counts differ by two. Selecting the next byte's encoding code so that it has the opposite imbalance corrects a previous imbalance.

Special Characters

An 8B/10B code encodes all 256 possible byte values while allowing other special codes that obey coding rules. Of these, three, referred to as *comma codes*, uniquely contain a bit string (001.1111) that never occurs elsewhere. Receivers use comma codes to synchronize their clocks to correct code word boundaries. SSA uses the remaining codes as special characters. They are:

- FLAG   A comma character delimiting *frame* ends.

- ABORT'   Prematurely aborts a frame's transmission. SAT Used with arbitration.

- SAT'   Used with SAT arbitration.

- DIS   A comma character indicating the disabled state.

- ACK   Acknowledges successful frame reception.

- RR   Indicates readiness to accept another frame.

- NUL   Used to "pad out" transmissions, for example when waiting for some response before proceeding. The NUL character is ignored.

The remaining comma character is invalid because, in certain circumstances, it can cause erroneous comma detection.

The three remaining special characters are available for application or higher level protocol use. The SSA-SCSI definition currently reserves two and the third is defined as the SYNC character, which synchronizes the disk drive rotation.

In summary, 8B/10B code exhibits the following advantages:

- The maximum number of consecutive bits without a bit value transition is five, making the clock always recoverable.

- AC-coupled signal processing and amplification is possible since signals contain little if any DC bias.

- Numerous signal bit encoding combinations and sequences are invalid, facilitating noise error detection through simple rule-based error checking

- Special characters exist for byte synchronization and special signaling—even within data sequences.

SSA Transmission

Despite SSA's serial bit-by-bit nature, bytes remain the transmitted information unit. Serialized eight-bit bytes transmit as a unit bit stream. However, serialized bytes generically require intervening control bits because:

- There are no byte begin and end delimiters.

- It is otherwise impossible to recover and synchronize clock data (timing).

- Any errors are undetected, hence uncorrected.

- If more bits of one type, say binary zero, are present than the other, say binary one, the first's electrical polarity DC biases the data signal, making transitions difficult to detect.

To address these problems, serialized bit stream transmissions usually proceed at fixed clock rates interspersed with control bits (e.g., Start, Stop and Parity) which trade some bandwidth in return for partially solving the first three problems.

However, DC bias complication is often ignored though it can preclude serial link speed increases. This is because as data rates increase, signal data increasingly contains higher frequency components (data bit value fluctuations). Extracting these signals reliably sometimes requires a receiver AC-coupled amplifiers, which cannot amplify DC biased signals.

SSA Frames

In SSA, data transmission is frame based. Any SSA node can transmit frames to any other network node and all frames contain routing *path addresses*. On their journey, frames may traverse several links. Data integrity across any link is the responsibility of the two nodes immediately involved, even if they are not the packet's original source and eventual destination.

A frame consists of a minimum of a 6-character sequence, with FLAGs delimiting each end. Adjoining frames may share a single FLAG. Referencing Figure 9-5, the remaining frame component descriptions follow.

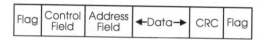

Figure 9-5. SSA Frame Format

Control

This 1 byte field contains a frame *sequence number,* important for lost frame detection, or indicates the frame type which can be:

- *Control frames* used for various types of reset
- *Privileged frames* for certain protocol related messages
- *Application frame* for sending normal data

Address

A 1 to 6 byte data field directing frames to correct nodes, using a *path* value, and to the correct node *channel*.

DATA

A 0 to 128 byte data field containing application data for application frames or a protocol message for privileged frames. Control frames do not have data fields. Except for message frames and frames containing the last data byte, the data field length must be a multiple of 16. Privileged message frame length is a maximum 32 bytes.

CRC

A four-byte error detection field immediately preceding a frame's trailing FLAG. CRCs accumulate over the control, address, and data fields but do not include FLAG characters or intervening special characters. It uses the FDDI and *Frame Check Sequence* (*FCS*) 32-degree polynomial which, by itself, detects one error in 10^{13} bytes on average.

For SSA link reliability, tight controls exist for node data flows. Each node must contain buffer space for at least one complete frame. After transmission, a transmitter must wait for a receiving node Acknowledge (ACK) before it can discard the frame. ACKs only arrive after passing all error checking. ACKs are sent twice to insure safe ACK signal reception.

Since error checking is not instantaneous, for maximum bandwidth utilization, a receiver can (with sufficient buffer space) request a second frame before acknowledging the first by sending two Receiver Ready (RR) characters to transmitters. It may do this when it has the buffer space, even if the transmitter has not completely transmitted the first frame. Even though RR characters signal a transmitter to send another frame before it receives the first frame's ACK, a transmitter still requires the acknowledge signal before discarding its first frame's copy. The ACK for the first frame must arrive before transmitting a third frame to allow correct ACK-frame association.

If transmitters do not receive an ACK before completing a second frame transmission, they insert NUL characters before the trailing FLAG. In this way, the received ACK appears between the two FLAG's of the frame following the one it acknowledges, allowing unambiguous ACK-frame association. If ACKs fail to appear within the ACK time-out period (currently 50 microseconds), an error occurs.

ACK and RR signals only occur between individual link nodes; if nodes simply pass data through to subsequent links, they must observe correct ACK and RR protocol. Finally, ACKs, RRs and CRCs are generated by each communicating node-pair and are not forwarded.

Cut-Through Routing

Because SSA link error rates are typically minuscule, SSA uses *cut-through routing* to accelerate frame forwarding. With cut-through routing, nodes forward arriving frames during reception without waiting to validate frame CRCs. This can reduce inter-node frame delays to 5–10 characters, or 0.5 microseconds at 20 MBytes/sec bandwidths.

If a node detects an inbound frame error while forwarding a frame, it transmits an ABORT character (followed by a FLAG) to the receiver. This receiver, in turn, sends an ABORT if it is forwarding the defective frame which would normally arrive with a valid CRC since transmitters generate each frame's CRCs. ABORT characters direct receivers to discard currently arriving frames, leaving the receiver that detects the error to initiate frame recovery.

Error Handling

Though SSA's few cable wires allow it high quality cable shielding, data errors are possible and if left uncorrected their consequences can be memorable, to say the least. In addition, SSA's *hot swapping* allows connecting or disconnecting nodes without powering the nodes down or providing other nodes with a warning. Links abruptly fail and reemerge later. Such *deliberate* errors must also be detected and corrected

SSA's Error Recovery Procedure (*ERP*) provides SSA with reliability beyond its 8B/10B code and 32-bit CRC, which are particularly proficient at detecting its estimated 1 error in every 10^{24} bytes. Other detection mechanisms include:

- Synchronization loss

- Frame sequence error

- ACK Time-out (50 microseconds)

- 8B/10B code violation protocol error

- Frame reject (too many data characters, invalid address, etc.) as well as any internal errors detected by the links themselves

Detecting an error invokes SSA's ERP, which attempts recovery. If successful, the recovery is transparent to higher level protocols other than with a slight bandwidth loss.

ERP first *resets* the link, which causes attached nodes to exchange their status. This provides error information and consequently determines whether the error is recoverable. If recoverable, transmitters *retransmit* corrupted frames. If retransmission is successful (before reaching a retry threshold), the link continues transparently without informing the higher level protocols. When errors are not recoverable, ERP *exits* with an *Asynchronous Alert* privileged message. This marks the link non-operational. However, with loop connections, traffic may be rerouted to avoid failing links. Correct protocol must be observed along *every link*. If receivers detect transmission errors, they must attempt error recovery. Thus each link only forwards good data.

Spatial Reuse

With bus topologies, nodes connect to the same wire. However, in some ring topologies, node links are separate, independent connections that can provide *Spatial Reuse*. Spatial reuse makes links that are not involved in a particular data transmission available for use with another transmission. Figure 9-6 depicts a spatial reuse example. Node 3 transmits to node 2 *while* node 4 transmits to node 1. The concurrent transmission is possible because the links are independent and the ACKs return along the same path.

Spatial reuse is applicable to strings as well as other topologies. As long as links are not transmitting (i.e., are not along a message's path), then the links are available for communication. If a node has a second message for an actively transmitting link, then a priority scheme must resolve what message to transmit first.

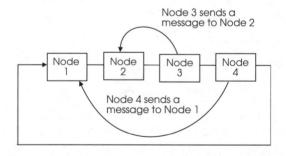

Figure 9-6. Spatial Reuse

SAT Algorithm

The SAT algorithm supports spatial reuse by providing a priority scheme to balance frame priorities. This algorithm nearly triples SSA loop throughput versus dual counter-rotating token ring technology. Here, tokens circulate *opposite* to data transfer directions. These tokens, referred to as *SATs*, allow possessors to originate assigned numbers of frames (SATisfy itself in one direction) in lieu of routing incoming port frames. After transmitting the originating frame count, SAT owning nodes must pass the token to another upstream node. Nodes that do not have a SAT token can always originate frames but must give priority to frame routings. Network configuration assigns these minimum and maximum numbers (called the *A_Quota* and the *B_Quota*). Finally, SSA uses complementary *SAT'* tokens, to control opposite direction transmissions.

Low-cost, Low-power Solution

Lower power requirements and fewer components mean higher reliability. Via industry-standard 3.3 volt CMOS, SSA is a low-cost and low-power serial solution. SSA is significantly less expensive than other high performance serial alternatives and should maintain its competitive advantage as technology progresses. Already SSA circuitry requires significantly less power than other high performance serial alternatives.

SSA's designs will integrate functions onto single silicon chips using the industry's lowest cost and power standard CMOS with low-cost and low-power requirements. Today's 80 MByte/sec systems use 0.8 micron CMOS circuits, the current industry standard. Future 0.5 micron CMOS circuits will provide 160 MByte/sec.

Standardization

To insure widespread SSA acceptance, SSA is designed as a *standard* disk drive interface available to numerous disk drive and subsystem manufacturers.

To this end, the American National Standards Institute (ANSI) has formed its X3T10.1 committee, with the intent of approving SSA-PH as an industry standard. Currently, the SSA specification is controlled by the *Serial Storage Architecture Industry Association* which is currently incorporating the *SSA - User's Industry Group (SSA-UIG)*. SSA-UIG comprises leading storage subsystem industry representatives that formed the organization in late 1992 with the intent to eventually hand over SSA-PH control to ANSI.

Finally, the ANSI X3T9.2 committee has accepted the SCSI-3 to SSA mapping project (Serial SCSI Protocol or SSP). The SCSI-2 mapping, or SSA-SCSI, remains with SSA-UIG.

SSA Summary

Serial Storage Architecture is an open, low-cost, high performance serial interface for disk drives and other devices that is extremely efficient. With many proposed enhancements such as SCSI-3 mapping, low power versions, multimedia-specific additions, and performance improvements, SSA is a strong contender to become the preferred serial link.

SSA is a powerful, efficient, low-power, high-performance, and responsive serial interface currently only for disk drives. It will eventually connect disk drives, optical drives, CD-ROMs, tape drives, printers, scanners, and other peripherals to personal computers, workstations, servers, and storage subsystems. SSA's fundamental building blocks are single ports capable of conducting two simultaneous 20 MByte/sec conversations—one inbound, one outbound. A typical SSA connection with two ports can conduct four simultaneous conversations, for a total bandwidth of 80 MBytes/sec.

SSA's dual-port, full-duplex architecture gives peripherals connections with no single point of failure. With SSA, multiple paths are natural, facilitating increased fault tolerance. SSA provides hot plugging and automatic reconfiguration when adding or deleting nodes that can be up to 20 meters apart using low-cost shielded twisted pair wiring.

SSA has multiple topology flexibility including strings, loops, and switch configurations based on a series of point-to-point links requiring no buses and or global arbitration. Typical individual loops can support 127 nodes (peripherals). In complex switched configurations containing multiple loops, the theoretical maximum number of nodes exceeds two million.

SSA links are extremely reliable and use a robust 8B/10B encoding method. Dual-port devices can achieve 80 MBytes/sec effective bandwidth and systems can vastly exceed this using spatial reuse. A SCSI mapping layer provides complete SCSI command compatibility, facilitating SCSI parallel bus migrations.

Data travels in small packets, each packet containing up to a 128 byte payload. Short frame lengths and exceedingly low protocol overheads, coupled with the high bandwidth, ensure excellent response and throughput under peak loading. Point-to-point full duplex linkage allows initiating nodes to talk to any other device in either direction with excellent signal quality and correspondingly low error rates. Each SSA node performs extensive error checking and provides transparent frame recovery if an error occurs.

SSA's exclusive spatial reuse capability enables separate SSA links to perform different operations simultaneously, delivering higher aggregate link throughput than provided by individual nodes. Serial link independence provides bandwidth multiplication depending on node relative link positioning. In effect, several initiators simultaneously can communicate on common loops, multiplying configuration bandwidth.

Since SSA configurations are self-configuring, device repair, insertion, and removal proceed without operational disruption or data loss. SSA's enhanced fault tolerance and resultant availability allows RAID implementations which would be impractical with parallel SCSI, since array configurations are independent of physical cabling.

Fibre Channel-Arbitrated Loop

The Fibre Channel architecture provides high performance links between computing nodes. Originally conceived of as a 1 Gigabit fiber optic point-to-point system, it evolved to include switch and loop topologies, and electrical interconnections. Of particular interest to the storage community is the Fibre Channel-Arbitrated Loop (FC-AL) topology, which promises low cost interconnects for disk drives. Because this book mainly deals with storage systems, it concentrates on FC-AL. However, to fully explain FC-AL requires including much of the material from the broader Fibre Channel standard.

Fibre Channel Topologies

The basic topologies consist of two nodes directly connected by a Fibre Channel link, or a group of nodes connected through a *Fabric*. As indicated in Figure 9-1, links to each node consist of two serial paths, one for each direction of transmission. The Fabric typically

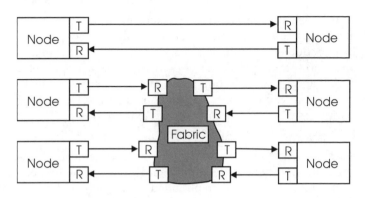

Figure 9-1. Basic Topologies of Fibre Channel

consists of switching hardware, whose internal details are not specified by the Fibre Channel standard. Because the Fabric requires a transceiver for each link between it and a node, the overall topology has twice as many transceivers per node as the point-to-point configuration.

In contrast to the basic topologies, the FC-AL topology arranges nodes in a ring, with the "in" link of one node connected to the "out" port of the adjacent node, as shown in Figure 9-2. Because no switch is required, the number of links and transceivers is cut in half, but any two nodes can still communicate by passing data through intermediate nodes. Each loop can optionally connect to a Fabric port at one point, allowing communication with nodes not on

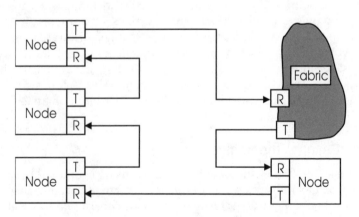

Figure 9-2. Fibre Channel Arbitrated Loop Technology

the loop. Loops are limited to 127 port addresses, including the Fabric port, if present.

In Fibre Channel nomenclature, ports which are part of a node are called *N-ports*, while ports which are part of the Fabric are called *F-ports*. Ports which can participate in an arbitrated loop have "L" included in their name, to become *NL-ports* and *FL-ports*. Such ports can still function as conventional N- and F-ports, but can support the additional protocol necessary for arbitrated loop operation.

Fibre Channel Characteristics

Fibre Channel is a layered protocol consisting of five levels, numbered FC-0 thorough FC-4, which are described by a set of standards documents. The first three levels are part of the FC-PH (or PHysical) standard. FC-0 defines media types, connectors, electrical and optical characteristics. FC-1 defines the signal encoding used for transmission, including the 8B/10B encoding scheme. FC-2 defines a number of link level protocols necessary for operation, including the framing and signaling protocol and the login protocol.

The next level is FC-3, the common services layer. At present there is no standard governing this level. Finally, the mapping of various command sets to Fibre Channel is governed by a set of standards at the FC-4 level. Mappings for a wide variety of popular protocols have been established, each with its own standards document. These include SCSI, HIPPI, IPI-3, SBCCS, IP, IEEE 802, and ATM.

In addition to the basic standards, levels FC-0 through FC-4, there is a separate standard for the FC-AL extension, which augments the FC-PH standard at the FC-1 and FC-2 levels, and a set of profiles to aid in interoperability. Profiles are not standards, but rather recommendations to simplify design and improve interoperability. By limiting the Fibre Channel options, profiles help to reduce costs in specialized applications which don't need the full flexibility of the Fibre Channel standard.

Most FC-0, FC-1, and FC-2 aspects are common to all topologies. At the FC-0 level, Fibre Channel has been defined over both single and multimode fiber optics, several types of electrical coax and twisted pair. Table 9-1 shows the currently defined speeds for Fibre Channel. Speeds range from 12.5 MBytes/sec to 100 MBytes/sec, with even faster speeds expected in the future. Obviously a given link must have compatible hardware on each end, which may pose

Table 9-1: Data Rates for Fibre Channel

Common Name	Baud Rate (Mb/sec)	Data Rate (MBytes/sec)
Eighth Speed	132.8	12.5
Quarter Speed	265.6	25
Half Speed	531.3	50
Full Speed	1062.5	100

interoperability problems (or require a large degree of flexibility by either or both ports).

All Fibre Channel variants use serial links, which are encoded according to the standards at the PH-1 level. This level specifies a serial encoding scheme which converts each 8-bit byte into a 10-bit *character* for transmission. The encoding scheme was originally developed by IBM and is also used in their ESCON and SSA storage interconnect systems. It is known as 8B/10B, and has several advantages for long distance, high speed serial transmission:

- The code allows easy clock recovery by maintaining frequent bit transitions.

- The number of ones and zeros transmitted, averaged over several bytes, remains equal.

- Several additional special characters, beyond the 256 needed to encode the incoming data, are available and can be used for signaling, bit synchronization and delimiters.

- There are a great many invalid codes which enhances error detection.

Maintaining roughly equal numbers of ones and zeros in the transmission stream has long been recognized as necessary for long distance and high speed communication. Technically, the count of ones versus zeros is known as the *disparity* of the bit stream, with an equal overall count termed *neutral disparity*. Maintaining a neutral disparity results in an overall average value of the transmitted signal (known as the Direct Current, or D.C. component) of zero. This allows the use of *A.C. coupled amplifiers*, which are much easier to build than *D.C. coupled*, especially for optical and very high speed electrical transmission systems. Since the 8B/10B code maintains an overall neutral disparity, it efficiently uses high speed electrical or fiber optic links which often cannot tolerate any D.C. signal.

Fibre Channel uses a set of four character long codes (called *ordered sets*) to provide various signaling functions. All of the ordered sets start with a specific character, whose bit pattern is such that it never occurs in any of the rest of the data. The rest of the four characters are chosen such that overall neutral disparity is maintained. Because the codes are unique, and maintain proper disparity, they can be sent outside of the normal framing protocol. Examples of ordered sets are *start of frame*, a frame delimiter; *Idle*, a primitive signal; and *Link_Reset*, a primitive sequence. Both the SCSI Mapping and the FC-AL standards define their own additional primitive signals and sequences which are used to implement necessary protocol extensions.

At the FC-2 level, Fibre Channel uses a protocol consisting of Frames, Sequences and Exchanges. Frames are the basic unit, consisting of up to 2112 bytes of data and optional header. It is expected that a port will be able to buffer at least one frame of data in high speed memory. The size of the buffer can be anywhere from 128 bytes to 2112 bytes, varying in 4 byte increments. Ports can only accept frames which fit in their frame buffers, so maximum frame size is the smallest of the frame buffer sizes at all the ports involved.

Groups of frames make up a *sequence*. Groups of sequences make up an *exchange*. Sequences are unidirectional, requiring that all data flows from the initiator of the sequence to the recipient of the sequence. Exchanges can have only one active sequence at a time, but the sequence initiator may change (or not) with each new sequence. Thus exchanges support bi-directional data flow, but only one direction at a time. For concurrent bi-directional flow, a pair of exchanges are required.

A complete frame consists of a Start of Frame (SOF), a 24 byte required header, optional 64 byte header, up to 2048 bytes of data, a 4 byte Cyclic Redundancy Check (CRC), and an End of Frame (EOF). Frames must be separated at the transmitter by a minimum of 6 ordered sets (e.g., Idles), which totals 24 bytes. A typical frame is shown in Figure 9-3. The required header gives information about the source and destination of the frame, sequence and exchange IDs, and the position of the frame within the sequence (sequence count). The required header also contains four control fields, which help the N_Port determine how to use the frame (Routing CTL and Type), whether there is an optional header (Data Field CTL) and other

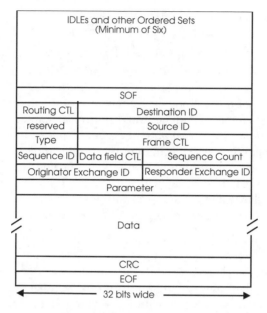

Figure 9-3. Typical Frame Format

information about the frame (Frame CTL). The CRC comes just before the EOF delimiter. The smallest possible frame (i.e., no data) occupies 64 bytes, including the IDLE primitive signals.

Fibre Channel initially defines three classes of service, and an option to intermix exchanges with different classes of service. There are also a couple of additional classes under consideration which may be included in future versions of the standard. Class one, the first class, is a dedicated connection which completely allocates the path between the nodes and guarantees full bandwidth across any intervening Fabric. Class one normally allocates the entire bandwidth of a port, but a port can support an *intermix* option which allows a single class one connection to coexist with frames from class two and class three exchanges. Class two is referred to by the Fibre Channel standard as *connectionless*, because it does not dedicate links to the exchange, though it still requires exchange set up for each pair of communicating nodes. Class two guarantees delivery or notification of non-delivery of frames. Finally, class three offers a datagram service with no delivery guarantee.

Frames are delimited by SOF and EOF ordered sets. Each Class of service has its own SOF for the first frame of a sequence and another one for the rest of the frames. There is also a special Fabric frame SOF (used for communication within a Fabric, but otherwise not defined). There are several different EOF ordered sets, indicating whether the frame is good or not, and whether it is the last frame in a sequence.

Fibre channel offers two forms of flow control for frames: end-to-end through acknowledgment (ACK) frames, and buffer-to-buffer through R_RDY primitive signals. Each of the three currently defined classes of service uses a different combination of flow control methods, summarized in Table 9-2. Class one, which assumes that the Fabric can always handle the full throughput, only uses end-to-end flow control. Class two uses both end-to-end and buffer-to-buffer flow control, while class three only uses buffer-to-buffer flow control. When a port is intermixing class one traffic with classes two and three, the class one traffic has priority and can use the full bandwidth of the link if necessary.

Table 9-2: Flow Control Usage by Service Class

	Buffer-to-Buffer	End-to-End
Service Class 1		*
Service Class 2	*	*
Service Class 3	*	

Class one and two frames are subject to end-to-end flow control thorough ACK frames. Three types of ACK frames are defined: ACK_0 acknowledges all frames of a sequence, ACK_1 acknowledges a single frame, and ACK_N acknowledges N consecutive frames. All ports must support ACK_1, support for the other two forms is optional, but they will be used in preference to ACK_1 if supported at both ends of the exchange.

Buffer-to-buffer flow control works with class two and three frames informing the sending port that the receiving port has space. To indicate such space, the receiving port sends R_RDY primitive signals to the sending port for each frame buffer available at the start of a sequence, and each time a frame buffer again becomes available. The sending port's count of net R_RDYs (received R_RDYs minus sent frames) is known as the port's *BB_Credit*. A port can send new frames as long as BB_Credit is greater than zero. Designs with sufficient frame buffers can offer *Login_BB_Credit* to the sending port, speeding up the beginning of a sequence by allowing the port to send frames before it receives any R_RDYs.

With so many optional features, how do a pair of communicating ports determine which to use? They do so by determining which features they have in common with a port *Login* protocol. Each port uses the protocol to determine the implemented features of the other port, then uses the most powerful of the jointly implemented features. To aid interoperability, Fibre Channel defines a set of base options which all ports must implement. The base set is sufficient for communications, though performance is often improved through use of optional features.

The login procedure returns a frame containing *Common Service Parameters*, which specify a variety of items, including Login_BB_Credit and implemented features. When ports are connected through a Fabric, each port must login with the F_Port to which it is attached, as well as with each N_Port with which it will communicate. For any pair of communicating ports, only features supported by both N_Ports and the Fabric (as communicated by the F_Port) can be used. Thus, each port must maintain a table of Fabric parameters and tables of N_Port parameters for each N_Port. Though logins are expected to be long lasting, port resource limits may require logging out of a port for which no active communication is in progress in order to login to a new port.

Fibre Channel-Arbitrated Loop Operation

The original Fibre Channel standard envisioned point-to-point links connecting a pair of ports which could either be node or Fabric ports. All routing and arbitration was relegated to the Fabric, whose details are outside of the scope of the Fibre Channel standard. However the arbitrated loop, as a shared communications medium, requires the addition of a routing and arbitration protocol, which is implemented in the NL- and FL- ports.

The Fibre Channel loop topology was developed to provide a low cost interconnection methodology for cost sensitive devices such as disk drives. The loop topology allows multiple nodes to communicate without the expense of an intervening Fabric. While the loop topology has lower aggregate bandwidth than a switched Fabric topology, there are many situations were it is quite adequate.

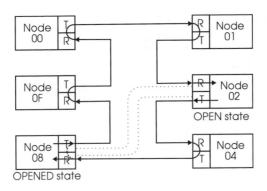

Figure 9-4. Operation of Arbitrated Loop During Data Transfer

As indicated in Figure 9-4, the FC-AL topology creates a virtual point-to-point connection between pairs of nodes, one pair at a time. The node which won arbitration opens the loop and enters the *OPEN* state, while the node with which it is communicating enters the *OPENED* state. These two nodes essentially break the loop, consuming almost all received frames and primitive signals and generating outbound traffic, just as though they had a dedicated link between them. All other nodes on the loop pass received bytes directly from their receivers to their transmitters, with minimal delay. Eventually the loop is closed and other nodes can arbitrate for it.

The basic primitive signals of Fibre channel, IDLE and R_RDY, are extended with the addition of eight new signals. Table 9-3 gives the names of the signals and a brief description. Normal FC-AL operation uses the ARBx, ARB(F0), OPNyx, OPNyy, and CLS primitive signals, which are the only ones which will be further discussed in this book.

Table 9-3: Primitive Signals for FC-AL

ARBx	Arbitrate for access to the loop for node x.
ARB(F0)	ARBs with hex F0 for "x." Used by fairness algorithm.
OPNyx	Open Full Duplex, from node x to node y.
OPNyy	Open Half Duplex to node y.
OPNfr	Open with broadcast replication.
OPNyr	Open with selective replication.
CLS	Close the loop.
MRKtx	Special synchronization signal.

Each node in the loop is assigned a one byte Physical Address (AL_PA) during loop initialization. The addresses are chosen such that they result in neutral disparity. The addresses are used in arbitrate and open primitive signals to indicate which nodes are involved. Address 00_{16} is the highest priority, and is used by the FL_Port, if present. The node addresses continue down to EF_{16}, skipping those which do not exhibit neutral disparity, for a total of 127 node addresses. Several additional addresses beyond EF_{16} also have neutral disparity, but those are reserved for other FC-AL functions.

FC-AL Arbitration Scheme

Ports on an arbitrated loop which have data to send place ARBx primitive signals on the loop in place of Idles or lower priority ARBs. The "x" in ARBx is the physical address of the arbitrating node. A port will continue to send ARBx's until it receives its own ARBx, indicating that the ARBx has completely circled the loop without being intercepted by a higher priority node or the previous arbitration winner. Once in receipt of its ARBx, the port becomes the arbitration winner, and is allowed to open the loop.

The port which acquired the loop must now select another port on the loop with which to communicate. It does this by immediately sending an OPNyx or OPNyy primitive signal addressed to the other port and entering the OPEN state. The port receiving the OPNyx or OPNyy primitive signal then enters the OPENED state. All intervening nodes simply pass through frames, creating a virtual direct link between the OPEN and OPENED ports. In addition to exchanging frames and R_RDY's with the opened port, the OPEN port will discard any ARBx's received from the loop, preventing other nodes from acquiring it. A polite port will note that another port is trying to acquire the loop, however, and release the loop in a timely fashion. A fair port will then wait until other lower priority ports have had a chance to acquire the loop, using a defined fairness algorithm.

The OPNyx signal opens the loop in full duplex mode. In this mode either node may send data to the other, following the exchange and sequence rules of the basic Fibre Channel standard. Alternatively, the loop may be opened using an OPNyy signal, which specifies half duplex operation where only the node transmitting the OPNyy can send data. Either node actively communicating on the loop may end communication by transmitting a CLS primitive signal. The node which won arbitration may immediately open communication with another node after receiving or sending a CLS by entering a TRANS-FER state and then sending a new OPNyx or OPNyy.

Since the basic arbitration algorithm grants port priority based on the physical loop address, higher priority ports could potentially prevent lower priority ports from ever gaining access. To prevent this, a fairness algorithm is defined (though not required) which prevents a node from attempting to gain access until all lower priority nodes have had a chance to acquire the loop.

The fairness algorithm defines an access window, during which all nodes obeying the algorithm are only allowed access to the bus one time. An access window lasts until each node trying to access the bus has gained access, at which time a new access window begins. An ARBx for a node with AL_PA of $F0_{16}$ (which doesn't actually exist but would be the lowest priority node if it did) along with the Idle primitive signal are used to define the access window. The details of the protocol can be obtained by studying the state tables in the FC-AL standard, Revision 4.5, clauses 8.4 and 9.

Arbitration can be fairly expensive, especially in a large loop. This is because the winning port's ARBx must completely traverse the loop, which only happens once the previous arbitration winner relinquishes control of the loop. The previous winner will not relinquish control until it has ended its currently open circuit with receipt of a CLS. Essentially the loop must become free of data frames before it can be acquired by the new winner and a new circuit established. This results in a gap in data transmission equivalent to one to two full loop transits during the close-arbitrate-open process of establishing a new port as arbitration winner. While the pass through delay in each port is small, it still can add up to a significant amount of time in a loop with many ports.

Because the arbitration periods subtract from available loop bandwidth, FC-AL contains several provisions to reduce the amount of arbitration required. One example has already been given, the ability to open a loop in full-duplex mode. This allows bi-directional flow of data frames without having to close and re-open the loop for each change in direction. Another arbitration reduction feature is the ability of an arbitration winner to close and re-open the loop to a different port without relinquishing the loop. This is done using the port's *Transfer* state, which maintains control of the loop while a new circuit is being established. The port must transmit CLS, and enter the transfer state while the CLS circles the loop. Once it receives the CLS, the port can immediately open the loop without arbitrating for it.

FC-AL Initialization

Ports on a loop obtain their physical addresses during the loop initialization process. This is a multi-phase process where a loop master is first assigned, and then addresses are assigned to the rest of the ports. Several loop initialization sequences are assigned to handle the loop initialization, which are inspected and modified by each port as they pass around the loop. The sequences contain information about which possible addresses are still available, so each port can pick one which does not conflict with any other port.

The first phase of initialization determines the loop master. If an FL-port exists, it indicates in the sequence that it should be loop master and discards sequences from any NL-ports trying to become loop master. Once its sequence returns, it assumes mastership. Meanwhile, all NL-ports capable of assuming loop mastership send their own sequences identifying themselves and offering their services. Each such NL-port discards any received sequences whose senders have an algebraically lower port name than its own. Thus, if no FL-port exists, the NL-port with the algebraically highest port name eventually receives back its own sequence, becoming the loop master.

Once a master has been chosen, it initiates four additional phases, each identified by its own loop initialization sequence. In each case, a 16 byte bit map of already assigned AL_PAs is passed around the loop, with each Port grabbing its desired address, if possible. If the desired address is available, the port sets the corresponding bit in the bit map, and saves the address internally for later use. Otherwise, it defers to future phases.

The first of the four port address assignment phases allows ports to grab AL_PAs that were assigned to them previously by the Fabric. If a port never had a Fabric assigned address, but saved its previous address, it can attempt to grab that address during the second phase. If it does not have a previous address saved, it can attempt to grab an address which has been hard coded into it (e.g., through switch settings). If a port has not been able to obtain an address by the fourth phase, it picks one from the set of free addresses, which becomes its soft assigned address. If there are more than 127 ports on a loop, some end up without addresses, and become non-participating ports. At the end of the fourth phase, the loop master may request a complete map of AL_PA assignments using two more loop initialization sequences. Finally, the master transmits the special primitive signal, ARB(F0), to enter normal loop operation.

SCSI Protocol

The SCSI Fibre Channel Protocol (FCP) is one of a number of FC-4 Level mappings for Fibre Channel. The underlying Fibre Channel implementation adheres to the standards described above, and may include point-to-point, Fabric, and Arbitrated Loop topologies. The SCSI FCP maps an I/O operation (as defined in the SCSI Architecture Model (SAM)) to a Fibre Channel exchange, and each request/response primitive of the SAM I/O operation into an FCP Information Unit (IU) sent as a Fibre Channel Sequence.

While various I/O operations are defined, the two most common are *read* and *write*. If a SCSI initiator wishes to begin a read operation, it sends an FCP_CMND payload with the SCSI read command to the target in an unsolicited command IU. The target, when it is ready to return the requested data, sends a data descriptor IU containing the FCP_XFER_RDY payload with a description of the data to be transferred followed by the data in an FCP_DATA IU. If more than one FCP_DATA IU is required, each is preceded by an FCP_XFER_RDY. However, none of the FCP_XFER_RDYs are required if the initiator can determine which data is being sent by other means. When all the data has been transferred, the Exchange ends with an FCP_RSP IU from the target to the initiator.

When a SCSI initiator wishes to begin a write operation, it sends an FCP_CMND payload with the SCSI write command to the target in an unsolicited command IU. The target, when it is ready to receive the proffered data, sends a data descriptor IU containing the FCP_XFER_RDY payload with a description of the data to be transferred. The initiator then sends the data in an FCP_DATA IU. If more than one FCP_DATA IU is required, each is preceded by an FCP_XFER_RDY. However, as with reads, none of the FCP_XFER_RDYs are required if the initiator can determine which data to send by other means. When all the data has been transferred, the Exchange ends with an FCP_RSP IU from the target to the initiator.

Since multiple concurrent exchanges are allowed, multiple commands may be queued up at the target(s), just as in parallel SCSI. The FCP standard allows up to 65535 concurrent exchanges, allowing significant queuing. The number of possible targets depends on the topology, varying from 1 for point-to-point to thousands for a Fabric topology. In addition, FCP has mechanisms for addressing logical units within a port and an extended login sequence to allow SCSI initiators and targets to exchange information about SCSI related capabilities.

Disk Attach Profile

For SCSI storage subsystems using FC-AL for interconnection, a disk attach profile has been developed. The disk attach profile assumes that the SCSI initiators and targets are located on the same Loop. This allows some simplifications in the design of the hardware and the protocols used. Some of the key simplifications loops allow are:

- Only Class 3 frames are allowed. Since FC-AL acts as a point-to-point link once a pair of ports have opened it for communication, only the low overhead R_RDY buffer-to-buffer flow control is required for correct operation. Thus the end-to-end flow control of Classes 1 and 2 is not needed.

- Only Continuous Relative Offsets of data are allowed on reads.

- Read XFER_RDY IUs are not used. Because only Continuous Relative Offsets are allowed, and the initiator is already expecting data from the target, there is no need to send XFER_RDYs on reads. However, write XFER_RDY IUs are still required, because the target may not be ready to receive data immediately after receipt of an FCP_CMND IU from the initiator. The initiator waits for an FCP_XFER_RDY IU before sending FCP_DATA.

There are many other restrictions listed in the profile which attempt to simplify the design and increase the likelihood of interoperability. A few of the other restrictions in the profile are:

- Use of the Transfer state is allowed for SCSI Initiators, but not for SCSI targets.

- Multicast/Selective replicate is prohibited.

- The alternate BB_Credit model is required.

- Login_BB_Credit can be greater than zero, but all ports must support Login_BB_Credit of zero.

■ Mixing of Data and Response in the same sequence on a read or Command and Data in the same sequence on a write is prohibited.

Use of FC-AL for Connecting Disk Drives to Computer Systems

As a concrete example of the above standards, the operation of a Fibre Channel-Arbitrated Loop with a SCSI Fibre Channel Protocol which conforms to the Disk Attach Profile follows. Specifically, both a read and a write operation are presented using the basic half-duplex mode of operation found in the initial implementations. Allowed enhancements to the protocol will be discussed at the end of this section.

For reads, Figure 9-5 illustrates the basic sequence:

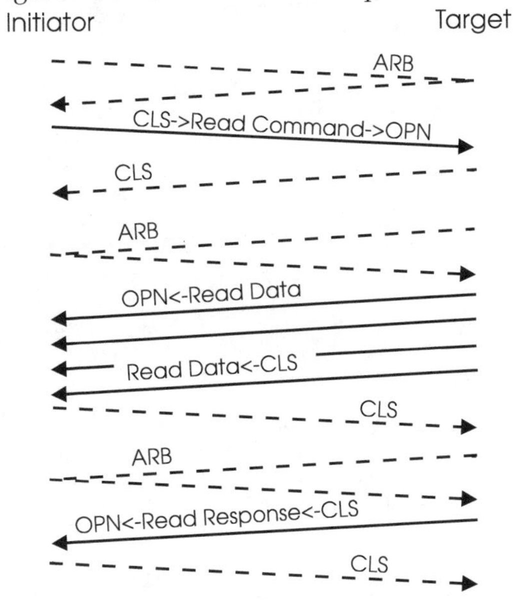

Figure 9-5. SCSI Read Protocol on Fibre Channel

1 The Initiator arbitrates for the loop by sending ARBx, and acquires the loop when it receives its own ARBx. Then the initiator opens the loop to a target in half-duplex mode by sending OPNy, sends a read command as a single frame FCP_CMND IU sequence, then closes the loop with a CLS.

2 The target, when it has the data ready, arbitrates for the loop, opens the loop to the initiator, sends the data as one or more frames in at least one FCP_DATA IU sequence, then closes the loop.

3 Finally, when the target is finished, it arbitrates for the loop, opens the loop to the initiator, sends a response with an FCP_RSP IU, then closes the loop.

For writes, Figure 9-6 illustrates the basic sequence:

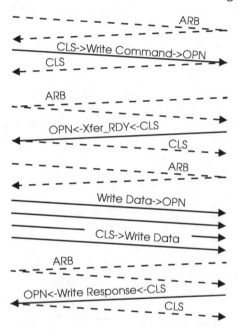

Figure 9-6. SCSI Write Protocol on Fibre Channel

1 The Initiator arbitrates for the loop by sending ARBx, and acquires the loop when it receives its own ARBx. Then the initiator opens the loop to a target with OPNy, sends a write command as a single frame FCP_CMND IU sequence, then closes the loop with a CLS.

2 The target, when it is ready for data, arbitrates for the loop, opens the loop to the initiator in half-duplex, sends an XFER_RDY IU, then closes the loop.

3 The Initiator, when it has the data, arbitrates for the loop, opens the loop to the target in half-duplex, sends the data as one or more frames in an FCP_DATA IU sequence, then closes the loop. If more data is requested than can fit in a single sequence, steps 2 and 3 will be repeated until all data is transferred.

4 Finally, when the target is finished, it arbitrates for the loop, opens the loop to the initiator in half-duplex, sends a response with an FCP_RSP IU, then closes the loop.

On average, each of the arbitrations in these two examples adds 1.5 loop delays. In addition, if Login BB_Credit of Zero is provided, an additional 1 loop delay is added to each arbitration. For large loops, this can result in a considerable loop bandwidth reduction, as each loop delay represents a period of time when no useful data is transmitted. However, use of Login BB_Credit by either or both ports, the Transfer state by the initiator, opening the loop in full-duplex rather than half, and other features, (all of which are allowed in the profile) can significantly reduce the amount of loop delays required to implement the SCSI protocol.

To summarize, Fibre Channel is a serial data transport standard offering high performance and significant implementation flexibility. For the cost sensitive disk drive interconnect market, a combination of the FC-4 layer SCSI protocol with the FC-1 and FC-2 layer Arbitrated Loop extensions and FC-0 GigaBaud electrical cable specifications, and optimized through the Disk Attach Profile exists. SCSI initiator and target implementations which conform to these standards are emerging from a number of vendors to satisfy the bandwidth requirements of the high performance disk subsystem market.

Chapter Questions

1 IEEE 1394 proposes

    a 100 MBit/sec data rate

    b 200 MBit/sec data rate

    c 400 MBit/sec data rate

    d All of the above

2 IEEE 1394 Isochronous traffic

   a Is slower than Asynchronous traffic

   b Is good for multimedia

   c Supports hot-plugging

   d Is obsolete

3 IEEE 1394

   a Uses full duplex transmissions

   b Requires manual configuration

   c Eliminates GAP Times

   d Uses half duplex transmissions

4 IEEE 1394 Root nodes

   a Are selected by jumper settings

   b Determine maximum transmission rates

   c Communicate with other network root nodes peer-to-peer

   d None of the above

5 IEEE 1394 resets typically occur following

   a Node addition or removal

   b Applying bus power

   c ID assignments but only after two consecutive subaction gaps

   d a and b

6 SSA provides

   a Full duplex communication

   b Half duplex communication

   c File Store and Forward functions

   d a and b

7 Valid SSA topologies are

   a Loops

   b Strings

   c Switched Loops

d All of the above

e Only a and c

8 Valid SSA Nodes are

a Dual Port

b Single Port

c Switches

d b and c only

9 FLAGs

a Start and end SSA frames

b Vary in length depending on topology

c May be shared between successive frames

d a and c

10 Spatial Reuse

a Recovers unused network topology for subsequent reuse

b Permits multiple independent simultaneous transmissions whenever possible

c Requires serial link clean up, so SSA avoids its use pervasively

d Is essential to virtual addressing

❐

PC I/O System Software

What This Chapter Is About

This chapter discusses how operating systems and other software interact with hard disks and their controllers, including how they superimpose organization on disk sectors to create data storage repositories.

Eight Miles High

When applications begin processing stored data, they first *open* a data file for *reading, writing,* or both. To open a data file, applications identify the specific data file using a unique name and disk location such as a drive and directory. Operating systems must therefore devise and provide standard ways for naming drives, defining data set locations, and naming data files. This allows applications written on one user's machine to operate predictably on other machines that use the same operating systems.

In a nutshell, applications view a file as a logical data sequence they open, close, read, and write using file system functions. File systems are operating system components that store and retrieve file information using mass storage devices as storage repositories. File systems:

- Manage physical data locations within storage devices

- Manage file I/O operations for applications

- Maintain device, volume, directory, and file information for the operating system

MS-DOS/Windows 95 File System Architecture

With only minor differences (such as Windows 95 longer file names) Microsoft Windows 95 uses the same basic file architecture MS-DOS systems. Under MS-DOS, PCs usually provide a maximum of two floppy disk drives. MS-DOS refers to the first floppy drive as *drive A:* (MS-DOS assigns this drive the *drive letter* "A"), which has a hexadecimal zero BIOS hardware designator. MS-DOS refers to the second diskette drive, if present, as *drive B:*, which has a hexadecimal one BIOS hardware designator. MS-DOS 5.0 and beyond supports up to seven physical hard drives that distinguish among themselves using hardware considerations such as cable locations or jumper settings. MS-DOS logically refers to each physical hard disk drive, in whole or in part, as the *C:* drive, *D:* drive, etc. and internally as *Drive 1*, *Drive 2*, etc. the BIOS addresses these drives using hexadecimal address *80, 81*, etc.

When a diskette or hard disk is first manufactured, it contains no disk sectors—just blank media. Placing sectors on storage media is referred to as *low-level formatting*. In the early PC days, users low-level formatted both diskettes and new hard disks. For diskettes, users ran the MS-DOS FORMAT program which performed low-level formatting and other *high-level formatting* housekeeping activities. However low-level formatting hard disks required special utilities and required users to perform further organizing procedures before MS-DOS could high-level format the device.

Specifically, low-level formatted disks require *partitioning* using the MS-DOS *FDISK* program. Partitioning divides a disk drive into mutually exclusive, contiguous-cylinder groupings called *partitions*. MS-DOS distinguishes between several types of partitions:

- MS-DOS Primary Partitions for various MS-DOS versions

- MS-DOS Extended Partitions

- Non MS-DOS Partition which MS-DOS reserves for other operating systems

MS-DOS primary partitions often encompasses an entire hard disk's capacity—particularly after MS-DOS 4.0 was released. Alternately, an MS-DOS primary partition can consume a portion of a hard disk's capacity as the first partition, leaving the remainder available for designation as an MS-DOS extended partition and/or non MS-DOS partition. The maximum primary partition size varies by

MS-DOS version and the term primary refers to the fact that the system can boot off such a partition if it is on drive zero and properly initialized.

Using the FDISK program, users can divide an extended partition into MS-DOS *logical volumes* which MS-DOS subsequently assigns a system-wide unique drive letter so applications can consider them hard drives. Finally, users specify which hard drive disk partition, if any, is bootable. Only one partition is bootable within any partition table.

Drive Letter Assignments

MS-DOS assigns each disk drive's MS-DOS primary partition the drive's assigned drive letter (Figure 10-1). After assigning drive letters to each hard disk's primary partition, MS-DOS assigns the next available drive letter to the first logical volume within the first drive's extended partition, the next letter to the next logical volume on the first drive, etc. When all logical volumes within the first drive's extended partition have assigned drive letters, MS-DOS repeats the process in increasing drive order for each extended partition. Since the English alphabet has 26 letters and MS-DOS reserves two letters for diskette drives, MS-DOS systems can reference 24 storage volumes (primary partitions, logical volumes, CD-ROMs, network Drives, etc. using drive letters.

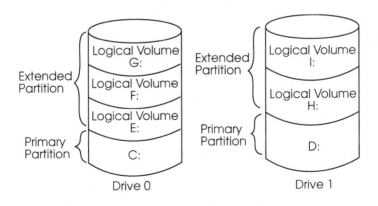

Figure 10-1. MS-DOS Drive Name Assignments

Partition Information Storage

FDISK stores a drive's user-specified partition and logical volume strategy in reserved sectors on the associated drive. Cylinder zero, track zero's sector one contains a drive's *partition table*. This sector provides each partition's starting/stopping cylinders and whether a partition is bootable. A small program that inspects the partition table to determine which partition, if any, is a bootable partition, precedes the partition table. The program only operates if it resides on the MS-DOS drive zero primary partition (logical C: drive).

During the boot sequence, BIOS first attempts to boot from diskette, though many motherboard CMOS implementations allow this to be optional. If a diskette is in the A: drive, PC BIOS attempts to read side zero, track zero, sector zero into PC memory at hexadecimal address 7C00. If the sector ends with a hexadecimal 55AA value, PC BIOS executes it as a program. Formatted diskettes that do not have a bootable operating system do contain a small program that, when executed, indicates to users the diskette is a non-system diskette. MS-DOS FORMAT writes this program after a non-system diskette format operation. If the format operation did place an OS on the diskette, the small program contains the logic to load the OS from the diskette, enabling it to boot from diskette.

If no diskette is in the A: drive, PC BIOS attempts to boot from the C: drive's primary partition. PC BIOS reads the partition table's sector into PC memory at hexadecimal address 7C00 and inspects it to be sure it is not empty. If it does not contain all zeros, PC BIOS executes it as a program. This small program inspects its appended partition table, selects the bootable partition, and reads its first sector in, referred to as the *boot record*. If this sector ends with a hexadecimal 55AA value, the master partition table's program executes it as a program, beginning the boot process.

Storage Volume Organization

Applications reference data files by drive letter, and file name. Each storage volume therefore maintains a directory, referred to as a *root directory*, that contains 512 32-byte entries. Each in-use entry is associated with a file the volume contains. An in-use entry contains a *file name* which consists of up to eight characters for the file name and up to three characters for the *file extension*, referred to as the *8.3 naming convention*. A directory entry indicates whether its associated file is a system file, hidden (invisible to the MS-DOS *DIR* command), is read-only, has been backed-up since last use, and whether the file is a *subdirectory* that provides a named extension to the root directory. Finally, the directory entry contains file size, file time-stamp information the MS-DOS DIR command displays, as well as a *File Allocation Table* or *FAT* entry value MS-DOS uses to calculate where to find the file's first sectors within the volume.

The MS-DOS FAT

MS-DOS allows applications to create files on storage volumes. To prevent two files from simultaneously attempting to occupy the same physical sectors and one overwriting the other in the process, MS-DOS maintains a table within each logical volume and primary partition that reflects what sectors are already in use and which ones are available for use. Historically, the number of entries in this table varied over time with MS-DOS releases. Early MS-DOS version FATs only contained 4,096 entries. Current MS-DOS versions provide 4,096 entries for volumes smaller than approximately 15 MBytes and 64K entries for volumes larger than this size.

Uniquely associated with each FAT entry is one or more physical sectors collectively called a *cluster* or *allocation unit* depending on the MS_DOS version. All FAT entries have a constant number of associated sectors (indicated in the volume's partition table). To calculate the approximate sector count associated with a given FAT's individual entries, divide the volume's total bytes by 65,536 (64K) and round up to the nearest power of two (2, 4, 8, 16, 32, or 64). While the maximum number theoretically is any power of two up to 256, MS-DOS only allows a maximum of 64 sectors to associate with each FAT entry. Sixty-four sectors per cluster provides a theoretical maximum total volume capacity of 65,536*64*512 bytes or 2 GBytes per volume. The following table partially summarizes the FAT evolution.

DOS Version	Cluster Index Size	Max Available Cluster Subset	Sectors Per Cluster	Max Supported Partition Size
<3.0	12 Bits	4,096	8	16 MBytes
3.0 to <4.0	12 or 16 Bits	4,096 or 16,384	4	32 MBytes
4.0 to <5.0	12 or 16 Bits	4,096 or 65,536	4	128 MBytes
5.0+	12 or 16 Bits	4,096 or 65,536	4 to 64	2,048 MBytes

Note that PC BIOS and IDE architecture impose other constraints that collectively limit a drive's capacity to 512 MBytes as summarized below. Enhanced IDE (EIDE) designs abandon CHS (Cylinder/Head/Sector) addressing and use LBA (Logical Block Addressing) to circumvent this limit.

Design Point	Max Cylinders	Max Heads	Max Sectors/ Track	Data Sector Size	Max Disk Size
BIOS	1,024	255	63	512 Bytes	8.4 GBytes
IDE/AT-A	65,536	16	255	512 Bytes	136.9 GBytes
Lowest Common Denominator	1,024	16	63	512 Bytes	0.5 GBytes

Using the FAT

Today, hard disk FAT tables usually contain 16-bit entries. The following table indicates allowable FAT entry values and their interpretation.

FAT Value	Meaning
0000h	Unused Cluster
0001h–FFEFh	Pointer
FFF0h–FFF6	Reserved
FFF7	Bad Cluster
FFF8–FFFF	Last Cluster

When MS-DOS opens a file listed within a volume's root directory, it uses the file's size value to determine how many clusters the file owns. It then uses the first cluster's value found in the directory entry, say hexadecimal value 0006, to calculate the file's first sector location (Figure 10-2). Next, it uses this cluster value as a FAT index and fetches the FAT entry at that FAT location, say entry 0006. If entry 0006 has a value from hexadecimal FFF8 to hexadecimal FFFF, no more file sectors exist. Otherwise, entry 0006 contains a *pointer* value ranging from hexadecimal value 0001 to FFEF which MS-DOS uses to locate the next file cluster and index again into the FAT. This continues until MS-DOS eventually finds an entry with a hexadecimal value of FFF8 to FFFF, indicating no more file clusters exist. The clusters MS-DOS traverses comprise the file's FAT *cluster chain*.

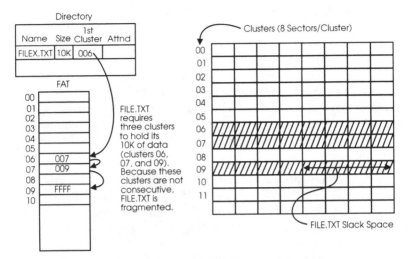

Figure 10-2. FAT Cluster

FAT Problems

MS-DOS's cluster-oriented FAT file system is simple and straight-forward. However, it induces a few problems:

- File fragmentation
- Capacity utilization
- FAT referencing
- Directory searching
- Physical geometry vulnerability
- Lack of a file transaction log or other recovery mechanism

File Fragmentation

MS-DOS views any storage volume as a linear sector pool (numbered sector zero through the last sector) it parcels out to files in cluster allocation units consisting of one or more sectors. When MS-DOS superimposes linear structure on a volume, it uses the first few sectors to describe the volume, the next few for a fixed-size File Allocation Table, the next few for the root directory and the remainder for the data files which include subdirectories.

When applications create files, MS-DOS finds the first unused FAT entry and allocates it for the file. If the file consumes this space and requires additional space, MS-DOS finds the next unused FAT entry and allocates it to the file, and so on. With each activity, MS-DOS updates the cluster chain pointers correctly. For best performance, the clusters should be physically adjacent on the same disk track. To assist in this placement, MS-DOS remembers where it found the last available cluster and begins searching from there for the next. On empty disks, this allows MS-DOS 5.0 and above to attempt sequential allocation.

However, when applications delete files, MS-DOS marks the directory entry as empty and zeros out the file's FAT chain. This later allows MS-DOS to reuse the space for other files. Since MS-DOS maintains a *cluster high-water mark* this available space is not used until MS-DOS is restarted or is forced to start at the beginning of the FAT after reaching the end.

Over time, MS-DOS's continual freeing and reallocation of space forces it to use non-adjacent clusters for file allocations. When files do not fit in available chunks, MS-DOS places the overlap in one or more other chunks. This results in performance degrading *file fragmentation* which forces MS-DOS to skip to various disk areas to read files. Popular disk utilities, including MS-DOS's DEFRAG utility temporarily eliminates file fragmentation by reorganizing disk file placement, often providing significant improvement in file I/O operations by reducing seeks and rotations required to access data. This procedure must be repeated periodically

Capacity Utilization

With the cluster-based FAT file system, a cluster is the minimum allocation unit. Therefore, each file wastes an average of one half cluster per file as unused *slack space* within the file's last cluster (Figure 10-3). Since desktop systems often have a few thousand files, wasted capacity can equal the space consumed by a thousand or more clusters and consume significant space.

An odd side effect can occur when moving all data from a smaller disk to a slightly larger disk. If the smaller disk is nearly full and the larger disk uses more sectors per cluster, all the data on the smaller disk may not fit on the larger disk. This is because the larger disk's increased slack space reduces its effective capacity below the smaller disk's effective capacity.

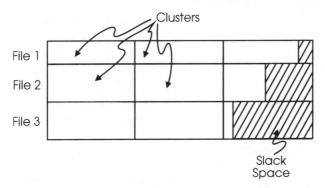

Figure 10-3. File Slack Space

FAT Referencing

MS-DOS provides a rudimentary software buffer utility. The
CONFIG.SYS BUFFERS parameter controls the maximum number
of hard disk sectors MS-DOS caches at any time. As MS-DOS reads
disk sectors, the data replaces the buffer's contents, eventually flushing previous contents. Since the cache also stores FAT sectors and an
entire hard disk FAT is too large to keep in memory, flushing FAT
sectors for file data forces MS-DOS to re-read the FAT table for subsequent cluster address resolution activities. This generates significant disk seek activity as MS-DOS alternates between FAT and file
accesses. Microsoft's SMARTDRV.EXE utility can mitigate this to
some degree.

Directory Searching

As MS-DOS creates files, it uses the first 32 byte file entry it finds
within the root directory or appropriate subdirectory. Since applications create files in varying order and MS-DOS has no provision to
order directory file entries, MS-DOS exhaustively searches directories for file information. When files reside within subdirectories
nested several levels deep as subdirectories of subdirectories of subdirectories etc., the searching consumes significant time, particularly
when the subdirectories are fragmented themselves. The searching
is an unfortunate file system side effect so the only performance
strategy is to avoid deep subdirectory nesting and to perform periodic disk defragmentation.

Physical Geometry Vulnerability

Like all operating systems, MS-DOS has no visibility into a translating disk's true cylinder, track, and sector geometry. So, while software may implement well-intended disk activity optimizations to minimize seek delays, the attempt may be in vain since it uses invalid information necessary to bypass BIOS and hard disk compatibility problems. This situation is not usually solvable unless disks provide actual geometry to operating system software.

Windows Family

When MS-DOS begins execution, the PC system unit processor operates in *real mode*. In real mode, 80386, 80486, Pentium, etc. processors emulate 8086 processors. They provide segmented memory addressing within 1 MByte address spaces using 16 bit registers. In this environment, there is no memory protection that prevents one application from disrupting the system by inappropriately changing memory values or I/O register settings.

When *Microsoft Windows 3.1* or *Windows for Workgroups* begins execution on an Intel 80386, 80486, Pentium, or Pentium-Pro, they usually quickly switch to *386 enhanced mode* which provides application memory protection within a 4 GByte address space. This prevents applications from capriciously modifying I/O control registers and provides rudimentary (cooperative) multitasking support whose effectiveness depends on applications being well behaved. Literature refers to this as *32-bit mode*. However, various problems arise when applications begin accessing devices.

First, Windows does not provide all BIOS support nor device drivers that are available for MS-DOS applications. Second, I/O activities typically manipulate I/O registers that Windows controls and protects. To solve these problems and simultaneously provide MS-DOS compatibility, Windows supports existing device drivers using *Virtual 8086 Mode*.

The 80386 and subsequent follow-on processor architecture allows operating systems to set aside 1 MByte virtual address space ranges and designate them as *Virtual 8086* or *V86* machines. In the case of the MS-DOS, Windows sets up an MS-DOS virtual 8086 machine that executes necessary MS-DOS FAT file, hardware BIOS and device drivers support loaded during MS-DOS initialization.

Programs executing in V86 mode execute in what is referred to as *16-bit mode*. When Windows applications access devices that the MS-DOS V86 device drivers control, Windows passes control to MS-DOS in 16-bit mode and the device driver programming eventually executes. However, when the device drivers attempt to access an I/O register or manipulate interrupts, a hardware exception occurs.

Programming exceptions reactivate Windows control code which references privilege tables to determine if the exception should be allowed. If so, Windows performs the operation for the V86 machine and programming resumes execution following the interruption point. There is significant complexity here, but the essential point is that V86 programming generates repeated hardware exceptions that require measurable CPU computing bandwidth overhead to resolve. Moreover, processor instruction pipelines and caches flush each time before executing several instructions to service the individual instructions generating the exceptions.

To eliminate this, Microsoft and hardware OEMs rewrote their 16-bit BIOS and device drivers as 32-bit mode modules. For disks, such BIOS programming support is referred to as *32-bit disk access*. While 32-bit disk access provides measurable performance benefit, the most significant benefit results from native 32-bit MS-DOS VFAT support and its consequences.

Native 32-Bit VFAT Support

Since Windows applications use MS-DOS FAT file systems, Microsoft rewrote MS-DOS FAT services for Windows For Workgroups to allow native Windows 32-bit mode programming to access FAT file volumes without resorting to MS-DOS V86 mode machines. This 32-bit support is referred to as *32-bit file support* or *VFAT* support and first appeared in Windows For Workgroups 3.11.

Prior to VFAT support, Windows used a 4 KByte MS-DOS V86 area as an I/O buffer area. Windows decomposed application I/O requests larger than 4 KBytes into more than one 4 KByte request which it sequentially passed to the MS-DOS V86 machine. Each such file I/O required moving data an additional time from the V86 machine to the correct protected mode memory area. The performance degradation compared to native 32-Bit VFAT Support was *devastating*.

Benchmark Devastation

Further increasing 32-bit file support's advantage over MS-DOS, Microsoft replaced MS-DOS's SMARTDRV.EXE caching program with the native 32-bit protected mode caching program VCACHE.386. Needless to say the performance difference was dramatic when Microsoft also bundled 32-bit IDE BIOS support with Windows for Workgroups 3.11. Since this bundling does not automatically include 32-bit SCSI disk support, vigilant benchmark reviewers must determine whether benchmarks actually provide head-to-head comparisons using 32-bit support for both SCSI and IDE. On occasion they do not and lead to sensational, but misleading and erroneous, reviews.

For example, many I/O subsystem benchmarks issue 64 KByte data requests when VCACHE is present. Prior to 32-bit file support, Windows decomposed these requests into sixteen 4 KByte requests. This meant 64 KByte requests executed various code paths 15 times more under MS-DOS V86 machines. The V86 mode code also generated exceptions not experienced by 32-bit programming.

Benchmarks show that 32-bit applications emerging for Windows 95 and Microsoft NT can be 40 to 50 percent faster than their 16-bit counterparts depending on depending on the application and type processing it performs. File I/O performance alone improves by as much as 60 percent.

OS/2 High Performance File System (HPFS)

When IBM and Microsoft began work on OS/2, a primary goal was to improve MS-DOS's FAT file system. Ray Duncan's September 1989 *Microsoft Systems Journal* article titled "Design Goals and Implementation of the New High Performance File System" outlined their approach which conceded that the MS-DOS FAT system was originally designed to optimize diskette file access and that even as early as 1987 the FAT file systems fundamental data structures were "simply not well suited to large random access devices." So, they applied their best minds to solve the problem.

Gordon Letwin, Microsoft's Chief OS/2 Architect, formulated the HPFS design which significantly differs from the MS-DOS FAT approach. While MS-DOS's file system was embedded in and inseparable from MS-DOS, OS/2's file system was an *installable file system* (*IFS*)—external to its native host operating system which loads it as the operating system begins operation after examining the system's CONFIG.SYS. For compatibility and diskette file interchange considerations, HPFS only supports hard disks, not diskette drives.

OS/2 permits multiple file systems to be active simultaneously. For example, one hard disk may require HPFS while another may require the OS/2 FAT file system. The OS/2 FAT file system emulates MS-DOS's FAT file system to control floppy disk storage and, optionally, hard drive storage. During OS/2 installation, users elect to format drives using HPFS which HPFS subsequently manages. If other hard drives use the FAT file system the OS/2 FAT file system manages them and all diskette drives.   When applications call *DosOpen* to open HPFS controlled files, OS/2 directs the requests to HPFS. Alternately, when applications call *DosOpen* to open FAT controlled files, OS/2 directs the requests to its OS/2 FAT file system.

OS/2 HPFS Components

OS/2 installs file system components after referencing the CONFIG.SYS file system component specifications. OS/2 file system software consists of:

- Device drivers which access storage devices

- Dynamic link libraries which control device information format and manage data flows to and from devices

DEVICE parameters control device driver loading and *IFS* parameters specifies dynamic link libraries.

OS/2's High Performance File System consists of:

- The HPFS driver: HPFS.IFS

- The HPFS write cache (*lazy-write*) utility: CACHE.EXE

- The HPFS lazy-write startup program: STARTLW.DLL

- The HPFS utilities: UHPFS.DLL

When the operating system initialization code encounters a CONFIG.SYS IFS specification, it loads the specified installable file system. The operating system also loads device drivers similarly specified by DEVICE parameter specifications and initializes specific devices for use by their file system.

HPFS Feature Overview

In many cases, HPFS file operations improve upon FAT file system operations because of HPFS's features which include:

- Sorted long file names within directories
- OS/2 multi-threaded I/O support
- File system data structure caching
- Write-behind logic with optional write-through caching
- Strategic directory structure allocation
- Highly contiguous file allocation
- Enhanced recoverability
- Extended attribute support

Long File Name Support

HPFS file names can contain 255 characters, including characters the FAT file system considers invalid—spaces for example. Hierarchical subdirectory names can also have up to 255 characters but a total path including drive, directories, and file name cannot exceed 259 characters.

Multi-threaded I/O Operations

OS/2's improved (preemptive) native multithreading support allows processors to continue application processing during I/O delays. As indicated in the SCSI Overview chapter, this can greatly accelerate application processing. Since it was designed to do this from the outset without many of MS-DOS's restrictions, it is more successful than Windows 3.1 in achieving overlapped I/O.

Write-Behind Logic With Optional Write-Through Caching

HPFS accesses disk volumes using a memory cache accessed as 2 KByte *blocks*. Data travels to and from disks through this cache, improving frequently used data cache availability. When requested data is not in the cache, HPFS selects the least-recently used expendable block and fills it with the requested data. HPFS copies deferrable write requests into cache blocks and signals I/O completion to the system without actually performing the disk-write operation.

HPFS later writes the data to disk using a background thread which appears to accelerate write operations more than file systems only using synchronous write operations. HPFS refers to deferred writes as *lazy writes*. Users select lazy-write support levels by specifying CACHE.EXE command line parameters:

- MaxAge: When cache data block residencies exceed this time specification, blocks queue for disk writing. This reduces lost data from unexpected system shutdowns.

- DiskIdle and BufferIdle: When I/O requests (non-lazy-write) do not appear for *DiskIdle* milliseconds, all cache blocks (oldest first) untouched for *BufferIdle* milliseconds queue for disk writing. This enables HPFS to write data during relatively inactive disk periods, reducing heavily used cached block rewrites.

HPFS supports a different hierarchical directory structure than the MS-DOS FAT file system. Therefore, the MS-DOS FAT file system cannot recognize HPFS files. However, MS-DOS applications running in a MS-DOS Session under the OS/2 operating system do recognize files and directories on both FAT and HPFS disks because the OS/2 FAT file system handles MS-DOS Session I/O.

HPFS Space Management

Gordon Letwin initially designed HPFS with a clean slate, intending to exploit OS/2's multitasking ability fully. HPFS uses a new type partition (*HPFS Partitions*) to distinguish them from previous MS-DOS FAT partitions.

Bands

HPFS partitions use 512 byte sector allocations. This single aspect makes HPFS partition space utilization vastly more efficient than FAT partitions but limits maximum storage addressing. HPFS allocates the first 8 KBytes (sectors zero to 15) to a boot block. The next two sectors are referred to as the SuperBlock and SpareBlock (Figure 10-4), and are discussed later. System functions maintains the SuperBlock which points to:

- Free space bit maps
- Bad sector map
- Root directory
- Directory Block Band

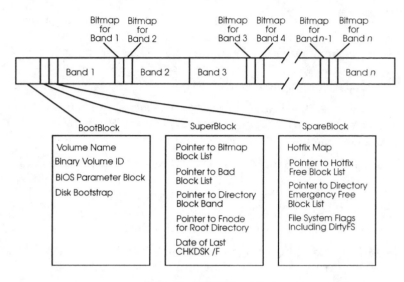

Figure 10-4. HPFS Structure

HPFS divides the remaining partition space into 8 MByte *bands*. Each contains its own free space bit-map. Adjacent band pairs have adjacent bit-map bands, allowing maximum 16 MByte contiguous allocation areas. One band, referred to as the *Directory Block Band* resides near or at the partition's center.

Fnodes

Fnodes are fundamental file system objects. Every file and directory has an associated Fnode which resides in a complete sector. Fnodes contain:

- Historical control and access information HPFS uses

- Extended file attribute information

- Access control lists for file security

- Allocation structure

- File length

- The object name's first 15 characters

File Extents

HPFS files comprise one or more contiguous sectors individually referred to as *extents*. HPFS describes extents using two 32 bit values containing the start and end sectors respectively. Fnode *allocation structures* hold 8 extent descriptors, usually allowing a single-sector Fnode to completely describe a small file's extents or a large contiguous file with eight or fewer extents. In other instances, Fnodes point to as many as 12 *allocation sectors* which contain as many as 40 paired start and end sector values—one pair per extent. If this is insufficient, intermediate allocation sectors can individually point to as many as 60 other allocation sectors which individually point to as many 40 extents, and so on. This arrangement allows fast file offset translation to extent locations.

Directories

Fnodes also describe directories which consist of one or more contiguous 2 KByte *directory blocks*. HPFS attempts to locate directory blocks in a band's center but can locate them anywhere. Directory entries are variable length but with 13 character names, each holds about 40 entries which appear in alphabetical order. When a directory block has no more space, the directory structure becomes hierarchical, which accelerates searching activities. At 40 entries per block, a two-level directory block hierarchy can hold as many as 1,640 entries and a three-level can hold as many as 65,640 entries. Beyond that, to avoid directory reorganization space problems, HPFS can use available blocks in the SpareBlock.

Extended Attributes

MS-DOS had few file attributes because it was never designed for networking or security. HPFS allows each file to have up to 64 KBytes of associated file attribute information referred to as *extended attributes*. Extended attributes can reside within the file's Fnode or within an extended attribute hierarchical structure. Applications and OS/2 can use extended attributes to determine whether applications use files in sequential or random mode and apply appropriate caching strategies.

HPFS Performance

The September 1989 HPFS *Microsoft Systems Journal* article stated "...the fundamental data structures used by the FAT file system are simply not well suited to large random access devices....The HPFS solves all the historical problems of the FAT file system." It did this using multitasking-enabled lazy writes, caching, sophisticated data structures, consecutive sector file allocation, space management information located near associated sectors, and sophisticated file allocation strategies.

When HPFS allocates files, it scatters them across separate bands where possible to minimize interleaved file extents (fragmentation). New files also obtain extra space for expansion. The HPFS file close operation reclaims unused space. Finally, applications can help HPFS by indicating at file creation time how large the file will eventually be. This allows HPFS to create maximum size extents, reducing subsequent fragmentation.

When Microsoft published the 1989 HPFS article, HPFS was not yet completely operational. With HPFS now fully implemented and on millions of desktops, Microsoft has apparently reconsidered OS/2's HPFS design advantages and now does not consider HPFS particularly interesting, perhaps even an experiment that failed. One suggested major flaw is its metadata, written at 16 MByte intervals throughout a partition, which was originally intended to decrease head movement. Since file system control data tends to cache, localizing it in the partition's front like MS-DOS does is "a more effective architecture" particularly with zoned bit recording where lower addressed sectors have the best access rates, hence fewer seeks per sector.

It is interesting to see how well-intended efforts by some of industry's finest minds eventually produce unanticipated results, such as using the FAT file system in Windows 95. With performance, there's always another surprise.

Microsoft Windows NT and NT File System (NTFS)

DOS and Windows were originally designed with 16-bit Intel processors in mind. As such, they dealt with Intel's segmented architecture, 20-bit address limits, and the tendency of many early DOS programs to access hardware resources directly which the operating system was supposed to manage. But Windows NT is a totally new design which exploits 32-bit addresses and paging hardware provided by newer Intel processors (80386 and higher) and other RISC processors. This gives each user program and the operating system a full 32 bit linear address space, greatly simplifying programming. The paging hardware also allows efficient virtual memory and protection implementation, an ability Windows NT exploits.

Since Windows NT is a totally new design, its specification includes numerous other ambitious goals. Most of Windows NT is written in C, with only a small portion of processor specific machine code. This, plus a modular and flexible architecture allows relatively easy porting to a variety of processors. The modularity also assists in achieving extensibility to support new uses and new hardware. In addition, Windows NT designers recognize that PCs are being used in ever more critical applications, so the design goals included achieving high robustness and security levels.

Early personal computer operating systems allowed one program to run at a time. But as applications have grown more sophisticated, it is recognized that allowing multiple programs to run concurrently is quite useful. At a minimum, background tasks such as printing should operate while interactive applications (such as word processors) run in the foreground. The Windows NT designers decided to provide a full *multitasking* operating system (also referred to as *multiprogramming*), a scheme which allows a wide range of applications and background tasks to share the computer. They even went one step further by providing a finer grain of multitasking known as *multithreading*, which allows a single program to use multiple execution streams.

The DOS and Windows operating systems have existed over a decade and millions of copies and compatible applications are in use. Providing these old applications some compatibility mode under Windows NT was an obvious requirement. But compatibility was extended to two other popular PC and workstation operating system environments: OS/2 (a PC operating system developed by IBM and Microsoft) and POSIX (an international standard for UNIX style operating system interfaces). Finally, it was necessary to provide these features without sacrificing overall performance. Compatibility requirements, combined with the robustness and security requirements, dictated a new file system structure, NTFS.

Modular Structure

Many older operating systems are *monolithic*—consisting of one large, complicated program which manages all system resources. Monolithic operating systems are very difficult to debug and enhance. Typically there is great interdependence between various OS sections and seemingly innocuous changes in one part can cause serious problems to appear in another. Though some potential performance advantages exist with the monolithic approach, it has been losing favor to designs which isolate components.

In the modular approach, operating system components communicate through well defined interfaces. Often some components are run as user level processes in isolated address spaces, further protecting them from external damage and preventing them from causing external damage. Windows NT does run *User Subsystems* (which provide various OS "personalities" to the users) as *user mode* processes. However, the remaining operating system, including the I/O subsystem, runs at *kernel level*, were it has full access to the computing resources. Individual drivers and system services constituting the operating system kernel communicate through well defined interfaces, providing many of the benefits of a modular architecture.

I/O Subsystem

The I/O subsystem consists of an I/O System Services layer which communicates with the user subsystems to handle I/O requests. The requests are placed into *I/O Request Packets* (*IRPs*) which are then passed to the I/O Manager to distribute to the drivers. Windows NT allows layered drivers, with each layer handling a different aspect of a particular request. The I/O Manager is responsible for passing the IRPs between the layers as appropriate.

Using layered drivers allows great flexibility in processing I/O requests and sharing driver functionality at several levels. For example, Figure 10-5 shows how I/O requests for a CD and a two disk drives might proceed through the I/O system. CD-ROM requests pass through the CD file system driver (file systems are implemented as drivers), then are converted to a SCSI request in the CD-ROM SCSI *Class Driver*, arrive at the correct miniport driver via the SCSI port driver, and finally reach the left most host adapter. Disk0 requests pass through the NT file system, the Disk SCSI Class Driver, the SCSI port driver and finally the same miniport driver and host adapter as the CD-ROM request. Meanwhile, Disk1 requests pass through the same NTFS driver and SCSI class driver and SCSI port driver, but use the right-most miniport driver and host adapter.

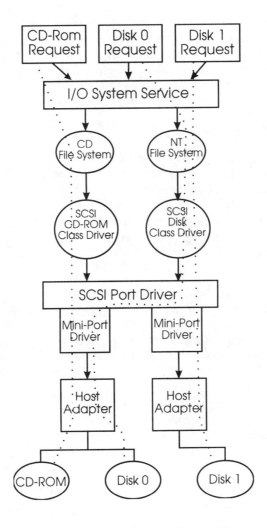

Figure 10-5. Layered Drivers in Windows NT

Because of the layered approach, additional drivers are easily added for new devices or when new functionality is required. Additional drivers, called *filter drivers*, may reside between layers to enhance functionality. For example, a disk performance monitor driver can reside between the file system layer and the SCSI class layer. Similarly, a SCSI printer might require adding a SCSI class printer driver. While I/O system drivers must install at boot time, some network system drivers can actually install at run time, allowing new protocol stack support without rebooting the machine.

Hardware Abstraction Layer

Many early operating systems, including MS-DOS, were written in assembly language and hence could only be used on the CPU family for which they were originally designed. But modern operating systems, Windows NT included, are written in higher level languages which can be compiled for almost any CPU family. Thus, it is possible to construct operating systems which can be ported to almost any CPU, provided that most of the operating system does not depend on CPU hardware details.

To simplify porting, Windows NT isolates hardware dependencies in its *Hardware Abstraction Layer* (*HAL*). The HAL provides a consistent interface to the remaining operating system, regardless of the hardware eccentricities. This is the hardware register's management layer that controls memory mapping, task switching and other specific hardware resources. By confining the lowest levels of these very hardware dependent activities to a single layer, porting programmers do not have to worry about making changes to the bulk of the operating system code. Windows NT has been ported to the PowerPC, MIPS, and ALPHA microprocessors, as well as the Intel 80x86 family.

Security and Reliability

Multi-user systems, such as servers, have long provided users protection from each other (security) and from the effects of failing hardware (reliability). In today's networked environment, even desktop PC users need protection from unauthorized program and data access, and users expect their systems to be far more reliable than ever. Thus Windows NT included security and reliability from the outset.

Initially, Windows NT provides security at the government defined C2 level (levels running from A1 to D, with A1 the most secure and D the least secure). At level C2, the operating system provides a secure logon facility, discretionary access control, auditing and memory protection. Windows NT allows system administrators to create user accounts with user names (identifiers) and passwords. Verification that the user name and password is correct is done by a protected subsystem with access to the security system's database. If the verification is successful, a user process is created, and an access token for the user is attached to it.

Access Control Lists (*ACL*), which list each user and group's allowed access to a resource, and how they may use the resource, provide discretionary access control. For example, a file owner might provide a specific co-worker read and write access to a particular file, and read access to all other department members. The ACL would include an entry for the co-worker's ID with the read and write privileges bits set, and an entry for the department's group ID with the read privileges bit set. Should someone whose ID or group is not in the file's ACL attempt access, the access will be denied and an entry will be made in the security audit log. The auditing feature, which records the ID of the user whose access was denied, helps system administrators detect deliberate attempts to thwart security.

Finally, a fundamental feature of any security system is the system's ability to protect the kernel from running processes and protect the running processes from each other. This is accomplished through memory protection provided by the virtual memory system and paging hardware. Besides preventing direct access from one user memory space to another (accept for regions of explicitly shared memory) the virtual memory system must "zero out" memory pages before reassigning them to new processes, to prevent information leakage between users.

The modular structure of Windows NT combined with the protection features of the security system provide reliability levels not seen in MS-DOS or earlier Windows versions. While a system running Windows NT is not fault-tolerant in the sense of surviving any single point of failure, it can detect and recover from many common forms of hardware and user software failure. For example, MS-DOS application bugs can easily crash the whole machine, while they only crash the particular user's process in Windows NT. Normally the system continues to run and other users are unaffected.

With the advent of large scale integration, logic component failure crashes are quite rare. But computers remain vulnerable to critical data losses due to disk drive media imperfections. The Windows NT file system, discussed later, protects key data structures from the effects of such imperfections, greatly reducing this common cause of system crashes. In addition, mirrored and other redundant file storage types are available to further reduce system crash and data loss risk.

Finally, Windows NT's modular structure and its well defined module interfaces make bug detection easier during development, because modules can detect erroneous requests from other subsystems. Such requests often indicate bugs in the calling subsystem, which can then be quickly fixed by the developers. While this approach to system design does not, in itself, result in bug free code, it does help, especially with large, complicated software projects such as an operating system.

Multi-threading and Multiprocessing

Windows NT supports:

- Concurrent multiple user processes (multitasking)

- Multiple execution threads within user processes

- Parallel computing through symmetric shared memory multiprocessing

This is partly possible through Windows NT's modular design, plus the memory management hardware found on current processors and consistently using locking to access critical data structures.

The basic computing entity is the *thread of execution* or *thread*. An execution thread consists of a:

- Unique identifier

- Volatile register set, including the program counter

- User mode stack

- Kernel mode stack

In other words, a thread consists of the basic execution state required to run a program. Each thread has a few private storage area pages reserved for this volatile state. Many threads can exist, but only one can execute on a given processor at a time. To resume a suspended thread's execution requires saving the current thread's volatile state and restoring the new thread's saved volatile state. The new thread resumes executing where it stopped. In this way, the operating system appears to run many independent threads simultaneously.

While threads keep track of execution sequences, other resources are necessary to support them. These resources are contained in a *process*, which consists of an address space (containing code and data), other system resources such as open files and communication ports, and at least one thread. In essence, a process is an executing program. Just as the operating system can have a number of threads in existence simultaneously, it may have a number of processes in existence, all of which share the available processor(s).

Providing each executing process with a large, private memory space protects all processes from each other. Windows NT implements a virtual memory scheme using paged memory management hardware that provides each process with a private two Gigabyte address space. In addition, processes have limited access to a two Gigabyte system address space. The private memory space serves to isolate processes and prevent them from damaging each other, while the system address space can control sharing between processes. An operating system's ability to protect processes from each other is a computer security cornerstone, though additional features are required for full security.

Having multiple threads concurrently executing on a single processor is a highly useful programming model, providing processors with work when some threads cannot run because they are waiting for an event to happen. For example, if only one thread existed at a time, and that thread was waiting for some disk I/O to finish, the processor would be unproductive. With multiple threads, a different thread can begin execution.

Multithreading really comes into play with shared memory multiprocessors. With multiprocessors, several threads can execute in parallel (i.e., simultaneously), so that more work is accomplished than possible with a single processor. Servers can especially exploit multiprocessing to handle larger request volumes than they could with a uniprocessor.

Compatibility

The modular Windows NT interface design can emulate other operating systems, providing applications with compatible interfaces. In Windows NT, *protected subsystems* provide this compatibility. Windows NT currently has MS-DOS, 16-bit Windows, OS/2, POSIX, and 32-bit Windows protected subsystems. These subsystems run in user mode, converting requests from applications into native Windows NT requests. However, each subsystem varies somewhat in operational details.

The fundamental protected subsystem is 32-bit Windows (abbreviated as *Win32*), which provides full access to Windows NT features. Applications written to use the Win32 API use the subsystem directly to handle graphical I/O and keyboard input, while other service requests are passed directly to the Windows NT kernel. An application linked Win32 DLL provides procedural interfaces which send requests to appropriate recipients.

The Win32 subsystem manages the screen display. Thus, screen output, even from other protected subsystems, passes through it. Because it is running in a private user space, it uses message passing. Windows NT implements a message passing mechanism set optimized for communication within a single computer, referred to as *Local Procedure Calls* (*LPC*). While these mechanisms are faster than the more general Remote Procedure Calls (RPC), they still involve a pair of context switches for each service request, which can hurt performance. However, many system calls can be sent directly to the Windows NT kernel, mitigating performance loss.

The OS/2 and POSIX environment implementations use protected subsystems as well. Here protected subsystems maintain the necessary data to fully emulate their APIs. The developers felt that providing generic NT kernel system calls sufficient to handle direct requests from all possible environments would be too cumbersome, so they chose to handle part of the task of emulating the API calls in the protected subsystems. As with Win32, a library linked to the application converts each call into a direct kernel request or an LPC to the OS/2 or POSIX protected subsystem. Unlike 32-bit Windows, graphical output requests must be passed on to the Win32 protected subsystem, so that it can manage the screen.

Finally, the MS-DOS and 16-bit Windows protected subsystems are implemented as user processes, but here applications run directly in the subsystem address space. Each MS-DOS application gets its own protected subsystem processes, complete with the machine environment emulations it expects. The processes run in Virtual mode on Intel platforms, which means applications see a virtual Intel 8086 processor just like the real 8086 processor they were originally written for. On the other hand, all 16-bit Windows applications share one multithreaded protected subsystem process, which emulates the original Windows environment. This helps with compatibility, but can allow one misbehaving 16-bit Windows application to crash all the others. In all cases, graphical output is passed on to the Win32 subsystem, while other system calls may be handled locally or passed directly to the Windows NT kernel.

Thus, through protected mode subsystems and a form of fast message passing known as LPC, Windows NT mimics four legacy operating system environments, as well as providing a new Windows NT native environment. Of course the native mode is the most efficient, encouraging applications writers to migrate their software to the new API.

Windows NT File System

The Windows NT File System (NTFS) contains many significant enhancements from the earlier HPFS and FAT file systems. Part of the change motivation is to support applications running in DOS, OS/2 and POSIX environments. Another motivation is to provide high performance support for large files and directories. Finally, Windows NT's improved security necessitated a secure and robust file system.

Features

Because NTFS is one of the newest commercial file systems, it incorporates some of the latest file system design approaches. These approaches allow NTFS to provide numerous features unavailable in previous PC operating systems. Some key NTFS features are:

- **Unicode based file names:** Allows full international character set encoding.

- **Long file names:** File names can be up to 255 characters long.

- **Multiple data streams:** Allows separate data block types to reside in one file. Each block can separately grow and shrink.

For example, a second data stream could store Macintosh file "resource forks."

- **POSIX support:** Hard links and case sensitivity provisions facilitate POSIX compliant program support.

- **FAT file system support:** Automatic 8.3 format file name generation from longer NTFS file names.

- **Fast file name indexing:** Directory entries are sorted by file name and organized into a fast access B+ tree. The design allows eventual indexing by other attributes than file name.

- **Built in security provisions:** NTFS's design includes file system attributes to support Windows NT security.

- **Bad cluster remapping:** If a cluster becomes unreadable due to disk problems, that file portion migrates to another cluster, which replaces the bad cluster. Of course, data may still be lost, but at least the majority of the file will be saved.

- **No fixed placement of file system data structures:** File system data structures may remap around bad clusters just like user files.

- **File system recovery logging:** Transaction processing techniques log file system data structure changes (not including user data) for system crash or other error recovery. These techniques quickly allow NT to return file systems to consistent states after a crash so operations can continue.

- **Support for RAID levels 0 and 1:** An added layered driver can provide mirroring and striping, the two simplest RAID approaches.

With these features, NTFS provides security, robustness, and extensibility far beyond that offered by previous PC operating systems. As seen from the features list, NTFS is a significant improvement over the FAT file system, especially with regard to robustness and long file names support. It also has some improvements over HPFS, notably in the recovery area.

Structure

The Windows NT file system divides the disk into *clusters*, where a cluster can consist of several disk sectors. Clusters are addressed by *Logical Cluster Number*, which is the logical sector number of the first sector in the cluster divided by the number of sectors per cluster (typically 1 sector for all but the largest disk drives).

The Windows NT file system replaces the File Allocation Table of the FAT system with the *Master File Table* (MFT). The MFT contains all pertinent file information needed to access the file including name and security information. Unlike many other file systems, the MFT is itself a file. In fact, all special file system data structures (termed *metadata*) are kept in files, even the boot program. A key advantage to this approach is that these structures (with the exception of the boot file) can reside anywhere on the disk and expand as needed. Full NTFS file system power is available to access metadata, including the ability to relocate portions away from bad disk sectors.

Figure 10-1 depicts relationships between some of the key data structures the file system uses. As mentioned above, the one fixed item is the *boot file*, which must reside at a specific disk address so BIOS can locate it during the boot processes. This file contains an MFT pointer. The MFT contains an entry for itself, then entries for such items as the mirror MFT, recovery log file, root directory, allocation bitmap file, the boot file and the bad cluster file. After these metadata files, the MFT contains entries for all the user files and directories.

Metadata files whose MFT entries are shown in Figure 10-1 serve critical NTFS operational roles. A brief description follows:

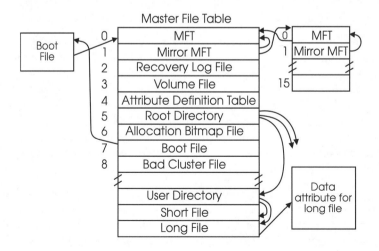

Figure 10-1. Key NTFS Data Structures

- **Mirror MFT:** A copy of the first 16 MFT entries resides in a different disk area than the MFT. This backup copy allows recovery in the event the main MFT sector fails.

- **Log File:** This file contains the file system modification (file create, delete, or rename) transaction log. It is a circular buffer, fixed length file, with old entries deleted when file system actions are fully written to disk.

- **Volume File:** Volume and NTFS version information written when the volume is first created.

- **Attribute Definition File:** MFT entries contain multiple attributes, some user-defined. This table contains information about each attribute type the volume uses.

- **Root Directory:** The "\" directory.

- **Bitmap File:** An in-use cluster bitmap.

- **Boot File:** The initial bootstrap code.

- **Bad Cluster File:** When NTFS detects unreadable clusters, the bad cluster address is added to this file. NTFS will not subsequently use the cluster.

Since MFT entries contain all information necessary to access files, MFT entry numbers can double as file "addresses." Hence directories consist of MFT entry number indexes for NT files. NTFS sorts the index by filename to enable fast searching of large directories.

In the standard installation, each MFT entry is 1 KByte long. This allows small directories and very small files to fit in the MFT entry. But larger files and directories must be stored in additional clusters on the disk, with the MFT containing pointers to the clusters. For files, the clusters are allocated in 2 KByte units called runs. By allocating a larger amount of space, NTFS is able to guarantee that disk reads can be at least 2 KBytes long, providing improved access efficiency (though further efficiency improvements could be gained with even longer runs).

When directories become too large to fit in the MFT, their entries are stored in a balanced tree, with the root being the MFT. The entries are sorted by file name, allowing an index search which avoids some of the disk reads that a linear search would require. Such indexing requires additional overhead during file creation, but can significantly speed up searches of large directories.

Recovery

As mentioned earlier, NTFS is designed for easy recovery in the event of a system crash or power failure. This means any file system state inconsistency can be detected and corrected when the system reboots. File systems become inconsistent after a crash or power failure because file system state changes require several different data structures writes. For example, to create a new file involves:

- Allocating an MFT record
- Adding a directory entry
- Possibly allocating a cluster from the Bitmap Table

If a power failure occurs before all disk modifications, the directory might point to an empty MFT, causing considerable confusion and, in previous operating systems, user excitement.

Many file systems, such as UNIX, invoke utility programs after a crash to scan the entire disk for such inconsistencies and fix them (e.g., remove the dangling directory entry). This can take a very long time on a large disk. NTFS uses a transaction processing style logging approach. Here, NTFS writes a full intended change record to a log file before the change commences and a commit record after the change is finished. By scanning the log file, NTFS determines which file system updates completed and which didn't, and concentrates on fixing the incomplete ones. This focused effort takes only a few seconds, rather than the minutes (or even hours) full disk searches take in other environments. Of course, writing the log file adds some overhead to file system operations, so this approach trades off a small drop in performance during normal operation for a large delay after a system crash.

Windows 95

Microsoft's Windows 95 introduces a new file system architecture. Adrian King's *Inside Windows 95*, available from Microsoft Press, indicates Windows 95's file system features support:

- Long file names
- Multithreaded FATs
- Network installable file systems
- Layered installable file systems (IFS)

Windows 95 file system design has many similarities to NTFS and later editions of this book will discuss them as they emerge from non-disclosure.

Novell® NetWare® File System

Each of the preceding file systems tends to service single users. In contrast, hundreds of network end users may simultaneously use a single server. So, network server operating systems such as Novell NetWare require heavier emphasis on I/O subsystem performance. Combined with read-ahead and lazy-writing, NetWare servers improve throughput and responsiveness by exploiting an insatiable memory appetite. Consequently, the Novell NetWare operating system file service caching algorithms are designed for large memory caches and directory searches are intentionally segregated and heavily optimized by hashing all directory file and subdirectory names.

Directory Hashing and Caching

With possibly thousands of files spanning dozens of disk Gigabytes, disk or cache file searches can be very slow. For example, a file name like:

\USERS\FRED\BEDROCK\DOCUMENTS\PAYROLL\401K.DOC

generates a search through the *USERS* directory, the *FRED* directory, etc.

Suppose the *DOCUMENTS* directory hadn't been referenced recently. In this instance, the search requires reading in at least a few *DOCUMENTS* directory blocks from disk. If the directory is large, even more blocks are read. Each read gives up the processor to let other NetWare processes run, and contributes to making file opens unacceptably slow. To avoid these delays while simultaneously making the file system more scalable, NetWare directory algorithms *hash* each file name.

Directory searches execute an algorithm similar to a Cyclic Redundancy Check for each file or subdirectory name. This creates a *signature* for that full name. Calculating signatures is fast, allowing searches to determine quickly from in-memory structures whether any files or directories hash to that signature. Because *collisions* (two names that hash to the same value) are possible, systems compare

Figure 10-2. Locating the Directory Entry

the complete requested name to all names that fall into that *hash bin* (share the same signature). Choosing a large enough hash table size minimizes collisions.

The same hash also quickly locates file portions already in cache memory. Because directory information is very likely accessed more often than file blocks, NetWare gives them cache precedence.

Hashing gives the most benefit when there are many files in a directory or many subdirectories. Directory entry insertion and deletion is faster, and searching doesn't slow down under heavy load. Compared to other techniques, hashing's improved memory utilization

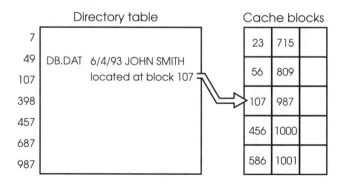

Figure 10-3. Locating the File in Cache Memory

allows it to keep a larger portion of a large directory tree in memory at once. Hashing also saves time during lazy writes, allowing servers to assume responsibility for disk writes, after quickly recording that *dirty* blocks need writing to disk.

Finally, during read-after-write, the dirty blocks for both the data and the directory (if any changes are needed in the file location data) can be safely written and verified to their addresses on the disk. For more information about the illusion of an ideal hard disk storage, see the sections below on logical disk address resolution and hot-fixing.

Unlike the sorted lists the preceding file systems use, hashing is fast both for lookup and for inserting new names into the list. Network directories can contain tens of thousands of files without noticeable performance degradation.

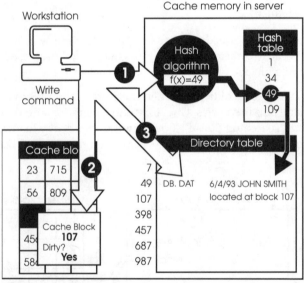

- ❶ Performs hash algorithm
- ❷ Writes file to cache blocks
- ❸ Updates directory table

Figure 10-4. Writing a File to Cache

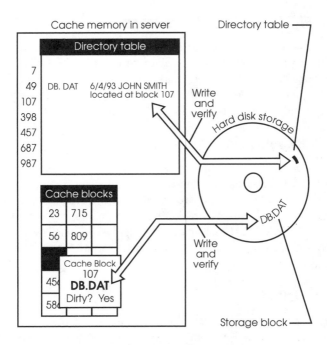

Figure 10-5. Cache Memory Write and Verify

Elevator Seeking

Novell NetWare engineers recognized that disk reads and writes for
hundreds of independent users could be serviced far more efficiently than simple arrival order. For a real-world example, imagine
how long you might wait on a hotel elevator if all riders arrived at
their floors in the order in which they pushed the elevator request
button.

NetWare's *elevator seeking* gives precedence to I/O read operations
that are near the current disk head position (or either head in the
case of head duplexing). Often, these operations are on the same
track as other pending I/O operations or so close that they can be
performed with minimum delay. Elevator seeking causes the file
system to become more efficient as the load becomes more random,
though quantifying the advantage with artificial benchmarks can
prove difficult.

Turbo-FAT for Fast Random Access

Random access reads into large files require complex FAT traversals to find appropriate disk extents. Therefore, large files (more than 64 blocks) use a Turbo-FAT index that groups together all of a file's FAT entries, greatly accelerating the process of calculating disk addresses for, say, random accesses into large databases.

Sub-Block Allocation

As disks became larger, the initial NetWare 2 Turbo-FAT technique eventually became insufficient. Larger block sizes in NetWare 3 dramatically improved volume size limits, but increased wasted slack space at file ends. In NetWare 4, Novell engineers implemented sub-block allocation. Hard disks can have block sizes as large as 64 KBytes, but single blocks can hold many small files that each consume as few as 512 bytes.

Scatter/Gather

Some of the most sophisticated adapter cards, like the Adaptec 1740 and successors, provide an advanced SCSI feature called scatter/gather. Scatter/gather provides both the ability to read contiguous data from disk and scatter (deliver) it to several non-contiguous buffers as well as the ability to gather data from non-contiguous memory buffers and write it to a contiguous disk area.

For example, a file server might receive 16 data blocks from its network media which it must sequentially write to a disk file. NetWare sequentially receives them and stores them in 16 memory buffers scattered throughout memory wherever space is available. When the file server takes responsibility for the data, it acknowledges each lazy write, allowing client workstations to continue working. In the optimum case, NetWare is busy performing other I/O operations so all 16 disk writes are waiting for service. NetWare's scatter/gather algorithm creates a single SCSI I/O operation for the entire contiguous disk area and services it with a single interrupt.

Even if only three or four disk writes can be gathered together, the interrupt reduction significantly improves the entire system's throughput. Because other NetWare subsystems also exploit scatter/gather, they can handle memory in convenient sizes (e.g., 4 KBytes), less than economical. A finely tuned network operating system therefore attains very high average I/O request sizes.

Read-Ahead

Read-ahead algorithms watch disk reads to see if they exhibit sequential behavior. A history of sequential block reads is a very strong predictor of future read requests. NetWare engineers therefore exploit massive caches to stay far enough ahead of current read requests to make subsequent contiguous reads virtually instantaneous. Care must be taken to give an appropriately low priority to reading the data and to the ability of the anticipatory data to stay in cache. After all, the data was speculatively read, and might never be requested.

Read-ahead algorithms are some of the best kept computer science secrets. Most of them are modulated by prior success. Each time an anticipated block is, in fact, requested from the file system, a success is accumulated. The read-ahead algorithm increases anticipation if reading ahead is succeeding and shrinks as memory gets exhausted.

Read-ahead and scatter/gather synergy makes extra reads nearly free. Since the read-ahead combines with actual reads, they are likely grouped into the same scatter/gather I/O operation and serviced by a single interrupt. Care must be taken to prevent thrashing, where recently read-ahead cached data is discarded to make room for other speculatively read data. NetWare limits anticipatory read growth in situations where the cache is turning over quickly.

Prioritized Disk I/O

The various I/O subsystem disk reads and writes have varied urgencies. When an end user needs to read a block of data, high priority is given since the end user is waiting until the block can be brought from disk into memory. Most other operations are lower priority. NetWare performs low priority operations like read-ahead, lazy writing, and re-mirroring mostly when the higher priority operations have been exhausted.

In order to guarantee reasonable progress for all tasks, there are four priority queues. During heavy activity periods, the highest priority queue is serviced over 80 percent of the time. But even the lowest priority queue is guaranteed at least one percent of the I/O operations.

Performance under Load

Directory hashing and caching, file caching, elevator seeking, and scatter/gather conspire to keep low priority work backlogged, hoping to combine it with other work to lower the cost of service. This is the single largest difference between desktop I/O systems versus file servers. File servers use algorithms designed to maintain acceptable performance under heavy loads. Desktop systems cannot afford algorithms intended to handle large caches and a high volume of asynchronous I/O coming from a large number of independent clients.

File-by-File Compression

NetWare 4 uses file-by-file compression by default. Seldom referenced files are transparently compressed on the hard disk. If a user accesses a compressed file, the image presented to the user is *bloated* (decompressed). If there have been multiple accesses to the file in less than the configured activity period (default: 1 week), the file decompresses to the hard disk. If not, the compression is retained. The administrator controls several server-wide settable parameters, and can easily monitor compression benefits and costs. Because very large file decompressions can cause heavy I/O loads, the user can set a file attribute to tell the system "don't compress."

Systems with numerous inactive files gain most of the space savings associated with compression, while only suffering the performance penalty when dormant files are accessed. Block-by-block compression was also considered, but would not have achieved the desired compression ratios.

Storage Management Engines (e.g., backup or Hierarchic Storage Management (HSM) programs) can choose to receive the file either compressed or bloated. For fast backup, the program requests compressed files. For interchange with other systems, archiving programs request copies that were uncompressed on the fly. In all cases, Storage Management Engine access uses the proper APIs so files are not unintentionally marked as newly accessed or otherwise unintentionally bloated onto the disk. This distinction between user accesses and storage management accesses (eventually even processes like virus checking, full content indexing, or text searching) keeps the file usage statistics valid so capacity planning and performance analysis do not become impossible.

System Fault Tolerance (SFT™)

System Fault Tolerance II (SFT II, disk mirroring and duplexing) provided excellent protection against hard disk crashes, hard disk defects, and controller failures. But it became clear during the evolution of NetWare 3 that more protection was needed against larger catastrophes that endangered whole servers or an entire room of servers.

SFT III makes a pair of file servers connected by a high-speed mirrored-server link appear as a single server. If an unforeseen disaster eliminates either server, the other server continues uninterrupted, perhaps several kilometers distant. Users connected to the server remain unaware of the outage—files need not be closed; connections are not lost. Although relatively expensive to deploy, the mirrored pair use the dedicated mirrored-server link to minimize performance degradation both to the Local Area Network and to the users of the files on the mirrored pair. In fact, the user level processes run in a mirrored server engine on both processors and each processor has its own, independent, I/O engine. Storage management processes like backup are very device-dependent and typically need to run in only one of the I/O engines.

The two processors in SFT III can be very far apart and can correctly function even with satellite transmission delays in the mirrored-server link. This far exceeds the design goal that the mirrored servers could be 10 kilometers apart. The assumption was that 10 kilometers was a reasonable distance for protection against fires, floods, and other catastrophes that will affect a whole room or building. Customers were pleasantly surprised that distances much longer than 10 kilometers are correctly supported. An Amsterdam hot spare server could be a secondary server for a primary server in Chicago, and a hot spare in Chicago could protect a primary in Amsterdam.

Hot Fix™

Disk sectors can be bad immediately after manufacturing, or they can wear out over time ("grown" defects). See the chapter on Hard Disk Controllers for a discussion of *defect mapping* and the chapter on Hard Disks for *bad sector management*. Repair strategies all have the common goal of making the media appear to be ideal. However, if the disk controller card continues to make the disk appear completely perfect when it is growing defects at an alarming rate, the network operating system may get no warning that the drive is failing.

Novell Engineers put an extra margin of safety into the process by allocating a portion of the drive to a Hot Fix area. Any defects that go beyond the number of defects that can be handled by the hard disk and controller are mapped to good sectors by NetWare. The statistics for Hot Fix usage can then be monitored by a centralized network management console along with all of the other symptoms it watches.

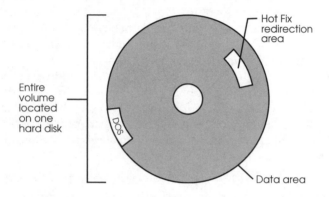

Figure 10-1. Hot Fix

Logical Disk Address Resolution

Hard disk addresses can go through several transformations to locate the correct physical block or blocks. NetWare generalizes these objects to allow the various storage management programs whichever view they need to see.

The *mirror object* sees a combination of redundant mirrored disks as though they were a single, ideal disk with a contiguous list of block numbers. If an application writes to mirror object block 107, the contents continue to appear to be in block 107 even if lower layers have to map around physical defects or crashed disks. A mirror object may have only one hot-fixed object, but still appears the same to outside applications. Mirroring is typically paired with duplexing, where each of two physical disks can be accessed asynchronously by two independent host adapters. Duplexing allows faster disk reads for two reasons: each disk can service half as many read requests, and, unless one disk is very idle, the disk with the head closest to the data receives the read request. Disk writes need to be done to each redundant hot-fixed object, but are typically almost as fast as a single write since the duplexed host adapters can handle the requests simultaneously.

The *Hot-Fix object* appears to be a single, safe, contiguous collection of disk blocks. See the section on Hot Fixing to see how grown defects on the disk may need to be mapped out. A hot-fixed object consists of one or more physical partitions that may be separate volume segments and may even be *spanned* across multiple physical disk drives. By expanding a partition or adding more partitions to a hot-fixed object, the hot-fixed object can be expanded. By gracefully growing, a storage administrator can add storage to a hot-fixed object without having to copy any of the existing data.

A *partition object* allows a storage application to see the true addresses of the data blocks on a single physical partition. Storage administration uses partition objects for statistics and to build up mirrored sets or span partitions into a single hot-fixed object, but application programs are not permitted direct access to physical file system reads and writes.

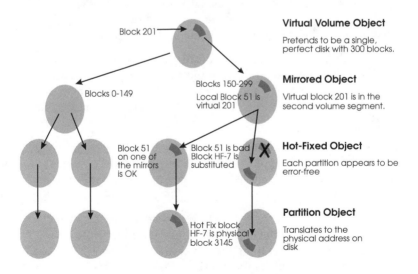

Figure 10-2. Translating Logical Addresses to Physical

Layered I/O Architecture

NetWare engineers wanted to make it easy to add new storage devices (hard disks, disk arrays, tape drives, optical disk jukeboxes, CD-ROM drives, etc.) independent of host adapters. To accomplish this requires several other objects:

An *Adapter Object* represents a host adapter card that supports physical devices. The Media Manager adds an Adapter Object to the database when it is automatically detected or manually registered. Each Adapter Object has an associated *Host Adapter Module* (*HAM*) that knows how to find and manage the adapter and knows how to pass I/O and IOCTL control blocks through the adapter to any device objects that may be connected to the adapter. For example, there is a HAM for each kind of SCSI host adapter or a HAM for an EIDE adapter. The HAM automatically detects attached devices.

A *Device Object* is a physical drive that holds media. The IOCTLs that control the device are sent to the device object for operations like mount, dismount, rewind, etc. A fixed disk device object is the parent of a fixed disk media object, but some devices can contain removable media.

The *Media Object* can either be Removable or Fixed. The architecture treats removable media like Magneto-Optical platters, CD-ROMs, or tapes in much the same manner as fixed disks. Media can be labeled, unlabeled, or a device can be requested to identify the media that it holds. Read and write I/O requests are sent to a media object.

An object detected by the HAM during the bus scan may be a *Changer Object* that contains one or more device objects. An auto-loader with 2 tape drives and 20 slots is a changer. A changer object will also have one or more slot objects and one or more magazine objects.

A *Slot Object* corresponds to a single media storage slot in a changer. A special case of a slot object is a mail slot that represents one or more import/export elements used to put media into the changer and take it out.

A *Magazine Object* represents a collection of media that move together. For example the tapes in a tape array might need to be grouped together. Or, moving the top side of a two-sided optical disk platter will also affect the location of the other side.

If a changer is not present, the jukebox functions are diverted to a set of human jukebox APIs that ask the console operator to insert or remove media from a particular storage device. Of course, this operation can be rather slow.

Once the devices have been automatically detected, the proper *Custom Device Modules* (*CDMs*) need to be automatically loaded. There is a Base CDM for each of the various formats for sending messages to a host adapter: a SCSI base CDM knows how to construct SCSI messages as opposed to EIDE messages. When the Media Manager performs a generic action, it calls the appropriate base CDM for that device object, and then chains through any filter CDMs that might be needed for added monitoring, address translations, or device-specific operations unique to a device sub-class. A particular tape drive may have a filter CDM that allows it to do faster seeks or allows it to emulate a more expensive tape drive that can do more complex operations.

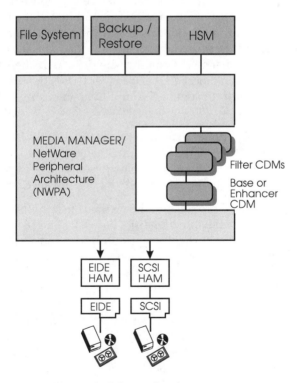

Figure 10-3. I/O System Overview

Host Adapter Module (HAM)

NetWare's I/O architecture separates the functions of the host adapter from modules that know details about the devices attached to the host adapter's bus. For example, an Adaptec SCSI *Host Adapter Module* knows how to find and manage the Adaptec SCSI controller card, and how to package a generic SCSI command through the Adaptec controller to a connected device. When Adaptec invents a new controller card with significant advantages, existing customers need only load the new HAM—old CDMs will be able to use the new functionality immediately.

Custom Device Module

There are several types of *Custom Device Modules* that act as drivers for the devices attached to a Host Adapter. For simple devices like generic disk drives or generic tape drives, there is a set of *Generic CDMs*. During auto-detection, each device's response to an *Identify* is compared to a list of *Specific CDMs* found in ASCII tables that can easily be read, printed, and updated by the network administrator. These tables tell NetWare which CDMs to load to take advantage of special features that go beyond the generic model. These CDMs can be Base CDMs, Enhancer CDMs, or Filter CDMs depending on whether they add functionality, simplify functionality, or re-distribute functionality.

The *Base CDM* supplies default methods for all of the basic functions of a class of devices. A Base CDM for changers would implement functions that are common to autoloaders and jukeboxes, but would return "Feature_Not_Implemented" for any advanced functions.

An *Enhancer CDM* provides all the methods needed for an enhanced service. It can overlay functions of a Base CDM and/or provide other functions. If a particular tape autoloader had a bar code reader and could identify tapes without having to load them into the tape drive, an Enhancer CDM would be used. The auto-detection recognizes the response to the identify request and loads the proper Enhancer CDMs based on ASCII DDI files. Each device must have a Base CDM, and a device can have several Enhancer CDMs that provide function implementations, but each function will either go to one of the Enhancer CDMs or to the device's Base CDM. For example, a request to Select a particular optical disk platter would go to an Enhancer CDM that overlaid that function pointer in the Device

Object, but a request to read from a platter would pass to the Base CDM for that Device Object.

A device can also have a chain of Filter CDMs. Each *Filter CDM* provides a single value-added function. A Filter CDM can take several messages and combine them into one (e.g., for scatter/gather operations), or it can take one message and change it (e.g., for hot-fixing), or it can take one message and split it into several (e.g., for mirroring). If a particular tape drive can find a block much quicker via an enhanced seek, a filter CDM could be used to implement a sequence of seek operations in a single operation.

NetWare Peripheral Architecture

The *NetWare Peripheral Architecture* collectively refers to the interfaces to HAMs and CDMs and the portion of the I/O subsystem that schedules messages, handles I/O compilation, and covers I/O aborts. It offers a framework that gives all of the infrastructure that used to make it hard to write device drivers for multi-processing operating systems.

Multiple Name Spaces

One of the central features of a local area network is heterogeneity. It is not uncommon to have personal computers attached to a file server that run the Macintosh OS, OS/2, Microsoft Windows, Windows NT, and DOS. Full interchange between these clients is a requirement. NetWare provides multiple, simultaneous name spaces and associated metadata. If a Macintosh user looks at a file he created, it has the appropriate naming conventions, icons and colors along with their resource forks. And it also has independent names in the DOS and UNICODE name spaces. Initial names default to reasonable names based on the creator name space and attributes like the code page. One disk can contain files freely shared among OS/2, DOS, NT, and Macintosh users.

This causes some unexpected requirements for storage management programs like backup/restore products, near-line storage, and content indexing. For example, a backup program would want to show a directory tree of the files on a tape. Should it show the file names and directory (folder) names the way they would look to a Macintosh user? Or the way they would look to a DOS user? To solve the problem, each file and directory also indicates its creator name space. As file naming has matured, there is reasonable convergence that new file systems throughout the industry will allow long leaf names (255 characters), long path names (no limits smaller than 1023 characters), UNICODE (16 bits per character to avoid problems in translating among international code pages), and a limited number of well-defined separator characters.

Disk Space Quotas

Shared disks have always had trouble deciding who to blame when a volume runs out of space. To better allocate disk space, NetWare 2 implemented user volume quotas. Each user could be assigned a quota so that no single user could overwhelm the disk and cause all of the other users to run out of disk space. If bad neighbors try to create or extend files that would exceed their personal quota, the file system returns an "out of space" error. A network administrator with sufficient rights can simply increase that user's quota.

It is common (and desirable) for the sum of the quotas to be larger than the disk. Statistically, some users will be under their quota. In NetWare 4, another mechanism put disk space quotas on directories regardless of which user owns the files. This prevents single sub-trees from being a bad neighbor, using up much more than a fair share of the on-line disk. Both mechanisms count elastic bytes—the small number of bytes actually present on-line after the effects of compression or migration. Users who are almost at their quota today may be well under quota tomorrow simply because of compression. An intelligent migration system can use quotas as part of its choice of which files to migrate to cheaper, near-line storage, assuming that users with a smaller quota were users who should have a smaller working set on-line.

Delayed Purge - Salvage Queue

One of the most common human errors is unintentional file deletion. NetWare uses a salvage queue to hold recently deleted files and provides users with a "Salvage" command. If the end user has sufficient permission, the salvage does not require embarrassed calls to network administrators. Some directories contain very short-lived files that are very unlikely to be salvaged, so NetWare allows the user to set an attribute on directories to bypass the salvage queue. NetWare uses this feature in many ways, if the user does not change the default configuration. For example, spool files for the printer are immediately purged upon deletion when their print job finishes.

The age of the oldest unpurged file in the salvage queue can be much better when unimportant files bypass the queue.

The salvage queue can consume virtually all free disk space. Because this space can be quickly reclaimed if the disk starts to fill up, it is one of the first systems to react when free space becomes critically low. This space does not count toward HSM volume fullness thresholds or trigger other compensating mechanisms to free up disk space.

When the user requests statistics on how full the volumes are, there is often a time lag between the time a file is deleted and the time the space appears as free. The extra processing increases the chance that a user can recover from an inadvertent deletion, but may be misunderstood by users trying to tell how much space is available.

Directory Services

Under NetWare 4, storage administration is done in a directory tree that can cover many servers. The directory is a global, distributed, replicated database that maintains information about, and provides access to, every resource on the network. Typical objects are users, groups, printers, volumes, or servers. Instead of logging in to individual servers, users login to the network. End user and group authentication and permissions are assigned by adding them into the tree, and the authority can be freely used throughout all of the servers in the tree.   There are a variety of benefits in making the network easier to administer, but this chapter focuses on the benefits with regard to fault tolerance and storage.

Partitions of the NetWare Directory Services™ (NDS™) tree are replicated to several servers in the tree to provide fault tolerance and improved performance. Lookups can be done from the nearest replica. There is a performance penalty when new users are added, since those changes have to be replicated to other servers. It is especially useful to have replicas that are geographically strategic—to avoid data loss in the event that one entire site suffered flood, fire or other major catastrophe. If there is a replica at another site, the users can continue to be authenticated and will still have rights and permissions on the running servers. When the disaster is over, the stale replica (or empty one if the data had been destroyed) can be updated (or recreated) from surviving off-site replicas.

Because NetWare Directory Services only has to protect object information (it does not replicate the data in user's files), the distributed database maintenance overhead is very low.

Directory Mapping

For capacity planning and performance analysis, using tree-based addresses allows the storage administrator the luxury of moving data from overburdened servers and volumes to idle ones without changing the way users address them. Users continue addressing applications that logically appeared on the "L:" drive letter, even though space and time force the storage administrator to move its programs or data to another server and/or volume. Changing network drive letter assignments via MAP statements in early NetWare versions achieved this (typically in either the system-wide login script or in user login scripts). NetWare 4 provides a directory mapping facility that provides a single place to administer directory mappings across many servers and many users.

Real Time Data Migration (RTDM)

NetWare provides an application programming interface (*API*) for third party vendors to register bulk storage farms like optical disk jukeboxes that would be inexpensive repositories for old, seldom used files. This Hierarchical Storage Management approach retains a Data Migration Key on the disk so that if a user opens the file (e.g., with dosOpen) it can be transparently demigrated. The hard disk is considered the on-line device and slower devices are considered the *near-line* devices. There can be several stages to the hierarchy with fast, duplexed disk, slow simplex disk, optical disks in the jukebox, tapes in the autoloader, and, eventually, even tapes on the shelf. If the data is so old that it spilled out of the robotic devices, humans may have to act as the robotic arm.

Thus, unlike compression (which is typically occurs when files have old access dates), migration may cause protracted delays. The delay for jukeboxes to grab optical platters, move them to drives, and retrieve files could be dozens of seconds or longer. For this reason, most migration systems wait until the on-line disk space is badly needed before they migrate files off of the disk.

Migration, of course, must be carefully integrated within storage management. When accessed using Novell's Storage Management Services, backup programs have the option of "peeking" at the data

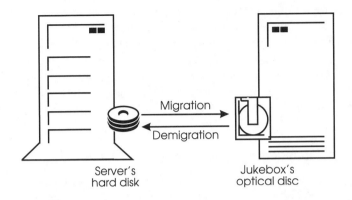

Figure 10-4. Migration and Demigration of the Requested File

from the near-line storage without triggering demigration. And, just as with compression, the storage usage statistics such as file access dates are crucial to the HSM decisions and should not be ruined by processes whose reading of the data is incidental to normal operations.

With compression and migration, a volume that physically holds 10 GBytes of data could (over time) seem to hold 100 GBytes or more. Imagine the problems from virus checkers using an undisciplined *dosOpen* approach to scan entire logical volumes, reading every file in ways that did not signal the operating system that this was not a typical user request. Some of the data that deserves to stay compressed would cross the threshold from "casually accessed less than once a week" to "active." Worse yet, for every megabyte of data recalled from near-line storage, a megabyte of data would have to be migrated off of on-line disk to make room.

Storage Management Engine (SME)

A *Storage Management Engine* is typically used for backup/restore operations or Software Distribution, but can be any program that wants to access files in a heterogeneous environment without end user access side-effects. SMEs need very little knowledge of the target's file system or security requirements, because the *Target Service Agent* (*TSA*) APIs make all Target Services look like a universal, generic file system. This allows programs to read files without unintentionally hurting metadata such as access dates, without unintentionally demigrating them or decompressing them, and without knowing details about how locking or naming is done at that target. The APIs allow direct reading and testing of the place holder files that the migrator leaves in place of the content of the file. Many SMEs are written by third-party vendors to provide value-added services like archiving, enhanced record-keeping, better scheduling, or hierarchical storage management. The Storage Management Services Software Developer's Kit provides the interface.

Storage Management Data Requester (SMDR)

The *Storage Management Data Requester* provides low-overhead communications to other SMDRs whether local or remote. For example, a SME would ask the local SMDR for a list of the hosts that need to be backed up. A SME that runs on one operating system can ask for an inventory of targets all over the network even if they are on other platforms. The communications between hosts is handled transparently by the local SMDR and the remote SMDR as though the TSA APIs were a remote procedure call.

Target Service Agent (TSA)

A *Target Service Agent* is responsible for all of the knowledge about the resources on a particular file system, service, or application. It provides TSA API implementations that SMEs call. The resources (e.g., a volume on hard disk) consist of objects. Each object is transported within a complete wrapper that includes its metadata and data in industry standard SIDF, ISO-14863. Each field is tagged with its field type so that systems that do not understand extended attributes or Macintosh resource forks can skip over those fields. Dates are recorded in ECMA international time stamps. Object names can be recorded in several redundant formats so that systems that expect 16-bit UNICODE names will not have to use the 8-bit ASCII name, and systems will not have to truncate HPFS or Macintosh names. This helps future-proof metadata so it is readable by other operating systems, or by future versions of the same operating system.

TSAs for databases like Btrieve, SQL, or Oracle can present a list of resources and objects that are named for tables and databases, rather than the native file system files. The TSA is responsible to interlock properly with applications to ensure the SME sees a consistent resource image with referential integrity. If such a TSA were asked to perform an incremental backup, the TSA might choose to backup audit files or transaction lists. The TSA must also be able to restore a whole resource (with correct locking and integrity testing) or only restore individual objects. An email system TSA might want to classify objects by user, so that a single user's email could be restored without changing any other user.

Through the Target Service Agent Software Developer's Kit, several third-party developers have written custom TSAs for file systems other than NetWare or for services that have special backup or restoration concerns.

System Independent Data Format (SIDF)

System Independent Data Format is ISO-14863 (and ECMA-208). Tapes and optical disks written with SIDF labels, sessions, and objects are structured to make data (and the metadata that describes it) transportable between a wide range of operating systems. The SIDF Association, http://www.sidf.org, provides certification and is the clearinghouse for interchange testing.

Since the standard is very new (adopted by ISO in October 1995), there are only a handful of vendors who use it as a native format. Other vendors can read SIDF tapes, but can still only write their own proprietary format. Obviously, a system that can create interchange tapes today is preferable to a system that can only use them to import data.

System Management Considerations

Initially, desktop systems were usually stand-alone devices. As previously discussed, their hardware and software configuration and support processes were difficult and became increasingly so. While today's Plug 'n' Play standards address configuration issues, reporting system configurations and operational problems generally remains a problem. This complicates software installation and support procedures for network administrators who must verify minimum hardware requirements are met for various applications and diagnose network node problems.

Since most business computing resources connect to networks, increasing network importance mandates a comprehensive and coherent management strategy that maintains accurate client and server system configuration information and monitors activities, vigilantly searching for problems. To address this situation, the Desktop Management Task Force (*DMTF*) is an open industry organization with over 90 key supplier members that exists to address desktop manageability issues. The DMTF's goal is to encourage PC product vendors to produce manageable products and to provide a standard management framework for these products. To this end, DMTF has developed the Desktop Management Interface (*DMI*). DMI is a powerful standards-based approach to managing PC systems. It usually requires no hardware and extends PC systems by increasing their ease of use and providing intelligence and manageability through real-time systems diagnostics and system component support.

A DMI implementation, called a *DMI Service Layer*, is a desktop background application that performs DMI activities such as collecting information from *manageable products* and storing it in a database, called the *Management Information Format* or *MIF* database. The MIF database is an ASCII text file that describes each manageable product's attributes in some meaningful way. The Service Layer passes information to management applications on request and delivers commands from *management applications* to manageable devices.

Manageable Products

Manageable products are DMI compliant software and hardware such as installation programs, operating systems, software applications, modems, hard disks, CD-ROM drives, printers, etc. operating in either desktop client servers and clients or attached directly to networks. The DMI service layer collects this information from manageable products through its standardized *component interface*. Manageable products also use the component interface to deliver *indications* to the DMI Service Layer. Indications signal *management applications* that significant events have occurred, such as manageable product installation, error, or failure.

Management Applications

Management applications are local or remote programs that change, track, interrogate, or enumerate desktop system components. They may range in complexity from simple MIF database browsers to advanced network analyzers. These applications can either diagnose components themselves or direct appropriate information across the network to a centralized support facility. DMI implementations provide a standard interface between themselves and management applications using the *management interface.* This interface allows management applications to interact with manageable components while shielding the management applications from having to know specific manageable product interaction details.

Adaptec CI/O Software

Adaptec CI/O software (Comprehensive I/O) is a Microsoft Windows software product that allows central support facilities to monitor and control Novell NetWare server SCSI subsystems. The enterprise-scalable software displays the status and performance of all SCSI devices connected to any NetWare server using Adaptec SCSI adapters. CI/O software automatically polls server SCSI busses and reports any status changes such as I/O subsystem configuration changes or failures. It also allows network managers to install new software drivers quickly and easily from a central location. Finally, CI/O software produces a customizable graphical performance profile for every monitored SCSI device. This provides network managers a clear view of server I/O loading, allowing them to spot bottlenecks and balance I/O loads by moving data to other SCSI devices.

CI/O software is based on the *HP OpenView* network management platform and uses the standardized *Simple Network Management Protocol (SNMP)* to communicate with monitored machines. SNMP transmits a single notice of an extraordinary event for management application action, called *trap-directed polling.* Low frequency polling is also used but trap-polling's single connection-less packet approach is most reliable during system stress.

Because SNMP products operate on many different types of machines, a formal network programming language called Abstract Syntax Notation One (ANS.1) exists to address byte-order problems. This standardizes the management protocol and the object definition for information being managed. SNMP is compatible with DMI which provides SNMP-based applications console support. Both technologies cooperate to deliver cohesive LAN administration information, allowing network managers to create a complete management environment with a consistent and integrated interface.

Summary

I/O subsystem software superimposes structure on disk sectors and provides application read/write access to data storage devices. Writing effective I/O subsystem software requires an intimate knowledge of storage devices and operating system services. High performance software optimizes frequently used instruction sequences to specific processors, exploiting hardware capabilities even further. Because I/O subsystem component interactions are complex, well-considered approaches can provide implementation disappointments and surprises, even to professional software architects. Finally, the number of performance features make it easy for benchmark administrators to inadvertently overlook one or more of them, producing invalid comparisons.

Chapter Questions

1 The FAT File system

   a Appears in Windows 95

   b Is efficient with the advent of effective caching

   c Is simple

   d All of the above

2 MS-DOS partitions

   a Are listed in the Master Partition Table

   b Are bootable or non-bootable

   c Are only for MS-DOS use

   d a and b

3 File fragmentation

   a Destroys disk heads after small particles dislodge

   b Is fixable with software utilities

   c Results in files spanning disk partitions

   d Is controlled by the cluster high-water mark found in the MS-DOS FDISK utility

4 Operating system disk caching strategies

   a May depend on thermal recalibration

   b Are hampered by Zone Recording because it hides the true disk geometry

   c Are not needed

   d May require compression utilities

5 Windows

   a Has the same File I/O software as Windows for Workgroups

   b Requires 32-bit I/O software

   c Uses MS-DOS file I/O software

   d Uses MS-DOS file architecture

6 HPFS write-back caching

   a Is dangerous

   b Is called lazy writes

   c Needs extensive hardware assists

   d Is based on MS-DOS FAT Architecture

7 In HPFS, hard disk bands are

   a 4 MBytes

   b 8 MBytes

   c 16 MBytes

   d User selectable depending on whether the drive is SCSI or IDE

8 Which of these statements about Windows NT is NOT true

   a Written in assembly language

   b Supports full multi-tasking

   c Has a layered I/O system

   d Can work with disks formatted for the FAT file system

9 In Windows NT, each process gets a region of private memory which is how large?

    a 64 KBytes

    b 1 MByte

    c 2 GBytes

    d 4 GBytes

10 Directory hashing

    a Converts file names from long names to FAT names

    b Speeds up the process of finding the location of a file on disk or in cache

    c Scrambles the contents of directories for encryption

    d None of the above

11 Elevator Seeking

    a Finds the next sequential file

    b Rearranges disk read and write requests to service the queue faster

    c Copies files to sequential locations

    d Rearranges files on disk to make them contiguous

12 NetWare Directory Services

    a Replicates all of the data on the disks

    b Replicates information about the resources

    c Allows users to log into the network instead of individual servers

    d b and c

13 In NetWare, Disk Space Quotas

    a Can be used to limit the disk space used by a subtree

    b Can be used to limit the disk space used by a particular user

    c Can cause programs to get "out of space" errors even though the disk is not full

    d All of the above

14 Directory mapping

   a Allows moving applications to other servers with minimum impact on users

   b Migrates data to near-line storage to free up disk space

   c Speeds up directory lookups

   d Replicates directories for fault tolerance

15 Compared to compression, migration

   a Is only used when disk space is needed

   b Typically takes longer to undo

   c Requires a large, cheap storage device

   d Is best used to make very large files take up very little on-line space

   e All of the above

❑

11

Performance Assist Considerations

What This Chapter Is About

Disk capacity and processor speeds are increasing dramatically. But to maximize system performance requires hardware assists to stage data closer to the processor. For example, in the case of disks, data rate, rotation rate and head positioning speed have only increased moderately because of mechanical and magnetic constraints. A general rule for disk activity is:

> *Reading or writing several blocks at once is more efficient than several smaller reads or writes.*

But avoiding disk reads is even more efficient! Based on these guidelines, *caching* attempts to satisfy request streams from local fast memory, called a *cache*, or at least tailor the request streams to the underlying hardware. Caches appear on hard disks and microprocessor chips as well as on motherboards in the form of second level caches and software buffers. When processors have more than one execution unit, such as the Intel Pentium, minimizing execution unit interference by optimizing instruction sequences provides substantial performance increases.

Caching

Caching exploits the fact that computer programs typically access a small amount and range of code and data at any given time. This is known as the principal of locality, and consists of two types of locality:

- Spatial
- Temporal

Spatial locality refers to the fact that computers often request data that is in nearby locations, such as the sequential locations fetched by the instruction execution unit. *Temporal* locality refers to the tendency for a computer to re-use recently used locations, such as a program instruction loop. Computers exploit locality of reference by migrating the most likely to be accessed data into faster memory (the cache), gaining significant speed without having to employ large amounts of faster and more expensive memory.

As Figure 11-1 indicates, caching appears at all computer system memory hierarchy levels. Processors use internal registers and small, very high speed on-chip caches to hold currently executing code and data. They often use larger off-chip caches to hold less frequently used code and data in readiness for quick access by the on-chip cache when it is not found (has a miss). Main memory holds disk drive code and data under explicit program control in older systems, but under automatic operating system control in newer systems. Disk controllers and drives may have local memories to cache recently accessed disk blocks or temporarily hold write data until the disk drives are free to accept it. Finally, the disk drives themselves serve as a cache for data in *tertiary* storage, though the management of tertiary storage, such as tape drives, is often done manually.

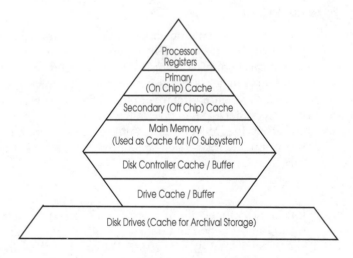

Figure 11-1. Levels of Caching in a Typical Computer System

How Caching Helps

Caching techniques allow smaller amounts of expensive, fast memory to hold frequently used portions of a much larger, cheaper and slower memory. Thus, the computer program performs as though it had large amounts of fast memory, for the price of small amounts. How well it actually performs depends on the *hit ratio*, the fraction of the total requests which are satisfied by data from the cache. High hit ratios are typically achieved through three general mechanisms:

- Existing data re-use

- Fetching large data blocks

- Pre-fetching the next sequential data block (Read Ahead)

Existing Data Re-Use

Typical computer access patterns exhibit temporal locality, where recently accessed locations are the most likely to be accessed in the near future. By moving the data stored in the requested location into a cache on the first access, it will be available for quick access from the cache on subsequent accesses. A processor will often re-use locations ten or more times in quick succession, so caching greatly improves performance.

While processors often have high re-use rates for main memory accesses, disk I/O is less likely to re-use blocks, especially in desktop environments. For example, launching applications involves reading most or all of the application in from the disk, but then that disk area is not referenced until the application is next loaded, perhaps days later.

Fetching Large Data Blocks

Although temporal locality may not be a big disk I/O factor, spatial locality is. Computer programs often read files sequentially, from file beginning to end. Even when the file is not read strictly sequentially, computers often use adjacent data regions within files. If large block sizes are used, there is a high probability that all data brought in eventually gets used.

Caches often load more data than initially requested. Usually the additional data's load time is short compared to the time it takes to fetch individually requested data. For example, processor caches typically receive requests for four data bytes, but read thirty-two bytes. It might take ten to fifteen clock cycles to send the request to main memory, access the memory, and return the four bytes, while only four to eight additional clock cycles to return an additional 28 bytes. Thus, fetching thirty-two bytes takes about 50% longer, but returns 700% more data. Since there is a high probability that the additional data will be used, the processor experiences significantly lower effective access times.

In the case of disk I/O, head positioning often involves seek and rotational latency with tens of millisecond delays. Yet the transfer time for even an 8 KByte block of data is less than one millisecond. Thus, it can take a long time to position heads, but relatively little time to actually transfer the data. By reading several sectors at once, subsequently requested data is readily available from main memory.

To be most effective, the disk sectors which comprise the file cache block should be adjacent to each other. In DOS, this is achieved by allocating space for new files in *clusters* of eight to thirty-two contiguous sectors. This allows four to sixteen kilobyte cache blocks to be used, resulting in a greatly reduced effective access time.

Prefetching the Next Sequential Data Block (Read Ahead)

Because Disk I/O is often sequential, additional performance can be obtained by reading the next sequential file portion into the file cache, even before the program accesses it. This allows file access to overlap program execution, especially when the host adapter is able to use DMA. Thus *read-ahead* (also called *prefetching*) has the potential to completely hide disk drive access times.

The read-ahead may be done on a disk address basis or on a file address basis. File address based read ahead is preferred, because the file system may not keep sequential file locations in sequential disk locations. But, depending on where caching is done, the file information may not be available. For example, disk drives often cache the most recently read sectors, and can perform read-ahead of the next physical disk sectors. But on many file systems, the data fetched by the read-ahead is often not even from the same file, and hence useless. On the other hand, file systems are aware of the logical addressing and can make sure a useful block is fetched by the read-ahead.

Cache Organization

Since caches hold a subset of the total memory space, they must be able to map the original (main) memory addresses to local cache addresses before they can access the data in the cache. Figure 11-2 illustrates the principle with a hypothetical four entry cache and sixteen location main memory or disk drive. Each cache entry has:

- Storage for a data block

- An address tag indicating where the data originally came from

- A set of state bits

Initially, no cache entries are usable, as illustrated by the *Invalid* (I) state of the fourth cache entry. During cache use, memory or disk data migrates into the cache, the tag is set to the address where the data came from, and the state of the entries is set to *Valid* (V).

As illustrated in Figure 11-2, the location of a main memory item in the cache does not necessarily have any relationship with the item's location in main memory. In order to keep track of the correspondence between cached locations and their main memory counterparts, a structure called the tag is used. The tag typically includes a portion of the original address, and some bits indicating the state of the data stored at that cache location.

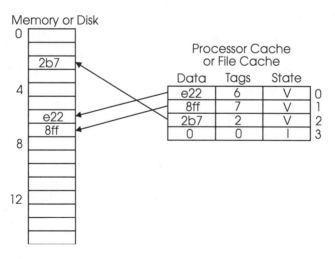

Figure 11-2. Basic Cache Operation

When the cache receives a request, one or more tag locations are searched for a match with the main memory address. If a match is found, and the state bits indicate the cached data is usable, then the cache location associated with the matching tag is used to satisfy the request, rather than main memory. The tags are stored in the same kind of memory elements as the cache data, and represent an overhead cost. The relative cost of the tags is particularly affected by choices of block size and associativity.

In general, the finer the grain of mapping and the more flexible the mapping, the more complicated (and costly) the mapping function becomes. For that reason, the actual cache organization often compromises between performance in terms of hit ratio and performance in terms of cache access time. Three key attributes of a cache are the:

- Total amount of data it can hold (*cache size*)

- Size of the individual data units (*block size*)

- Number of cache data units that a given location in the main memory can map to (*associativity*)

The cache size is the total number of data bytes which a cache can hold. For processor caches it is usually in the tens to hundreds of kilobytes, while for file system caches it is often in megabytes to tens of megabytes. Memory structure sizes at all hierarchy levels are increasing as memory density improves and costs drop.

Caches store information in blocks (also sometimes called *lines*) which range from 4 to 64 bytes for typical processor caches, and to 4 to 16 KBytes for file caches. Picking optimum block sizes is a fairly complicated procedure. Large block sizes reduce the relative tag cost (there is one tag for each block), and can improve hit ratios in some cases because one block can satisfy multiple adjacent requests. Too large a block size can reduce the hit ratio because it causes data that is never used to be read in, and reduces the cache block count. Memory access characteristics from which the cached data is taken also affect block size. Disk drives can read 4 KBytes to 16KBytes in about the same time as single 512 byte sectors, so using large cache blocks generally improves performance.

In ideal caches, each main memory location can map into any cache block. This is known as a *fully associative* cache, and achieves the best hit ratio for a given size cache. However, each request for data must be matched against all cache block tags, which can be too expensive in time or hardware. At the other extreme is the *direct mapped* cache which maps each main memory location to a specific cache block. The hit ratio is lower, but only one tag check determines if the location is in the cache. Compromises in which each memory location is allowed to be in one of two or four cache blocks are also frequently encountered, known respectively as *2-way* and *4-way set associativity.*

In the I/O world, the cache miss penalty is the time it takes to access a disk drive, often in the 10's of milliseconds, so maximizing hit ratios, even at the expense of searching numerous tags, is justified. Thus disk and file caches are usually fully associative, with software algorithms locating cache entries. Because using large block sizes results in relatively few tags to search, and because of the long time required to service a miss, even the time required by sequential tag searches is justifiable. But some systems combine the file cache with the virtual memory system, using the VM's translation look-aside buffer to assist locating cached file blocks.

Write-through vs. Write-back

Cache actions on reads are quite straightforward. Blocks are sent to requesters if present in the cache. Alternately, blocks are obtained from the next memory level and both stored in a cache block and forwarded to the requester.

However, cache writes have additional alternatives. If the block is present, it may be updated in the cache (*write-back*) and marked as a *dirty block* (not written to the lower hierarchy level). Alternately, it may also be sent on to the next level of memory (*write-through*). If the block is not present, it may be brought into the cache and then updated (*allocate on write-miss*), or written straight to memory, bypassing the cache (*no-allocate on write-miss*). If the size of the write equals the cache block size, a write-miss can place data in the cache without accessing memory at all. The most common combinations are:

- Write-back on write-hit with allocate on write-miss
- Write-through on write-hit with no-allocate on write-miss

Write-back caches can substantially reduce traffic to the next memory hierarchy level. For example, many programs will create short lived temporary files which are written, read, then deleted. Write-back caches could avoid sending such files to disk. However, write-back cache implementations require more overhead in either control logic or software and can substantially delay reads if dirty block replacement is required. To reduce the frequency of dirty block replacements, partially or wholly associative caches will try to preferentially replace clean blocks, but that can reduce cache hit ratios. Other techniques include writing dirty block contents back to disk whenever the disk subsystem is idle, or when dirty block populations exceed preset thresholds.

With processor caches, write-through caching can be faster due to the high frequency of dirty block replacement which occurs in set associative write-back caches. But in the I/O world, highly associative file caches benefit more from eliminating disk writes than from occasional dirty block replacements. A speed up technique both write-back and write-through caches can use temporarily stores writes in write-buffers, hiding much of the latency of writing back to the next level of the memory hierarchy.

However, there is a different problem with file caches, namely *volatility*. If the power fails, or the computer is turned off, dirty block data can be lost. Main memory file caches often try to minimize this problem by writing out dirty blocks within a few seconds or minutes of modification. Another option places file caches, or at least a large write-buffer, in a host adapter equipped with non-volatile RAM. Once in the non-volatile RAM, the data is nearly as safe as it is on disk and is available without disk access latency.

Replacement Policies

Since caches are small compared to system memories from which they fetch data, they are normally completely filled. Thus, when a cache miss requires reading new data into the cache, some old data block must be replaced. Ideally, the cache should evict the block with the longest expected time to re-use. Of course, in a direct-mapped cache there is no choice, but associative caches can choose, and often do so based on formulas which attempt to predict future usage based on past usage.

The principal of temporal locality suggests that blocks which have gone the longest since their last access are the ones least likely to be used in the immediate future. The Least Recently Used (LRU) replacement algorithm implements this strategy, and is typically the best performing scheme. For caches with a large degree of associativity, keeping track of complete usage history can be difficult, giving rise to approximate LRU algorithms, or the use of other replacement policies.

There are patterns, such as the cyclic access pattern commonly found in scientific programming, which cause LRU to perform very poorly (e.g., in a cyclic pattern the least recently used items are actually the most likely to be used next). Therefore, simpler algorithms, which are easier to implement, are often chosen. A couple of other commonly used ones are First In First Out (FIFO) and random.

With processor caches, speed considerations generally require small associativity amounts and simple replacement algorithms. Caches are typically direct mapped, or two- or four-way set associative and use LRU replacement for the associative caches. But disk I/O involves much longer time frames, so more sophisticated algorithms can be used. Also, the access patterns are often highly sequential, which favors different replacement policies than those used in processor caches. Thus, the cache blocks are often searched associatively, and adaptive algorithms are used for determining blocks to replace on misses. To give the flavor of an adaptive algorithm, one particular type will be described below.

Quite often, computer programs read disk files sequentially and only once. In such circumstances prefetching is helpful to overlap disk requests with computation, but there is no benefit to holding the disk blocks in the cache once they have been used. Other programs may treat the disk as a true random access device, reading and modifying locations throughout a file and benefiting from repeated access to the cached disk blocks but not from prefetching. It is a fairly simple matter to determine if the file is being accessed sequentially or not, and change prefetching and replacement strategies accordingly. When picking a candidate block for replacement, blocks which are part of a file being accessed sequentially would be taken before blocks which are part of a more randomly accessed file. In theory, this optimizes overall cache hit ratios and improves performance.

Access Time Equations

One way of looking at the effect of caches on computer performance is how they reduce the average access time to the lower levels of memory. This lower access time is also referred to as the *effective access time* (T_{EA}). For a given level of the memory hierarchy, n, T_{EA} is given by the following equation:

$$T_{EAn} = T_{An} + (1- h_n) * T_{EA(n+1)}$$

where T_{An} is the given memory level's intrinsic access time and h_n is the given level's hit ratio. The formula can be applied recursively to each layer of the memory hierarchy (provided the hit ratios are known for each level) to get the overall effective access time as seen by the processor. To illustrate the point, calculations for a typical disk I/O subsystem are now given.

Traces were taken of the disk accesses generated by a standard benchmark (SYSMRK93 from BAPCo), with and without a file cache. High performance disks currently have an average access time of 12 milliseconds and transfer data to the host at 10 MBytes/sec. Because read requests amounted to over 80% of the total requests, and the effects on performance of writes are difficult to calculate due to write-buffering strategies, only the read statistics will be used. For these traces they were:

	Count	Hit Ratio	KBytes Transferred	Avg. Length (KBytes)	Total Disk Access Time (ms)	Effective Disk Access Time (ms)
reads w/o cache	225,100	0.00	314,000	1.4	12.1	12.1
reads w. cache	33,600	0.85	360,000	10.7	13.1	2.0

Note the dramatic effective access time reduction due to the file cache, even though it actually fetched more disk data than the non-cache case. The cache reads many more data bytes with each disk request than the program asks for, but most data is subsequently used so the net effect is a reasonable hit ratio and good performance. The 6:1 ratio in access time is typical of the improvement caches provide.

If a program were *disk-bound* (constantly waiting on the disk), the 6:1 access time ratio could translate to a 6 times performance increase. Generally, however, a processor executes many instructions between disk accesses, so the effect is less dramatic. This example only looked at effects of an explicit file cache on disk accesses, not on overall main memory caching effects. If the number of processor instructions executed between disk requests were known, as well as other memory system details, then actual processor performance could be calculated.

Cache Coherence and Consistency Issues

Up to this point, described caches generally contain identical copies of locations in the next lower hierarchy layer. The one exception is when they operate as a write-back cache, and have some modified blocks. Even then, caches still contain the most current information. But, what happens if some external agent changes the data somewhere near the bottom of the hierarchy? That is where cache coherence and consistency issues arise.

The term "Cache Coherence" was originally applied to the issue of keeping the caches in multiprocessor computers in agreement on the contents of each memory location. If one processor changes the contents of a location in its cache, it must ensure that all other processor caches with copies of the location are notified of the change. As people designed and built multiprocessor systems, it became apparent that the order in which the modifications were observed was also important, and not necessarily guaranteed by many of the implementations. The issue of write ordering is known as the memory consistency.

In Uniprocessors, the agent making the change is often a DMA I/O device. Figure 11-3, which continues the example from Figure 11-2, cache location 1 contains an old copy of location 7, which has been

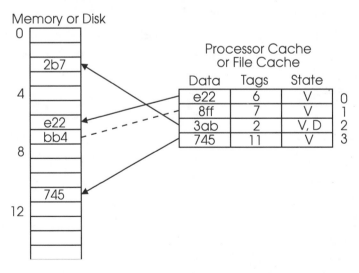

Figure 11-3. Cache Inconsistency Issues

updated through the actions of a DMA device. Such a device can dump large data amounts into main memory during I/O reads. But when the processor tries to read that data, it may get old cache data instead. With write-back caches, as illustrated by cache line 2 in Figure 11-3, the reverse problem occurs on I/O writes, where the data written out is the older main memory copy, not the newer cache copy.

One way to keep a uniprocessor's cache consistent with main memory is to flush caches before an I/O write and invalidate them after an I/O read. This maintains consistent copies, but usually flushes or invalidates many cache lines that aren't involved in the disk I/O. An alternative is to have cache lines selectively flushed or invalidated based on the specific addresses involved in the I/O transfer, such as by using a cache which monitors the memory's address bus for matches with cached locations.

Figure 11-4 illustrates the monitoring approach, also known as *snooping*. In such snooping caches, a *secondary tag store* often compares memory bus addresses with cache contents. The secondary tag store tracks primary tag store contents through cache coherence protocols. When a memory bus write is detected, tag matches cause corresponding cache locations to become invalid. When a memory bus read is detected, a tag match on a dirty line causes corresponding cache locations to flush to main memory and used in place of the memory data in satisfying the read.

In a multiprocessor system, not only do DMA devices create memory system inconsistencies, but so do the multiple processors. Fortunately,

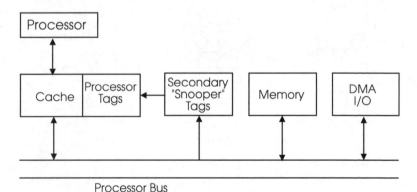

Processor Bus

Figure 11-4. Use of Cache Snooper to Maintain Cache Consistency

a small snooping protocol extension also keeps cache coherence between each processor cache. The extensions ensure that only one processor can modify a given location at a time by adding additional memory bus protocols. The most popular approach is for entities about to modify a location to request ownership of that location. The protocol then ensures only one entity can have ownership at a time. More sophisticated memory units, with sharing information kept in directories, can be used instead of the snooping tag stores.

While the preceding discusses processor and memory subsystems, main memory is also a cache for disk data, and so consistency issues also arise there. For example, several desktop (client) systems might connect to a file server. It would be nice to allow them to cache data in their local memories (or even on their local disks) to improve performance. But, if changes are made to the files, say by administrators loading new application versions on the server, or user programs modifying files cached on their machines, problems similar to the ones described for processor caches ensue. These problems can be solved by extending processor cache protocols to the file or disk I/O system.

In one possible application of coherence protocols to a server based file system, the server directory structures used would be expanded to include file sharing and caching information. Since all access requests initially go to the server, servers can redirect requests to the appropriate client processor, or request return of the modified blocks from the client with the latest version. Thus, clients always obtain the latest version of a file or disk block on each access, but several clients can cache the blocks locally, greatly improving performance. Similar schemes have been incorporated into several recent research projects.

Cache Summary

Caches greatly improve the performance of computer systems by providing rapid access to much of the requested information. Caches can achieve these performance benefits with a relatively small amount of memory because computer access patterns are often highly predictable, exhibiting spatial and temporal locality. In the I/O world, main memory is often used as a cache for remote and local disk storage. Disk drive caches are also used to exploit the built in prefetching provided by rotating media and the sequential nature of disk I/O. Appropriate combinations of both types of caches can dramatically improve the I/O performance of any computer system.

Pentium Superscaler Programming Considerations

Software executes on processors with designs that vary by model. So, it is generally impossible to select a specific instruction stream that is optimal for all processors within a single family. For example, optimum instruction streams for the Intel 80486 processor sometimes degrades Intel Pentium processor performance. Consequently, the following discussion only focuses on considerations that effect I/O subsystem performance for the Intel Pentium processor.

Pentium's U-Pipe and V-Pipe

Intel Pentium processors contain two instruction execution units that each have a five stage pipeline but share a common prefetch queue, qualifying it as a genuine *superscaler* processor. To achieve maximum performance, programming must observe the considerations necessary to allow both execution units simultaneous execution. Therefore, it is useful to understand what approaches trigger such conditions.

The Pentium contains one complete 80486 execution unit, referred to as the *U-pipe*, and a subordinate execution referred to as the *V-pipe*. The U-pipe and V-pipe can access the Pentium cache simultaneously and have individual write-back buffers to processor cache. In addition to superscalar architecture, Pentium processors provide reduced instruction cycle times. Many instructions now execute within a single clock cycle introducing even higher performance levels.

While the 80486 has a 32-byte instruction prefetch queue, the Pentium has a 128 byte instruction prefetch queue. In addition, the Pentium has a branch prediction feature that attempts to insure the correct branch path decodes within in the instruction prefetch queue, dramatically accelerating branch instances. However, Pentium's dual processors can interfere with one another causing pipeline stalls mentioned in Chapter 2.

Pentium Caching

Pentium performance depends heavily on high cache-hit rates which provide from two to fifty times reduction in processor fetch times.

Pentium contains separate 8 KByte instruction and data caches. This insures intensive data manipulation does not force instructions out of cache as happens in 80486 caches. The Pentium two-way set associative 8 KByte instruction cache consists of 256 32-byte cache lines, comprising eight *cache banks*. The first cache bank contains the first four bytes out of every cache line. The second cache bank contains the second four bytes out of every cache line etc.

Both the U-pipe and the V-pipe have simultaneous access to the single instruction cache which is fed by a 66 MHz 64-bit wide bus from the external secondary cache. The bus width and speed provides four time the bandwidth to secondary caches than an 80486 obtains. BIOS or other software can configure the Pentium cache as a write-back versus a write through cache, boosting access performance for variables such as loop counters.

Maximizing V-Pipe Execution

The V-pipe is subordinate to the U-pipe and its utilization can vary between zero percent to 100 percent. Avoiding U-pipe pipe stalls while insuring simultaneous V-Pipe execution is essential to achieve maximum Pentium performance. Otherwise, a Pentium executes approximately as fast as a similar speed 80486 processor rather than achieving its doubling potential.

When an instruction following a U-pipe instruction is valid for the V-pipe and is pairable with the U-pipe instruction but does not cause register contention, the V-pipe starts executing the instruction. Otherwise, the instruction waits for the U-pipe and the next instruction becomes a V-pipe candidate. An overview of some conditions necessary to achieve this follow:

- Memory operands should be properly boundary aligned.

- It is best to fall through branches whenever possible.

- The U-Pipe and V-pipe cannot access the same cache bank simultaneously without stalling the V-pipe.

- The V-pipe cannot execute an instruction that has not been executed out of cache at least once by the U-pipe.

- The U-pipe can execute all instructions.

- The V-pipe can only execute variants of 16 specific, but frequently executed, instructions and can only execute those concurrently when the U-pipe executes variants of 23 specific, but frequently executed, instructions.

- Decomposing more complicated CISC-type instructions into smaller RISC-type instruction sequences favors simultaneous U-pipe and V-pipe execution. However, this also expands code size, increasing cache misses and forcing trade-offs.

- If one instruction executes faster in one pipe than another simultaneously executing instruction, the pipe with the faster executing instruction remains stalled until the slower instruction completes.

If the above rules seem a bit complicated, they are. But since hand optimizing program instructions can triple or quadruple performance, high performance requirements may warrant the effort. However, optimization techniques that optimize instruction streams for one processor may not be valid on later versions or processor clones so optimizations may be best left to matched compilers designed to produce efficient instruction sequences for specific processors.

Chapter Questions

1 Where can caches be used?

   a Between the processor and main memory

   b In a disk drive

   c As part of a file system

   d All of the above

2 The Cache Hit Ratio is

   a The fraction of time that read data is found in a cache

   b The fraction of requests that go to the cache instead of CPU registers

   c The fraction of requests to data blocks already present in the cache

   d The fraction of requests to dirty blocks in the cache

3 Caches are effective due to

   a Amdahl's law

   b The principal of locality

c Volatility

d The degree of associativity

e Adler's law

4 The number of cache blocks into which each main memory location can map is known as

a Amdahl's law

b The principal of locality

c Volatility

d The degree of associativity

5 The address where a cache entry originally came from is called a

a Block

b Set

c Tag

d State

6 The data in each entry is stored in the cache

a Block

b Set

c Tag

d State

7 The valid bit is part of the cache

a Block

b Set

c Tag

d State

8 The least recently used algorithm refers to

a A method to decide which cache block to replace on a miss

b A policy which replaces the oldest item in the cache

c A good performer on programs with iterative access patterns

d All of the above

9 Given a file system cache which can deliver a disk block in 100 microseconds in a system with disk drives which average 10 milliseconds access time, what is the speedup (disk access time/effective cache access time. if the cache has an 0.80 hit rate?

    a 3

    b 5

    c 10

    d 100

10 In a cache system, what is a snooper?

    a A device to look for parity errors

    b A device for discovering why performance is poor

    c A device which enforces cache consistency

    d A device which detects illegal use of your computer

11 The Pentium

    a Benefits from the same optimization strategies as the 80486 processor

    b Has two execution units and processor pipelines

    c Has the same hardware cache as the 80486

    d Is not a genuine superscalar processor

❐

12

RAID Systems

What This Chapter Is About

This brief chapter discusses how various Redundant Array of Inexpensive Disks (*RAID*) designs achieve improved storage subsystem capabilities. In the past, they used the highest performance interfaces available. These designs now typically use SCSI in proprietary implementations because of its overlapped I/O capabilities. In the future, RAID systems will use serial I/O technology.

RAID Background

RAID is a family of techniques for managing collections of disks in such a way that desirable cost, availability, and performance properties are provided to host computing environments. RAID is a particularly exciting technique for delivering flawless mass storage performance at reasonable cost.

In 1988, University of California at Berkeley researchers David Patterson, Garth Gibson, and Randy Katz published a paper titled "A Case for Redundant Arrays of Inexpensive Disks." This landmark paper outlined five approaches that exploited inexpensive disks to create disk storage subsystems with varying

- Capacity
- Performance
- Fault Tolerance

The authors arbitrarily named the five designs RAID Level 1 through 5 which comprised various trade-offs among the three above aspects. In 1993, the RAID Advisory Board's *RAIDBook* formalized the five designs and added four more, designated RAID Level 0, RAID Level 6, RAID Level 10, and RAID Level 53.

Unlike MS-DOS's design that assigns one or more drive letters to individual hard disks, RAID *Array Management Software* (*AMS*) coordinates hard drives activities. This makes individual disk presence transparent to MS-DOS. Typically, AMS uses SCSI overlapped I/O capabilities for improved connectivity and performance. In addition, most RAID AMS systems distribute data across several hard disks, referred to as *data striping*, and may sometimes synchronize spindle rotations for improved throughput.

In such systems, system seek times equal the slowest individual seek time. But, once seeks are complete, throughput can proceed significantly faster depending on the RAID Level selected. However, simplistic data striping leaves systems vulnerable to single drive failures which disrupt the entire storage subsystem. Therefore, some RAID levels incorporate data redundancy provisions to compensate gracefully for individual drive failures.

RAID technology is sweeping the mass storage industry. Informed estimates place its expected usage rate at 40% or more of all storage over the next few years. Information technology professionals should be familiar with the benefits and costs of RAID technology so they can make informed decisions about strategically deploying it.

This following chapter is excerpted with permission from the RAID Advisory Board's *RAIDBook*, the definitive RAID reference work. Edited by Paul Massiglia, this easy to read, brilliantly presented, 200 page book provides extensive RAID information and is highly recommended.

The Motivation for RAID

Computer Systems Become Unbalanced

While improvements in the unit cost of mass storage capacity have generally kept pace with those in computers themselves, improvements in input-output (I/O) performance have not. Moreover, the reliability expectations for data are far greater than those on the computing components of the system. Even applications which tolerate service outages cannot tolerate permanent loss of data due to a component failure.

The mass storage industry's two biggest challenges in recent years have therefore been:

- To improve I/O performance at the pace of computing performance so that access to data does not become a limiting factor for applications

- To provide access to on-line data at levels of reliability well in excess of the expected lifetimes of the computer systems that process it

These challenges must be met cost-effectively so that solutions are affordable by most users.

These challenges are doubly difficult to meet because magnetic and optical disks, which are the most cost-effective mass storage technologies, have electromechanical components. These electromechanical components operate more slowly, require more power, and generate more heat, vibration, and noise than purely electronic devices. The disks in which they reside are therefore both inherently slower and more failure-prone.

While it is to the credit of disk designers that Mean Time Between Failure (MTBF[1]) values of hundreds of thousands of hours have been achieved, and data access times have been reduced to less than a third of what they were two decades ago, the reliability of data stored on disks remains a concern for many system users.

---

[1] The *Mean Time Between Failures* of a device is the average time from start of use to failure in a large population of identical devices. It is more appropriately used to assess the failure rate in a population of devices than the probable lifetime of a single device.

So the challenge for the mass storage industry is to start with devices that by themselves can be the limiting factor in system performance and reliability, and to build from them storage subsystems that make data the most reliable component of the system. In the course of doing this, storage is expected to become even more affordable and performance is expected to improve!

Solving the System Imbalance Problem

Disk I/O limits system performance for two reasons:

- Data must be located by the relatively slow processes of seeking and disk rotation.

- Once located, data must be transferred to or from the disk media in a one-bit wide stream.

Experienced system designers and managers have long known how to make slow disks keep up with fast computers—use lots of them in parallel. It is not uncommon for a large computer system to be connected to hundreds of disks—not just for the storage capacity they make available, but for the number of parallel I/O streams they permit. Even in departmental and smaller systems, multiple disks are becoming the rule.

On the surface, concurrent use of multiple disks is an attractive solution. If one disk can perform 50 I/O operations per second, two should be able to perform 100, and so on, up to the computer system's appetite for I/O.

Imbalance Persists...

But, as experienced system managers know, systems' I/O loads are rarely distributed neatly across the available disks. A far more likely scenario is that most of a system's I/O requests are addressed to a small fraction of its storage. One sometimes hears of an *80/20 rule*— 80% of the total I/O load is directed at 20% of the I/O resources. Applying this rule to 10 disks, each capable of 50 I/O operations per second:

- Two of the disks (20%) together deliver 100 I/O operations per second (all they are capable of).

- The remaining eight disks deliver a total of 25 I/O operations per second (20% of the overall I/O load), for an overall total of 125 I/O operations per second—far fewer than the 500 I/O operations per second one would expect with a perfectly balanced I/O load.[2]

Exploiting I/O Resources Effectively

The obvious solution to this sub-optimal use of resources is to *tune* the I/O system—to rearrange data on the disks until the most frequently accessed pieces of data are evenly distributed, or *balanced*, across the I/O resources. A considerable amount of system management effort today goes into I/O system tuning, and not without success. But tuning the I/O system has limits:

- It may be physically impossible to tune an entire I/O system perfectly. Using the example above, suppose that an application requires 100 I/O operations per second against a single file. Whatever disk contains that file will be a *hot* disk, i.e., it will be saturated with I/O requests, and the application's requirement will not be satisfied.

- Even when it *is* possible to balance the I/O load, there is no guarantee that it will stay balanced. In almost any system, the I/O load changes with time. Which data are hot depends on which applications and users are active. Even within a single application, as new data is created and old data deleted, the location of the system's active data changes.

Thus, while I/O system tuning is an important step toward optimizing I/O resource utilization, it is neither sufficiently precise nor sufficiently responsive to keep a dynamically changing system operating at peak efficiency. Some kind of *disk array* is usually a more effective solution to I/O tuning problems.

Disk Arrays

We begin with a few RAID Advisory board definitions.

- A *host computer* is any computer system to which disks are attached and accessible for data storage and I/O. Mainframes, and servers, as well as workstations and personal computers,

---

[2] There is some evidence from examination of actual systems that suggests that while the 80/20 rule is somewhat extreme, a 55/20 rule (i.e., 55% of the I/O load is directed at 20% of the resources) is not uncommon. Using a 55/20 rule, the ten disks in the example of this section could handle about 180 I/O requests per second, still only 36% of the hardware's potential.

can all be considered host computers in the context of this book, as long as they may have disks attached to them.

- A *RAID-related product* is any computer system mass storage product that implements or interfaces with RAID technology as defined in the *RAIDBook* in some significant way. RAID-related products may include storage controllers, disk sub-systems, software packages, and test equipment.

- A *disk* is any non-volatile, randomly accessible, block-addressable rewritable mass storage device. This definition includes both rotating magnetic and optical disks and *solid-state disks*, or non-volatile electronic storage elements. It does not include special-ized devices such as *write-once-read-many* (*WORM*) optical disks (which are not rewritable), nor does it include so-called *RAM disks* implemented using software to control a dedicated portion of a host computer's random access memory (because the storage they provide is volatile).

- A *disk subsystem* is a collection of disks and the hardware required to connect them to one or more host computers. The hardware may include a controller, or the disks may be con-nected directly to a host computer's I/O bus adapter. A disk subsystem which includes additional capabilities, such as tape or CD-ROM is called a *storage subsystem*. All of a computer sys-tem's storage subsystems collectively comprise its *I/O system*. The ANSI X3.T10 RAID Study Group refers to a disk sub-system as a *SCSI Disk Array* (SDA).[3]

- A *disk array* is a collection of disks from one or more commonly accessible disk subsystems, combined with a body of Array Management Software. Array Management Software controls the operation of the disks and presents them as one or more *virtual disks* to host operating environments.[4] The ANSI X3.T10

---

[3] At the time of writing, the ANSI X3.T10 RAID Study Group is engaged in the process of creating a standard governing SCSI-attached disk arrays. In the course of creating this standard, terminology similar to that defined here is being developed. Where the ANSI and RAID Advisory Board terms for similar concepts differ, the latter will be noted in the text.

[4] Array Management Software is often referred to as *firmware* when it resides and exe-cutes in a disk subsystem rather than a host computer.

RAID Study Group does not define a term for disk array in the sense in which it is used in this book.

■ A *virtual disk* is an abstract entity realized by Array Management Software. A virtual disk is functionally identical to a physical disk from the standpoint of applications.[5] Its cost[6], availability and performance may be quite different, however. The ANSI X3.T10 RAID Study Group refers to a virtual disk as a *volume set*.

■ A *member disk* or *member* is a disk which is under the control of Array Management Software. Disks may be array members for part of the time and be used as conventional disks at other times.

The RAID Advisory Board's definition of *disk array* permits considerable flexibility in configurations. In addition to disk arrays which consist of some or all of the disks within a single subsystem, the definition includes arrays whose Array Management Software executes in host computers and controls disks connected via multiple controllers or I/O. Figure 12-1 illustrates the disk array topologies accommodated by the RAID Advisory Board's definition.

Figure 12-1 illustrates an array comprising all of a subsystem's disks (Virtual Disk 1), an array comprising some of a subsystem's disks (Virtual Disk 2), and an array whose members reside on multiple subsystems (Virtual Disk 3). In actual practice, most disk arrays are implemented within a subsystem (Virtual Disk 1 or Virtual Disk 2 in Figure 12-1), making them self-contained *array subsystems*. It is important to recognize, however, that the essence of a disk array is not its implementation site, but the fact that it uses Array Management Software to manage several disks and present them to a host operating environment as virtual disks with different cost, availability, and performance characteristics than the underlying members.

---

[5] One important way in which an application's view of a disk differs from an operating system's is that the application is generally insensitive to whether I/O requests are handled one at a time or queued, whereas operating systems are intensely sensitive to this property for performance reasons. Acceptance and internal queuing of multiple I/O requests is one important way in which arrays differ functionally from disks. (Though this distinction is disappearing.)

---

[6] In this context, cost refers to the relative cost per MByte of storage available to applications.

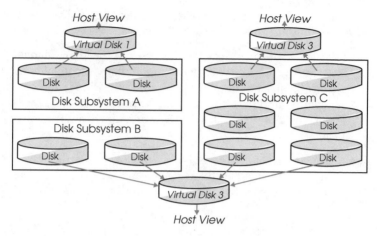

Figure 12-1. Common Disk Array Topologies

The Role of Array Management Software

Array Management Software may execute either in the disk subsystem or in a host computer. Its principal functions are to:

Map the storage space available to applications onto the array member disks *in a way that achieves some desired balance of cost, availability, and performance*

Present the storage to the operating environment as one or more virtual disks by transparently converting I/O requests directed to a virtual disk to I/O operations on the underlying member disks, and by performing whatever operations are required to provide any extraordinary data availability capabilities offered by the array

Figure 12-2 illustrates two common disk arrays:

- *Mirrored* arrays, in which two or more member disks contain identical images of user data

- *Striped* arrays, which interleave user data on two or more member disks

The models of Figure 12-2 are examples of disk arrays with different cost, availability, and I/O performance properties.

- A *mirrored array* presents very reliable virtual disks whose aggregate capacity is equal to that of the smallest of its member disks, and whose performance is usually measurably better

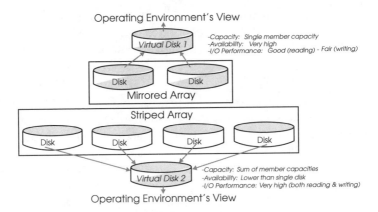

Figure 12-2. Two Common Disk Arrays

than that of a single member disk for reads and slightly lower
for writes.

- A *striped array* presents virtual disks whose aggregate capacity
  is approximately the sum of the capacities of its members, and
  whose read and write performance are both very high. The
  data reliability of a striped array's virtual disks, however, is
  less than that of the least reliable member disk.

Disk arrays may enhance some or all of three desirable storage properties compared to individual disks:

- They may improve *I/O performance* by balancing the I/O load
  evenly across the disks. Striped arrays have this property,
  because they cause streams of either sequential or random I/O
  requests[7] to be divided approximately evenly across the disks
  in the set. In many cases, a mirrored array can also improve
  read performance because each of its members can process a
  separate read request simultaneously, thereby reducing the
  average read queue length in a busy system.

- They may improve *data reliability* by replicating data so that it
  is not destroyed or inaccessible if the disk on which it is stored

---

[7] This book refers to streams of consecutively issued requests to read or write blocks of
data located at adjacent ascending disk addresses as *sequential* read or write requests.
Similarly, it refers to streams of consecutively issued I/O requests which to not have
this property as *random* I/O requests, without regard for whether the addresses of the
data requested are truly random.

fails. Mirrored arrays have this property, because they cause every block of data to be replicated on all members of the set. Striped arrays, on the other hand do not, because as a practical matter, the failure of one disk in a striped array renders all the data stored on the array's virtual disks inaccessible.

- They may simplify *storage management* by treating more storage capacity as a single manageable entity. A system manager who is managing arrays of four disks (each array presenting a single virtual disk) has one fourth as many directories to create, one fourth as many user disk space quotas to set, one fourth as many backup operations to schedule (although, alas, not one fourth as much data to back up!), etc. Striped arrays have this property, while mirrored arrays generally do not.

The principle of disk arrays is simple—trade a little of a relatively abundant resource (computing capacity required to execute the Array Management Software) to optimize the use of a scarce resource (data reliability and/or I/O performance). In most cases, the extra processing required is minor—formulating and issuing extra I/O requests, and is well spent to attain the benefits offered.[8]

Layered Arrays

It is sometimes possible to combine two disk array technologies to achieve a combination of their benefits. One way to do this is to *layer* one array on top of another. Perhaps the most popular example of layering is a striped array whose members are actually virtual disks presented by mirrored arrays, as illustrated in Figure 12-3.

Figure 12-3 illustrates six disks arranged as three mirrored arrays. Each mirrored array presents its operating environment with a virtual disk with a capacity equal to that of one member. In this case, however, the "operating environment" is another layer of Array Management Software, which creates a single striped array using the virtual disks presented by the three mirrored ones. This array's virtual disk is presented to the "real" operating environment for application use.

---

[8] This is not necessarily the case with RAID Levels 4 and 5. For many array implementations that use these technologies, the consumer must carefully consider the I/O workload to which the array will be subjected.

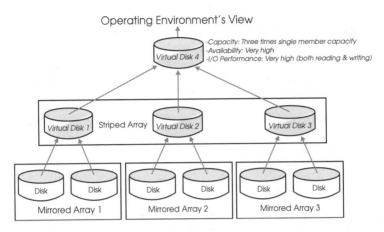

Figure 12-3. Layered Disk Arrays

The mirrored arrays in this example present very reliable virtual disks. The striped array balances the I/O load evenly across its mirrored members, providing high performance. This combination of striping and mirroring therefore offers both high data availability and high I/O performance, albeit at a fairly high cost (in the example of Figure 12-3, the user pays for 6 disks and host connections, but has usable storage capacity equal to that of only three disks).

Extending the Disk Array Concept: RAID

The striped and mirrored disk array models discussed above have been tremendously successful in the market. Most major system vendors offer mirroring and striping in some form.

The popularity of early disk arrays coupled with the growing imbalance between computing and I/O capabilities led researchers to examine other ways of combining disks into arrays with desirable combinations of affordability, data reliability and I/O performance. In 1988, David A. Patterson, Garth Gibson, and Randy H. Katz of the University of California at Berkeley published a paper entitled "A Case for Redundant Arrays of Inexpensive Disks," which outlined five disk array models, or *RAID Levels* that would achieve just this. They labeled their models RAID Levels 1 through 5, although no hierarchical relationship was implied.

A *Redundant Array of Independent Disks* (*RAID* or *RAID Array*) is a disk array in which part of the physical storage capacity is used to store redundant information about user data stored on the remainder of the storage capacity. The redundant information enables regeneration of user data in the event that one of the array's member disks or the access path to it fails.

The Berkeley RAID Levels are the five RAID Levels defined in the Berkeley paper "A Case for Redundant Arrays of Inexpensive Disks."

Three of the Berkeley RAID Levels have proven commercially attractive, and are found in a variety of disk array products:

- *RAID Level 1*, or disk mirroring as discussed above. RAID Level 1 offers the highest data reliability[9] of the Berkeley RAID Levels. Most implementations provide improved I/O performance when reading data (compared to the performance of one member disk). The primary drawback of RAID Level 1 is its inherent cost (because of the number of components required) compared to other forms of RAID.

- *RAID Level 3* uses a *parity disk* to store redundant information about the data on several data disks. Strictly speaking, the RAID Level 3 mapping algorithm is to distribute the data from each virtual disk block evenly across corresponding blocks of all array members but one (the *parity disk*), and to write the parity of the distributed data in the corresponding block of the parity disk. Many RAID Level 3 implementations approximate this behavior.

  RAID Level 3 provides excellent I/O performance for applications in which large blocks of sequentially located data must be transferred quickly, such as image processing, scientific data collection and reduction, and batch data processing. The data transfer rate and computing requirements of these applications all but preclude host-based implementations, so RAID Level 3 arrays are usually subsystem-based.

- *RAID Level 5* uses storage capacity equivalent to that of one disk in an array to store parity computed on user data stored on the array's remaining media capacity. In this respect is it

---

[9] for member disks of a given reliability (MTBF)

similar to RAID Level 3. It differs, however, in that the array's disks operate independently of each other, and in that the redundant information is distributed across all disks in the array.

For practical purposes, RAID Level 5 offers data reliability approaching that of mirroring,[10] with read performance bene-fits similar to those of striping. There is a substantial perfor-mance penalty compared to a single disk when data is written, however. Since this *write penalty* is inherent in RAID Level 5 data protection many designs incorporate features specifically designed to mitigate its effect.

RAID Level 5 is especially well suited for applications whose I/O loads consist predominantly of a large number of concurrent read requests. Transaction processing and office automation applications often fall into this category. It can also be also very good for data transfer-intensive applications, such as image analysis, which make mostly read requests. It is not as well suited for write-intensive applications such as data entry or scientific or engineering data collection.

Other RAID Levels

Since the publication of "A Case for Redundant Arrays of Inexpen-sive Disks," a sixth RAID Level has been described by the original authors.[11] RAID Level 6 incorporates a second disk containing inde-pendently computed redundant information. It is capable of protect-ing against data loss due to double as well as single disk failures. RAID Level 6 provides extremely high data reliability at relatively modest cost for large arrays, but exacts an even more substantial write penalty than RAID Level 5, and so virtually all implementa-tions include extensive features aimed at enhancing application write performance.

---

[10] Although numerically, it is substantially less, both are large compared to the typi-cally expected 3–5 year life of disk subsystems.

---

[11] A reference appears in a paper entitled "Disk System Architectures for High Perfor-mance Computing," *Proceedings of the IEEE*, Vol. 77, No. 12, December, 1989 [Katz89]. Some vendors have used the term *RAID Level 6* to refer to a combination of RAID Levels 0 and 1 (described later in this book). The RAID Advisory Board usage con-forms to the Berkeley definition.

In addition, the term *RAID Level 0* is often used to refer to disk striping because the data mapping is conceptually similar to that used in RAID implementations.[12] Strictly speaking, the absence of redundancy in a striped array, makes the term RAID a misnomer. Because it is in common use, however, the RAID Advisory Board endorses the term *RAID Level 0* to refer to disk striping. This book uses the terms disk striping and RAID Level 0 interchangeably.

RAID Level 0 and the original five Berkeley RAID Levels are described in more detail in the *RAIDBook*. Table 12-1 presents a brief cost, data reliability, and I/O performance comparison of the more common RAID Levels for reference. In Table 12-1, I/O performance is shown both in terms of *data transfer capacity*, or ability to move large amounts of data rapidly, and *I/O rate*, or ability to satisfy large numbers of I/O requests per unit time, since a given RAID Level may inherently provide different relative performance according to one of these metrics than the other. Each RAID Level's particular strong point is highlighted by shading.

Table 12-1: Summary Comparison of the Most Common RAID Levels

RAID Level	Common Name	Description	Disks Req'd (Cost)	Data Reliability	Data Transfer Capacity[1]	Maximum I/O Rate
0	Disk Striping	Data distributed across the disks in the array. No redundant information provided.	N	Lower than single-disk	Very high	Very high for both read and write
1	Mirroring	All data replicated on *N* separate disks. *N* is almost always 2.	2N, 3N, etc.	Higher than RAID Level 2, 3, 4, or 5; lower than RAID Level 6	Higher than single disk for read; similar to single disk for write	Up to twice that of a single disk for read; similar to single disk for write

---

[12] In fact, the Berkeley researchers recognized striped data mapping as a desirable feature for any RAID Level rather than a level in its own right.

Table 12-1: Summary Comparison of the Most Common RAID Levels (Continued)

RAID Level	Common Name	Description	Disks Req'd (Cost)	Data Reliability	Data Transfer Capacity[1]	Maximum I/O Rate
2		Data protected by a Hamming code. Redundant information is distributed across m disks, where m is a function of the number of data disks in the array.	N + m	Much higher than single disk; comparable to RAID 3, 4, or 5	Highest of all listed alternatives	Similar to twice that of a single disk
3	RAID 3, Parallel Transfer Disks w. Parity	Each data sector is subdivided and distributed across all data disks. Redundant information normally stored on a dedicated parity disk.	N + 1	Much higher than single disk; comparable to RAID 2, 4, or 5	Highest of all listed alternatives	Similar to twice that of a single disk
4		Data sectors are distributed as with disk striping. Redundant information is stored on a dedicated parity disk.	N + 1	Much higher than single disk; comparable to RAID 2, 3, or 5	Similar to disk striping for read; significantly lower than single disk for write	Similar to disk striping for read; significantly lower than single disk for write
5	RAID 5, RAID	Data sectors are distributed as with disk striping; redundant information is interspersed with user data.	N + 1	Much higher than single disk; comparable to RAID 2, 3, or 4	Similar to disk striping for read; lower than single disk for write	Similar to disk striping for read; generally lower than single disk for write
6	RAID 6	As RAID Level 5, but with additional independently computed redundant information.	N + 2	Highest of all listed alternatives	Similar to disk striping for read; lower than RAID Level 5 for write	Similar to disk striping for read; significantly lower than RAID Level 5 for write

[1] The Data Transfer Capacity and I/O Rate columns of this table reflect only the write performance inherently implied by RAID data mapping and protection, and do not include related performance enhancement features included in many implementations.

Still Other Forms of RAID

While RAID Levels 0, 1, 3, and 5 all represent useful data mapping models, each has its drawbacks when applied in products. Developers of RAID products therefore frequently improve upon the data mapping and protection models outlined in the original Berkeley paper, either by:

- Combining multiple RAID Levels into one product, often by layering; or,

- Combining some form of RAID data mapping and protection with other technologies, such as cache, redundant I/O paths, multiprocessing controller architectures, and others

The goal of such combinations is generally to improve I/O performance while retaining or improving on the data reliability characteristics that come from RAID data mapping and protection. One such combination that is available in several products is the combination of RAID Levels 0 and 1. This combination, whether layered or not has been referred to as *RAID 10*, *RAID Level 0+1*, and *RAID Level 0&1*, and possibly by other names.

Many RAID vendors use phrases like *"RAID n"* or *"RAID Level n"* (for some *n* not included in the Berkeley taxonomy) in their products' names or descriptions. *RAID 5+*, *RAID 6+*, *RAID 7*, *RAID 10*, and *RAID53* have all been used.

While such names might lead to an inference that the products incorporate some unique data mapping and protection model, this is usually not the case. What is more typical is for a product to either blend multiple Berkeley RAID Levels, or to add additional non-RAID features to a subsystem that implements one of the Berkeley RAID Levels.

To date, there has not been general industry-wide agreement on definition of data mapping and protection models other than the RAID Level 0 and the five Berkeley RAID Levels. This is not to say, however, that other useful data mappings will not be created and standardized. RAID continues to be the subject of substantial research and development. It is the RAID Advisory Board's intention to incorporate any such models into its nomenclature scheme and certification programs as they are developed and become generally accepted in the industry.

Another Disk Array Taxonomy[13]

Another way of classifying disk array data mapping and protection models is to observe that they are either:

- *Parallel Access Arrays*, in which all of the member disks participate concurrently in every I/O operation directed at the array; or

- *Independent Access Arrays*, in which the member disks may operate independently, even to the extent of satisfying multiple application I/O requests concurrently.

RAID Level 2 and 3 arrays are inherently parallel access arrays, because the data protection model assumes that all member disks operate in unison. Some parallel access array implementations require physical synchronization of member disk rotation. Others allow disks that are not rotationally synchronized, and approximate strictly parallel access behavior.

RAID Level 4 and 5 arrays are inherently independent access arrays. In principle, it is possible for every member of a RAID Level 5 array to be engaged in satisfying a separate application I/O request at any instant.

RAID Level 1 arrays (mirrored disks) may be implemented in either style, although in practice most RAID Level 1 arrays are independent access implementations.

In general, parallel access arrays are most suitable for applications requiring high data transfer capacity, while independent access arrays are most suitable for applications requiring high I/O request rates. This characterization becomes less clear-cut as vendors add advanced features, notably cache, to their products in an effort to improve I/O performance. Moreover, many array implementations adapt their behavior to approximate either parallel access or independent access, depending on the instantaneous I/O load.

For the purchaser and user of RAID technology, the independent access/parallel access classification is likely to be of more practical value than classification by Berkeley RAID Level, simply because it

---

[13] The concepts in this section were originally proposed by RAID Advisory Board member firm Formation, Inc., whose contribution is gratefully acknowledged.

relates an array's implementation technology to its suitability for use in given classes of applications.

Table 12-2: Summary of Disk Array Application Suitability

Array Type	Application Suitability	Examples
Parallel Access	High data transfer rate requirements	Seismic or telemetric data collection; batch processing of large sequential files
Independent Access	High data access rate requirements	Interactive transaction processing; multi-user file services (e.g., office environments).

Why Is RAID Important?

System managers who provide information handling services to their organizations, as well as information technology managers who make technology purchase and configuration decisions should be aware of the new richness of storage alternatives offered by RAID. RAID Level 3 and RAID Level 5, for example, offer data reliability comparable to that of disk mirroring (from a practical standpoint), at significantly lower *inherent cost*,[14] particularly when high capacity is required. There are trade-offs, however, in performance. Awareness of RAID and other mass storage technology options help with important decisions about storage alternatives.

Users of networked personal computers should also be concerned about the type of data storage services provided by their data servers. RAID technology, both in the form of host software and subsystems, is becoming readily available in the server market at modest cost. The material in this book can help make the personal computer user aware of the significance of the storage alternatives available for his server. Moreover, as disk size and cost continues to decline, the availability of RAID for the desktop itself is only a matter of time. Today, RAID is viewed as an added value option oriented toward larger disk subsystems. There is evidence that within a very few years the *average* disk will be part of a RAID array; in other words, non-arrayed disks will be the exception rather than the rule.

---

[14] Inherent cost is the cost of a product expressed in terms of the number of components contained in it. This book uses inherent cost as a way of normalizing the cost of various alternatives. Vendors of products which implement the various RAID technologies may set prices on some basis other than a pure inherent cost.

Comparing Storage Options

Figure 12-4 illustrates the mass storage *cost-availability-performance* (*CAP*) *triangle*—a convenient device for visually comparing the properties of various mass storage options. The CAP triangle is a useful way of looking at mass storage in general; not just disk arrays.

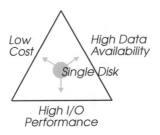

Figure 12-4. The Mass Storage *Cost-Availability-Performance* (*CAP*) Triangle

Purchasers of mass storage seek an optimal balance of the three basic mass storage properties:

- Low cost per MByte

- High I/O performance[15]

- High data reliability

Of course, the optimal balance of these properties is different for each user and for each application. The challenge for mass storage purchasers is to determine the correct balance of cost, availability, and performance each time they make a storage purchase.

The CAP triangle may be thought of as representing a continuum of affordability (low cost), availability, and I/O performance, with the extremes of these properties represented by its edges. Every mass storage product may be regarded as occupying a point within this

---

[15] I/O performance may mean either data transfer performance and I/O request performance depending on the context. For detailed evaluation purposes, it is usually necessary to distinguish between the two, since both application demands and array capabilities tend to tunable to favor one performance requirement over others. As a device for concisely summarizing mass storage characteristics, however, the CAP triangle does not attempt to do so.

continuum—closer to an edge if it possesses a property in greater degree, and further from that edge if less. Figure 12-5 illustrates the use of the CAP triangle to position a conventional disk, a striped array, and a mirrored array relative to each other.

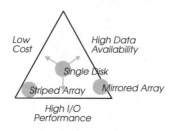

Figure 12-5. Using the CAP Triangle to Position Storage Technologies

In Figure 12-5, the single disk occupies the center of the triangle. As the most common on-line mass storage media in use today, it arguably represents the "norm" of cost, availability, and performance. Of course, different disk products have different properties, but compared to arrays and other alternatives, it is fair to regard conventional disks as a single class of storage.

The striped array is positioned close to the low cost and high I/O performance edges, because it is a low cost means of achieving high I/O performance. It is far from the high availability edge, however, because its net data reliability is less than that of a single disk.

The mirrored array, on the other hand, offers considerably greater data reliability than a comparable single disk, so it is closer to the high availability edge of the triangle. Moreover, since it offers higher I/O performance than a single disk, it is closer to the high I/O performance edge as well (although not as close as the striped array). The cost of mirroring, however, is relatively high—twice the cost of basic storage capacity—so the mirrored array is far from the low cost edge.

This CAP triangle is used in the *RAIDBook* to position various array technologies relative to each other in terms of their affordability, availability, and I/O performance.

Clearing up the Confusion...

To assist purchasers of RAID products in understanding the characteristics of different vendors' offerings, the RAID Advisory Board offers certification programs to vendors of RAID-related products. By subjecting their products to various forms of examination by the RAID Advisory Board or its agents, vendors may earn certification that their products comply with the definitions of RAID functionality set forth in Part 2 of the *RAIDBook*. Vendors of certified products may indicate their products' compliance by displaying the RAID Advisory Board trademark which looks similar to

Descriptive Legend

in their product literature or other descriptions. The "Descriptive Legend" attached to the trademark indicates the type of the RAID Advisory Board examination the product has undergone. Authorized use of the RAID Advisory Board's trademark means that a product has been examined by the RAID Advisory Board, and found to exhibit the characteristics of the designated RAID Level(s) as they are defined in the *RAIDBook*. No inference should be made about other product features.

The RAID Advisory Board trademarks, the criteria by which license to use them is granted, and the rules under which they may be displayed are described in the publication *RABInfo*, available from the RAID Advisory Board.

Chapter Questions

1 AMS stands for

   a Access Method Sequence

   b Adaptive Maintenance Software

   c Array Management Software

   d Adaptec Management System

2 RAID now stands for

   a Redundant Array of Inexpensive Disks

   b Redundant Array of Independent Disks

   c A popular insecticide aerosol

   d None of the above

3 Mirrored arrays

   a Have plated media which reflect light through their glass housings

   b Interleave user data on two or more member disks

   c Have two or more disks which contain identical images of user data

   d Are characterized by framed sector boundaries

4 Striped arrays

   a Have plated media which reflect light through their glass housings

   b Interleave user data on two or more member disks

   c Have two or more disks which contain identical images of user data

   d Are characterized by framed sector boundaries

5 Disk arrays may

   a Improve I/O performance

   b Simplify storage management

   c Improve data reliability

   d All of the above

   e None of the above

6 The three Berkeley RAID Levels that have proven commercially attractive are

   a Levels 1, 2, and 5

   b Levels 2, 3, and 5

   c Levels 1, 2, and 3

   d None of the above

7 In Parallel Access Arrays

   a Member disks may operate independently, even to the extent of satisfying multiple I/O requests concurrently

   b Member disks may participate concurrently in every I/O operation directed to the array

   c Member disks may use parallel SCSI connections

   d b and c

8 RAID attempts to balance

   a Cost per Mbyte, I/O performance, data reliability

   b Physical space, I/O performance, data reliability

   c Cost per Mbyte, Physical space, data reliability

   d Cost per Mbyte, I/O performance, Physical space

9 RAID Levels 2 and 3 are

   a Inherently parallel access arrays

   b Inherently independent access arrays

   c Suitable for high data transfer application

   d a and c

10 RAID Level 4 and 5 arrays are

   a Inherently parallel access arrays

   b Inherently independent access arrays

   c Suitable for high data transfer application

   d a and c

   e All of the above

❒

▼▼▼▼ 13

Benchmarks

Overview

Benchmarks are computing's performance yardsticks. Performance is most often considered to be throughput, but other metrics such as latency or security may also be employed. Regardless of the metric chosen, benchmarks need to provide the most accurate and meaningful measurements possible.

There are many reasons for measuring a computer system's performance. The measurements can be used to select between competing systems, eliminating some and determining which of the remainder have the best cost/performance ratio. Once a system has been bought, performance measurements can reveal bottlenecks and indicate where upgrades would be useful. For the computer designer, measurements of existing systems can indicate areas where redesign could provide a large performance gain, and more detailed measurements of internal system traffic can drive future computer architectures.

The ideal benchmark would be one which accurately predicts the performance users will obtain from normal computer use. It would be portable to all computer hardware and operating systems, easy to use, and immune to rigging by computer manufacturers. Unfortunately, such an ideal benchmark does not, and cannot, exist. In order to illustrate the point, this chapter will provide an introduction to the many issues and trade-offs encountered when designing and using benchmarks.

Benchmark Design Issues

There are many factors to consider in benchmark design. How wide a usage range (i.e., the application domain) should it attempt to cover? Should it use real applications, portions of real applications, or representative samples of application operations? Understanding the difficulties involved in creating good benchmarks puts the results of those benchmarks in better perspective.

Selecting the Workload

The closer benchmark workloads duplicate actual usage patterns, the more the results reflect actual performance. In the best case, workloads consist of actual applications used to accomplish real work. But convenience, cost, and repeatability issues argue for approximations to actual usage.

It is well known that different application domains stress very different computer parts. For example, most engineering applications heavily use computer floating point units, while database programs heavily use disk subsystems. A computer which scores well on floating point benchmarks might perform very poorly at database tasks. Consequently, most new benchmarks target increasingly more specific application domains.

Target Application(s)

An important aspect of producing a system workload which approximates an anticipated one is the applications selected for the workload. Typical application categories are:

- Office automation
- Program development
- Scientific, engineering
- On-line transaction processing

Application characteristics vary dramatically between categories, so care should be taken to only pick from categories that match anticipated usage. Most benchmarks will be targeted at a specific category, or even subcategory, as it simplifies result interpretation.

While the target category is often obvious, selecting the "right" application mix within the category is not. For example, the office automation category contains numerous spreadsheet, word processing and graphics programs. Approaches historically used include:

- Picking the benchmark developer's favorites
- Selecting the top selling applications
- Selecting the most used applications (e.g., through surveys)

The survey approach is probably the most accurate, but also the most difficult.

Once a set of applications is chosen, it is also necessary to supply them with realistic inputs. Depending on the applications, these are either keystroke scripts or sample data files. These scripts or data files should closely approximate actual expected usage. Sometimes, as with scientific applications, sample data files which are typical of normal usage are fairly easy to obtain. But in other cases, such as office automation, even defining what typical usage is, let alone collecting typical keystroke scripts, is very difficult. As with picking the applications themselves, surveys can used to determine typical usage patterns though survey response accuracy can vary.

Targeting Individual Components

Another benchmarking approach measures specific computer system components. The component specific benchmark workloads are chosen so that they mostly exercise the chosen component in isolation from other components. Such a benchmark might consist of a set of display or disk operations, and nothing else. A detailed knowledge of the targeted computer system is essential to properly construct such a benchmark.

Engineers often use component specific benchmarks to determine if particular subsystems are meeting performance expectations, and hence whether design improvements might be warranted. While component specific benchmarks can be very useful for discovering critical system bottlenecks, they also tend to exaggerate the importance of the targeted component. Thus, take care in interpreting their results. System benchmarks give you a better idea of how the user will perceive system performance, and hence are more appropriate for such activities as choosing a computer to purchase.

Modeling the Workload

The process of developing an approximation of the actual workload for use in a benchmark is known as modeling the workload. Modeling is an abstraction process which varies widely in its authenticity to original workloads. This section discusses some issues surrounding modeling.

Applications vs. Kernels vs. Synthetic

Benchmarks consisting of actual applications and typical user data or scripts are said to have an *application* workload. Benchmarks which consist of the most heavily used fragments of actual applications are said to have a *kernel* workload. Benchmarks which attempt to model the behavior of the applications without using the actual applications are said to have a *synthetic* workload. Of course, the scripts used in application and kernel workloads are often themselves synthetic, and many synthetic benchmarks are based very closely on real application behavior, so these categories describe how the workload is constructed more than the level of realism, but they are still a useful workload metric.

In general, application workload benchmarks are much larger, more difficult to port, and more time consuming to install and run than kernel or synthetic, but provide more accurate performance predictions. Kernel workloads are often so small that their performance can be exaggerated by typical hardware and compiler optimizations, causing them to overstate the performance the actual applications would receive. Synthetic workloads can also be too small to be representative of real application behavior. But synthetic workloads do have the advantage of targeting specific computer subsystems and can be very useful for understanding a particular computer's limitations or strengths. Both kernel and synthetic workloads are usually small enough to be easily ported to many machines and operating systems.

While some synthetic workloads are highly artificial, many others are based on traces or profiles of actual applications. Some examples include the Whetstone benchmark, based on instruction execution profiles of 1960's FORTRAN programs, and Dhrystones, based on execution profiles of "C" code from UNIX system utilities. Others, in particular component specific workloads, measure a few isolated operations with little attempt to model real usage. Many early CPU performance benchmarks simply measured the number of "add" operations that could be done in a second. A big danger of this type of synthetic workload is that it exaggerates the importance of the particular operations measured, giving a poor indication of the real performance that can be expected from the computer system.

In computer I/O realms, synthetic benchmarks based on I/O traffic traces or profiles produced by applications are popular. They can produce a very realistic workload for the I/O subsystem without the other overheads associated with real applications. Thus, they can be very useful for comparing different I/O configurations. However, it must be remembered that large score differences on such benchmarks are unlikely to be reflected in the actual performance experienced by users, because other computer subsystems often dominate the overall performance.

Because each benchmark category has its particular advantages and disadvantages, they all have utility. The performance analyst needs to pick from the category that best meets the goals of his or her performance measurement study. Thus, having a clear set of goals is very important for a successful study.

Workload Size

A common benchmark workload problem, especially kernel and synthetic ones, is the small size of the workload. For example, the code for many kernel benchmarks fits in primary cache, leading to unreasonably fast execution. In the I/O realm, workload-accessed file sizes may be small enough to fit entirely in main memory cache, leading to unrealistically high performance. Hence, the overall file sizes and the number of blocks most frequently accessed (their *working set*) must exceed typical file system cache sizes.

For I/O subsystems the workload size has an additional effect because of varying disk drive access times. Disk drives position their read/write heads over accessed disk sectors, which takes longer as radial distance between successive accesses increases. Hence a workload which uses small disk space amounts has unrealistically short access times.

Another problem with a workloads that use small fractions of available disk space is that transfer rates vary by distance from the center of the platter, due to zone bit recording. If the total file size a workload uses is small, the files may all fit in a single zone, allowing vendors to place them in the highest speed zone to create artificially high performance numbers.

So, for reasons of caching, seek time, and zone effects it is necessary for disk workloads to access a fairly large number of blocks during their execution. However, creating the large files required may interfere with the normal computer system use or prevent the benchmark from being run on some systems. So, some compromise is needed to access a large enough disk block range without making the workload so large that it becomes impractical to run.

Fidelity of Model

Regardless of the technique chosen to model the workload, the closeness with which the model's behavior approximates that of the target workload (the model's *fidelity*) is critical to accurate interpretation of the benchmark's results. A number of factors affect model fidelity:

- **Bugs:** Even a simple, synthetic model can have programming errors. Especially with synthetic models, take care to ascertain that resulting benchmark programs exhibit expected behaviors. For disk subsystems, this could mean monitoring the storage bus with a logic analyzer to verify correct benchmark operation.

- **Statistical Distribution Use:** Often, synthetic benchmarks will model a workload as a function of a random distribution. To produce these random numbers, a pseudo-random number generator (so called because the sequence of numbers produced by the generator meet certain statistical properties for randomness, even though the actual generation process is deterministic) is used. The random number generator should produce as close to an ideal uniform random distribution as possible. There are a number of general techniques for constructing pseudo-random number generators, each of which has many possible implementations. Determining whether a proposed generator function has good randomness properties requires a sophisticated set of statistical tests. *Many early generators, some of which were included in the run-time libraries of popular programming languages, are now considered to have poor properties.* Even with a good generator, the desired distribution may be considerably different from uniform, requiring the use of appropriate mapping functions. There are cases, such as caching situations, where the results can be very sensitive to nuances of the access pattern, which can be hard to capture with distribution mapping functions. *Cache simulation studies [A. Wilson] have shown that random distribution functions, even when derived from actual access patterns, produce significantly different results from the original patterns.*

- **Application Weighting:** For benchmarks which either consist of, or are modeled after, a set of real applications, there are still issues with regards to the weighting of the component applications in the final result. Since benchmarks attempt to model actual usage patterns, the portion of the overall result due to each application should be representative of the typical portion of usage given each application. Of course, determining what is typical is very difficult, and is also subject to change over time. One benchmark supplier bases the weightings on unit sales, another on customer surveys.

- **Script Validity:** Even when the workload consists of actual applications driven from scripts, the scripts must be representative of actual usage. For example, an office automation workload might include a word processing program. The script should represent typical editing operations on typical documents, but just determining what is a typical editing session could require a major research effort!

- **Think Time:** For interactive applications, simulating the response time of typical users (known as "think time") becomes an issue. For many office applications on personal computers, the think time easily dominates all other performance factors, so including it would hide most of the performance differences that the benchmark is intended to measure. On the other hand, not including the think time will place unrealistic performance demands on certain subsystems and indicate bottlenecks that don't really exist. There are also some performance enhancement algorithms that will work fundamentally differently under the high traffic scenario than they will under a normal traffic scenario.

Over the years, benchmark designs have become more sophisticated, taking more of these issues into account, hence improving fidelity. However, with the large variety of applications, and the rapid changes in the applications mix, it is very difficult to determine realistic weightings and scripts. Hence, while benchmarks are improving, the old adage "your mileage may vary" is very appropriate.

Benchmark Vulnerabilities

Many computer system aspects affect benchmarks, even ones targeted at a specific subsystem. Often these aspects produce unexpected, and even contradictory results. This section lists some of the more common ones to watch out for when performing I/O or system benchmarking.

Zones

Disk subsystem benchmarks, and to a lesser extent application domain benchmarks, are affected by disk drive media transfer rates. With modern, zoned drives, transfer rates vary with radial distance from platter centers. While this packs more data onto drives, it results in higher disk performance at the outer platter edge than near the center. This phenomena affects benchmark results in the following ways:

Partition and/or test file placement affects performance: If a separate benchmarking partition exists, results are lower when the partition consists of inner cylinders (higher cylinder numbers) rather than on outer cylinders (lower cylinder numbers). When a benchmark which creates test files is used, the file system may place them on inner cylinders, especially if the disk is nearly full. Of course, it is best to use a separate drive dedicated for use by the benchmarks, and re-initialize it for each benchmark run, which should prevent poor test file placement, but that cannot always be done.

Disk drive capacity can affect performance: Larger capacity disk drives can store more data in given zones than smaller capacity drives. Since some benchmarks operate with fixed size test files, those files may span more zones in a smaller capacity drive, resulting in lower measured media transfer rate, though per-zone rates are identical for the two drives.

There can be very subtle effects as well. One sequential access benchmark did not reset its block pointer between runs and ran a test suite with increasing transfer sizes. The short transfers, which are mostly affected by overhead, were done on the outer, high data rate tracks, while the longer transfers, which are mostly affected by media data rate, where performed on the slower inner tracks. Thus, the long transfer sequential access performance appeared to be less than it actually was.

Modern disk drives' use of zones create significant problems for performance analysts, especially when the type of disk drive is one of the test parameters. But the dramatic capacity and peak performance improvements they allow ensures zoning will exist for some time to come.

Hidden, Unknown Parameters

There are an impressive number of parameters affecting even simple PC system performance and many are relatively difficult to access or modify. For instance they may be affected by internal PC cabinet switch settings. Regardless, performance analysts must know all the parameters that can be changed.

Though rare, there are cases where hardware or software design deficiencies prevent parameter changes from actually taking effect. For example, software may be able to change a parameter by writing a system value to a register, but only if the change isn't overridden by a hardware switch setting. In the worst case, the fact that the change didn't actually occur is not reported to the software, so the person running the tests is not aware that the old parameter value is still in effect.

An example comes from SCSI. There are several speeds at which the SCSI bus can be run, asynchronous, 5 MHz synchronous and 10 MHz synchronous. Both devices in a transaction (e.g., host adapter and disk drive) negotiate the actual speed used, which is the highest both support. Thus, even though the host adapter is set for 10 MHz operation, the actual transfers may only occur at 5 MHz. The only way to tell for sure is to use a scope or logic analyzer to measure the actual timing used.

There is a computer industry tendency for software to change more parameter values. Some changes are automatic and are neither settable nor visible to end users. Even when users can set them, it isn't always true they can verify the changes have taken place. Unfortunately, write-only system configuration registers are all too common. Thus, the diligent performance analyst must run side tests just to determine what some parameters of interest actually are.

File Fragmentation

File systems must be able to manage disk storage efficiently in environments where files are constantly being created, enlarged and deleted. As operations continue, disk free space becomes fragmented, eventually resulting in file fragmentation and more frequent seeks. While it is possible to consolidate newly released disk blocks, preventing fragmentation, such free block consolidation is very time consuming, requiring considerable file copying, so it is not normally done by operating systems (though utility programs are often provided to de-fragment file systems).

Instead of preventing file fragmentation, file systems usually try to minimize it. Numerous strategies exist to reduce file fragmentation, with trade-offs between simplicity, computation cost, and ability to minimize fragmentation. However, as a file system continues running (without using a de-fragmentation utility), particularly if it is near capacity, file fragmentation is unavoidable and usually becomes severe. A particular problem in most cases is that file systems don't know the file's ultimate size at creation time, so they can't place it in the optimum location for its size. The situation is even worse in a multi-user system, where several files can be created and expanded concurrently.

File fragmentation is part of normal system operation, but the extra (and longer) seeks it causes will gradually reduce disk subsystem performance. This can affect benchmark repeatability, unless care is taken to remove the fragmentation before each run. Since de-fragmentation before each test in a suite of tests may not be possible, the performance analyst should be aware of several file system practices which especially promote fragmentation. In particular, simple allocation strategies for new or expanded files which pick the first available block (as practiced by many early operating systems) and retention of deleted files until all available free space is used up (becoming more common with PC operating systems) are particularly pernicious.

Simple Free Block Allocation

There are several free block allocation variants which cause trouble. They are all characterized by a lack of attempting to optimize new file block placement among existing free blocks. Instead, free blocks are allocated from a list or table in a "first one found" strategy. For example, disk space might always be allocated from the head of the free list, regardless of the size of a particular entry in the list. Or, a table might be used with files allocated from the first available found on a scan of the table. A variation of the table approach, used by MS-DOS, scans from the end of the last block allocated, which initially promotes contiguous files, but tends to spread usage across the entire disk surface, creating longer than necessary seeks. While these algorithms are simple to implement, they result in highly fragmented files after the system has run for a time. Ultimately, new files end up as a collection of individual disk blocks, scattered throughout the disk drive.

To see how this happens, consider the progression a disk volume undergoes after initialization when using a first one found scan from the last allocated block. At first, new files are allocated from the large, contiguous chunk of free space on the inner tracks of the drive and would tend to be contiguous. (Though if several files were being written concurrently, there would be some intermingling of blocks allocated to each). While new file block allocation progresses through the disk, deleted file free blocks begin accumulating on previously used disk portions. These free space chunks are often the size of the original files.

Eventually, these previously used free space chunks are the ones allocated for new files. Although the algorithm treats adjacent deleted files as one free space chunk, many chunks are from non-adjacent small files, causing the algorithm to split larger files into several small chunks. As these fragmented large files are deleted, the free space is returned as small chunks, maintaining the free space fragmentation state. As files continued to be created and deleted, the individual chunks tend to get smaller, and hence files become more fragmented.

Delayed Purge

More advanced disk allocation methods can reduce fragmentation caused by simple free list approaches. However, a new feature of some file systems, which keeps deleted files until there is no more free space in case someone might have deleted a file by mistake, is becoming more popular. This delayed purge tends to defeat fragmentation reduction attempts by creating an allocation pattern similar to the simple free list. Initially, files will become spread further apart as the disk becomes filled with deleted files. Then as the oldest deleted files are reclaimed, new files will be fragmented to fit the available free space chunks. Both effects greatly increase seek time amounts, thus reducing disk throughput.

The delayed purge effect is particularly pronounced during benchmarks. Benchmarks which either consist of real applications, or are closely based on the behavior of real applications, tend to create and manipulate numerous files while running. At the end of a run, they delete all created files, supposedly returning the file system to the same state it was in before the benchmark was run. However, if delayed purge is in effect, deleted files still exist, causing the disk partition to fill up with obsolete files and encouraging very rapid file fragmentation. In one study, NetWare's delayed purge caused a 30% performance decrease in the second benchmark of a two benchmark suite, which disappeared when delayed purge was disabled.

Inaccurate or Low Resolution Clock

Most operating systems provide an internal time of day clock, which system calls can access. Most benchmarks must use this time source as part of their performance measurement task. Unfortunately, these clocks are implemented in software and driven by a fairly low frequency clock interrupt. Two things to watch out for are:

- **Skipped clock ticks:** There are sections of operating systems where interrupts, including the clock interrupt, are disabled. If disabled for too long, one or more clock interrupts may be missed, leading to a slower clock. If the clock is being used to determine the time a task takes as part of a benchmark, the task will appear to execute more quickly than it actually should, leading to exaggerated performance numbers.

- **Low clock resolution:** Because clock interrupt processing consumes computing resources, the clock interrupt rate is usually kept low (sixty or fewer times a second). In addition, because interrupt latency is variable, the interval between successive clock ticks varies randomly about the mean rate. Thus, small time intervals measurements can be quite inaccurate. As system speeds continue to increase, benchmarks take less time to run, increasing their susceptibility to low clock resolution caused inaccuracies.

Hardware timing boards avoid these problems, but since no standard hardware timing boards exist and most systems don't have any, widely distributed benchmarks can't use them. However, some performance departments take the trouble to modify benchmarks to use hardware timing boards to obtain very accurate benchmark timing.

OS / Platform Limitations

Many benchmarks are limited to a specific operating system or specific hardware (e.g., instruction set). This limits their usefulness for cross system comparisons. Whenever possible, select a benchmark that works with all operating system and hardware combinations of interest. Of course, sometimes outside factors dictate the benchmark choice, for example, when the benchmark with the most appropriate workload to model your application is only available on a limited set of platforms, or you are only interested in a limited set of platforms. In such cases, a benchmark which only runs on a limited set of platforms is acceptable.

Computer Usage Changes Over Time

As computers evolve, so do the applications running on them. Benchmarks based on computer usage of just a few years ago may be quite dated. On the other hand, if benchmarks are changed frequently, they become less useful for comparing different systems. There are no good solutions to this problem.

Some simpler benchmarks have fixed usage patterns which have not changed over time. There are several benchmarks in the disk I/O realm that do sequential or random reads of fixed size blocks. Results taken from several years ago could be directly compared with those from systems to see how much disk I/O performance has improved. However, the simple workloads employed do not necessarily reflect well what a typical user will experience, so the reported improvements may be much different than those actually experienced by users.

On the other hand, trying to use application based benchmarks may not work because the proportions of different disk operation types have changed over the years, and the applications based benchmark you are using may track those changes. To compare accurately the performance gain of a new system over an old requires that both benchmark runs be done with the same benchmark version (presumably the older version that was used on the older system). Unfortunately, the old benchmark version may no longer be available.

Of course, the fact that computer usage patterns change over time reduces the usefulness of old versus new system comparisons anyway. Computer systems tend to be optimized for the usage pattern prevalent at their design time, so the performance improvement of the new system over the old, on the old usage pattern, may understate the performance improvement perceived by the users. Your performance measurement project goals dictate what the most meaningful comparisons actually are.

System Tuning

A benchmark's performance can usually improve by tuning the test systems. This is especially true of application benchmarks, which test the whole system. How much of this tuning is legitimate is often the subject of debate. The overall subject is too large to be adequately explored here, but a few examples follow.

Most current single user applications have Graphical User Interfaces (GUI), which make heavy use of the system's display card. Thus, display cards often have a bigger impact on system performance than any other component, causing system level benchmarks based on those applications to be strongly affected by display card performance. Thus benchmark performance significantly improves by optimizing system parameters to obtain maximum display card speed. In general, setting the display resolution and number of colors to the minimum the benchmark requires results in fastest display card speed and, subsequently, best benchmark numbers.

Modern disk drives strive to place the maximum possible amount of data on each disk surface by maintaining the bit density at near the maximum allowed by the head and coating technology. Since the linear velocity at the outer edge of a disk is much higher than that near the center, the data rate is also higher. Rather than continuously vary the data rate, the surface is divided into a number of zones, with each zone consisting of a group of contiguous cylinders all operating at the same data rate. The data rate typically varies by about a factor of two between the slowest inner zone and the fastest outer zone. Obviously, arranging for the benchmark to access sectors located in the outer zone of the disk maximizes benchmark performance.

A large variety of system parameters can influence application based benchmark performance, just as with the actual applications. Sophisticated users who predominately run one application often tune system parameters to get the best performance. Therefor it is reasonable for a performance analyst to do similar tuning before running benchmarks. An example is the TPC on-line transaction processing benchmarks. Improvements of more than 50% are commonly obtained through system parameter tuning. Since dedicated systems are usually used to do transaction processing, and the TPC benchmark results report the actual system parameters used, the practice is considered legitimate. But it does impose a burden on a potential system purchaser to carefully examine reported results for unrealistic tuning instances.

Measurement Procedures

Obtaining a good benchmark suite isn't enough for a successful performance study. It is also necessary to follow good measurement procedure, including such steps as understanding test objectives, ensuring desired information is not obscured by bottlenecks in other system parts, that all parameters are properly set and recorded, and that the experiments are carefully designed to yield maximum useful information with minimum measurements. This is only a brief introduction, but provides some insight into the many ways in which performance evaluations can be poorly done, leading to incorrect conclusions.

Understanding Test Objectives

Typically, performance studies compare several alternatives "to see which one is fastest." However, there are usually many measurable performance metrics. The appropriate metric often depends on the application or applications intended to be run on the machine. If you are simply comparing a set of complete systems, then determining the one which achieves the highest marks on the appropriate benchmark may suffice. If you are trying to improve the performance of an existing system by comparing alternate subcomponents, you should ensure the subcomponents directly affect the benchmark results. Also, the approach may be different if you are looking for specific bottlenecks for future engineering enhancement opportunities rather than a general comparative analysis.

Throughput vs. Latency

Throughput is the total work amount that can be done in a given time period, while *latency* is the amount of time it takes to get a given piece of work done. While it might seem latency is throughput's inverse, many systems overlap operations, allowing some independence between the two. For example, disk drives typically take about 10 milliseconds for average length seeks. Adding a second drive doubles the number of seeks that can be performed (the throughput), but does not change the time it takes to do a given seek (the latency). A multi-user server generally exploits the extra throughput by doubling the number of users, while a single user workstation would not. Thus, it is necessary to understand whether latency or throughput is more important for the intended use, and whether the proposed benchmarks measure latency or throughput.

Latency consists of inherent processing time plus time waiting in queues for processing. As system throughput approaches maximum sustainable rates, the observed latency begins to increase rapidly. The point at which latency begins to increase rapidly is known as the *saturation point*. In the above server example, if the server was operating near saturation, doubling the number of users without adding a second drive could easily double the observed latency (from the user's perspective) without increasing the throughput. However, if a second drive were added to the same system while keeping the number of users constant, there might only be a small effect on observed latency.

Most benchmarks report throughput results, such as MBytes per second. Some multi-user system benchmarks will try to measure latency directly, such as mean and worst case response time. Total throughput is fairly easy to measure, with the benchmark either running for a fixed amount of time and recording the amount of work done, or doing a fixed amount of work and recording the amount of time it takes. Multi-user latency requires recording the time each work request takes, which may be fairly short. Thus time measurement granularity issues come into play, and constructing an accurate benchmark may be more difficult. But such benchmarks are particularly useful in determining whether large variations in latency are present, which is generally not desired.

Burst (or Peak) vs. Sustained

Typical PCs are complicated systems with many performance influencing factors. Simple benchmarks which stress hardware or software subsets often report performance considerably higher than obtainable under normal operation. Yet the normal case is what most users are really interested in. In fact, measuring peak rates often hides serious overall performance deficiencies.

Some peak rate effect examples:

- **Caches:** If workloads are small enough to fit in caches, obtained performance far exceeds the typical. For example, processor caches are often as much as 10 times faster than main memory. If the typical hit ratio is 80%, but the benchmark achieves 100%, the measured performance is triple the typical performance. But real applications can't sustain such high hit ratios or obtain such a high performance.

- **Disk Drives:** Sequential accessing of large numbers of blocks can give very high performance. But typical real usage involves frequent seeks and requests for small numbers of blocks with an order of magnitude difference. Thus it is very important that the mix of non-sequential accesses and access sizes are similar to that expected in the actual application.

- **Pipelining:** Execution unit pipelining is a common technique for increasing computer system throughput, but it only works well if the pipeline can be kept full. A classic example is the floating point unit on a typical processor. It can often achieve one floating point operation per clock cycle, provided the operands can be supplied to it at that rate. But if intervening fixed point computations are required, or many of the operands must be fetched from main memory, the performance can drop dramatically. It is possible to write benchmarks that achieve the full rate, but they are unrepresentative of typical workloads.

The difference between the peak and sustained performance can be larger than a factor of two in many cases. Thus, peak performance numbers are not regarded as reliable indicators of actual performance. However, they are frequently cited by vendors, since they are much more impressive than sustained rates. Before selecting computer systems, sophisticated purchasers obtain benchmarks results that report sustained rates.

Recognizing Bottlenecks

Often benchmarking attempts try to measure the effect of changing a specific computer system component. However, throughput is often limited by a single, slowest component—known as the *bottleneck*. If component changes leave the bottleneck unaffected, then testing indicates little or no performance difference. Worse yet, there can be cases where *improvements* in one component actually *reduce* bottleneck component performance. Therefore, it is imperative to identify the limiting factor so that result can be properly analyzed.

As an example of an unexpected interaction between components caused by a severe bottleneck, consider the case of a server system whose performance is limited by CPU utilization. Installing a host adapter which has *higher* potential throughput but whose driver has a slightly *higher* CPU utilization actually *reduces* performance in this situation. Yet if the study goal is to measure the maximum host adapter transfer rates rather than driver overhead, the study results are misleading. Even when the CPU is not saturated, service latency differences still make such interactions possible.

Start from a Known State

The recent usage history can affect current performance in many subtle ways. To interpret benchmarking results properly and compare individual runs to each other, each run must start from a known, identical state. It is generally necessary to eliminate the history component by starting with "fresh" systems. This is the subject of system and benchmark initialization, which this subsection covers.

Proper Initialization

In short, everything must be initialized to a known state. And, computer systems contain a lot of state information. Internal registers, caches and main memory maintain the computation state. Mass storage systems, such as disk drives, maintain long term state. Some state information is even kept in nonvolatile RAM. Even such external "state" as machine temperature can potentially effect performance, though it is usually considered insignificant. So proper procedure involves recording the initial state of the system, and resetting the machine to that state prior to each measurement run.

The file system represents significant machine state which affects I/O system performance. Many disk I/O and system benchmarks create and manipulate a set of disk files during execution. For example, applications used by some benchmarks create, modify and delete files, just as happens during normal use. Under many operating systems, file systems become increasingly fragmented, which increases head movement observed during *subsequent* runs. To fix this requires running a defragmentation program or destroying and then rebuilding the file system portion the benchmark uses before each run. To facilitate reloading, many analysts run benchmarks from individual partitions (or volumes) taking care to compensate for zone bit recording considerations.

Just like file systems, main memory often becomes fragmented during operation. While the fragmentation severity varies with operating systems, it is best to reboot machines before each run to ensure no deleterious fragmentation occurred. Rebooting usually cleans up other machine states, ensuring benchmarks see an identical initial state each time.

However, sometimes a reset does not effect all of the state information. An example is the sector caches most hard drives use. These caches often use adaptive algorithms to decide how to manage their caches, and are unaffected by system reboots. Whether failure to reset the adaptive algorithm has significant impact depends on the particular benchmark and the particular system. If a possibly uninitialized adaptive algorithm is a potential problem, power cycle the machine.

When doing a set of measurement runs at one time, the preceding procedures provide consistent benchmarking conditions. However, if the study extends a previous one, and it is desired to compare the new results with the old, it is necessary to ensure all parameters are set to previous values. In the time since the previous study was done, many parameter values set by scripts and non-volatile memory may have changed. Not only should CONFIG.SYS and AUTOEXEC.BAT be checked, but stored BIOS settings in nonvolatile motherboard memory and adapter card settings must be checked. Basically all parameters that were recorded when the previous study was done need verification.

Cold vs. Warm Start

Starting from a fully reset, or "clean" state is known as "cold" starting, while starting from a more typical operating state is known as "warm" starting. While there are many good reasons for starting from a "clean" initial state, normal operating conditions are anything but clean. Thus, while straight forward approaches of resetting everything to the initial boot up state is part of good measurement procedure, it leads to somewhat unrealistic test conditions. Some unrealistic aspects include:

- **Initial Cache Fill:** Caches experience exceptionally low hit ratios when first enabled because they are totally empty and must be filled with current data before they stabilize at normal hit ratios. Most benchmarks run for long enough that processor cache impacts are minor, but file and disk caches are completely different matters. Caches might very well contain previously loaded program portions, reducing the disk activity needed to reload the program. Thus, starting with a completely "clean" slate may result in a measured performance that is less than what would typically be encountered in actual usage.

- **Fragmentation:** As already mentioned, file systems fragment over time, leading to poorer performance. Other computer system resources can also become fragmented over time. Some operating systems suffer main memory fragmentation, resulting in slower allocation of free memory. A typical system spends most of its operation in the lower performance state. This means that a benchmark starting from a "clean" state exaggerates the performance.

- **Adaptive Behavior:** It is becoming more popular to use adaptive algorithms within computer systems. These algorithms attempt to optimize their behavior based on the type of workload they have most recently processing. Thus, such systems may exhibit poor performance until the benchmark has been running for a while.

So, resetting systems back to the "just booted" state produces differences from normal operation which can both help and hurt performance, though on the whole they tend to help. To reflect real operation most accurately, benchmarks should start from a warm system state. However, if comparisons are being made between systems having similar cache sizes, memory amounts, and running the same operating system, it probably doesn't matter whether the warm or cold start approach is done. But, if different file systems or cache organizations are being compared, providing a realistic warm start is highly desirable.

Because each measurement must be done from a state which only differs from the other measurements in the specific parameters under investigation, achieving warm start conditions requires as much care as developing the actual benchmark. A script of work would be written, using similar methodologies to those used by applications based benchmarks. This script would be run after reset, so that each candidate system was brought to the same point. Since achieving a warm system state in a repeatable manner is difficult and time consuming, it is seldom done.

Recording Configuration Options

Measurement runs need to be repeatable over time. Another lab may want to verify or extend the measurements, or you may want to extend the measurements. Thus, accurately recording *all* parameter and configuration options is essential. With the typical PC, there are numerous configuration options to record. Examples are:

- BIOS version

- Operating system type and version (i.e., MS-DOS 6.2)

- Any installed drivers with their parameters

- Software disk cache version and size

- Benchmark version

- CPU type and speed

- Processor cache size and main memory size

- Graphics, disk and network card types, model numbers and option settings

- Disk drive manufacturer, model, firmware revision, drive layout and mode page settings

- Drive interconnect cable type and speed (i.e., Narrow SCSI; synchronous 10 MHz)

- File system layout such as disk partitioning, block size and striping

Given systems may have additional configuration options, which should also be recorded. Not only does the record of configuration options allow future measurement extensions, it also helps in explaining particular results. So don't overlook this important benchmarking aspect.

Experimental Design

One of the biggest performance analysis problems is containing the number of benchmark runs (experiments) that need performing. In general, system performance is affected by many parameters, each of which can assume a range of values. A number of techniques are known for reducing the number of runs required, a couple of which will be summarized here. For a more detailed treatment, see [Jain].

One popular approach establishes a base parameter set, then individually varies each parameter and records the results. While this approach is very effective if there is little interaction between parameters, this is often not the case. Moreover, you may miss some very important combinations. For example, two parameters may have to be increased together to get increased performance, while increasing either one separately gives little improvement. Thus the "one parameter at a time" approach indicates both parameters have negligible performance impact, when the combination has a large impact.

Another approach limits the values assumed by each parameter to two, then tries all combinations. The values chosen should be at or near reasonable usage extremes. Using linear regression, the relative performance impact of each parameter, separately and in combination, can be determined. This shows which parameters and parameter combinations are important to further study. A second measurement round can be done, only varying those parameters shown to have significant impact.

This approach still fails if one or more of the parameters has a non-linear relationship to the overall performance. For example, a typical time sharing system parameter is the number of users. Often throughput rises to a peak, then begins falling as the number of users increases. If the number of users parameter is only tested at its extreme points, it appears to have much less effect on performance than it actually does with intermediate values.

If analysts have some expected behavior knowledge, they can tailor the experiments to gain the most information for the least effort. For example, parameters known to be relatively independent can vary in isolation. Parameters suspected of highly non-linear effects can be sampled at more than two points. Non linear regression techniques or piece-wise linear approximations might be then used. In the time sharing example, measurements from the region with too many users could simply be considered out of range and be ignored (though the fact that performance decreases over a certain number of users is itself interesting).

Statistical Analysis

Once a set of measurements has been made, it will be necessary to draw conclusions from the results. Statistical approaches can be used to develop numbers which succinctly summarize the results, to determine the accuracy of the results, and to produce valid comparisons between results. While a detailed treatment of the statistical approaches available is beyond the scope of this book, a brief introduction to the basic approach of calculating a sample mean and sample standard deviation will be given.

Picking a Representative Value

Most performance study readers like to have one (or a very few) numbers to summarize the overall findings. What they are looking for is some kind of *average* of the data, which represents the typical values of the measurements. Some commonly used ones are the arithmetic mean, median, mode, geometric mean and harmonic mean. Since picking the correct approach is important, a brief description of the types will be given.

The *arithmetic mean*, calculated by summing all data measurements and dividing the sum by the number of measurements is probably the most commonly used averaging technique, even when it is appropriate to use different ones. The arithmetic mean only makes sense when the sum of the measurements is a meaningful number. For example, saying that the total time spent seeking in ten disk accesses was 80 milliseconds, and hence that the average was 10 milliseconds is meaningful, while saying that the mean color of diskettes is green because 10 were blue and 10 were yellow is not meaningful. The arithmetic mean uses all data points but is overly influenced by outliers. Thus, if the data has a wide spread between minimum and maximum values (e.g., one seek took 53 ms while the other nine took 3 ms), an average may be rather misleading.

The *median* is calculated by ordering all the results and then picking the one whose location in the ordered list falls exactly in the middle. For data which varies widely from maximum to minimum, the median may provide a more representative number. In the disk seek example mentioned above, with one seek of 53 ms and nine of 3 ms, the arithmetic mean would be 8 ms, while the median would be 3 ms. Clearly 3 ms is more typical of the actual performance than 8 ms, which is strongly influenced by the one long seek.

The *mode* is simply the most likely value or values of the data. It is formed by sorting the results and reporting the value that appears the most often. Data sets may have zero to many modes, depending on the distribution shape. For example, uniform distributions have no peaks and hence no modes, while data communication patterns commonly have bi-modal distributions (i.e., distributions with two peaks). The mode is appropriate when comparing categories, or when distributions have several distinct peaks.

The *geometric mean* is calculated by multiplying all the n values together and then taking the nth root. It is appropriate where the product of the values is a meaningful number, such as in an electronic amplifier, where the overall gain is the product of the gains of the individual stages.

The *harmonic mean* is used when the sum of the inverse of a set of values is a meaningful number. It is defined as: $1/x = (1/n) \sum 1/x_i$.

Multiple Runs

It has long been recognized in experimental science that when you perform a measurement on a system several times, each measurement yields different results. These differences are due to random parameter variation or even finite measurement precision, and are known as experimental error. Experimental error is inherent in the experimental processes, and differs from experimental mistakes. However, because digital systems are so deterministic, and the large number of digits in answers impart great accuracy illusions, experimental error is often overlooked when performing digital system measurements. In fact, there are sources of variation which cannot be controlled, resulting in measurable differences from test run to test run. If large enough, such variations produce misleading results.

To reduce experimental error uncertainty requires multiple test runs for each parameter combination. The set of results from a batch of runs with identical parameters is know as a sample. Statistical techniques can then determine the best actual value estimate (i.e., the mean value μ obtained with infinite measurements) and the extent of variation (the standard deviation σ obtained with infinite measurements).

Statistical Treatment

Let n be the number of measurements x_i (one measurement per test run) included in the sample. Then the best estimate of μ is the sample mean, $\bar{x} = \Sigma\, x_i/n$. The best estimate of σ is the sample standard deviation $s = \sqrt{(1/(n-1))}\, \Sigma\, (x_i - \bar{x})$. Intuitively, we expect the more measurements we take in a sample, the closer the sample mean is to the actual mean μ. This is indeed the case, and estimates of the closeness (known as *confidence intervals*) can be calculated.

Confidence intervals allow the specification of the probability that the measured mean, $\bar{x}$, falls within an interval from the actual mean μ. The interval can be calculated because, as long as each measurement in the sample is truly independent, it can be shown by the central limit theorem that the measurements that make up the sample will tend to be normally distributed with the mean μ and standard deviation σ/n. The probability density function for a normal random variable with mean μ and standard deviation σ/n can then be used to calculate the interval required to contain the mean with a given probability. The probabilities (called confidence levels) used typically range from 90% to 99%, though confidence intervals for any probability less than 100% can be calculated.

When comparing the results from two samples, confidence intervals can be used to determine whether any difference in performance is due to specified parameter changes, or just due to experimental error. Confidence intervals for the means of both samples should be calculated, and a check made to see if the difference of the means is less than the largest of the two confidence intervals. If so, the difference should be considered a measurement *artifact* (i.e., *statistically insignificant*). Otherwise it is considered to represent a real phenomena. Since confidence interval size increases with confidence levels, the selected confidence interval value can effect whether differences are considered statistically significant. The general practice reports confidence levels used along with the determination, e.g., "statistically significant at the 90% confidence level."

Remember, confidence interval calculations are only valid if the variations from run to run are statistically independent. If not, (e.g., the result steadily declines due to file fragmentation), then attempting to calculate a confidence interval could produce very misleading results. In this case, try to eliminate the dependence. For example, reboot systems before every test run within a sample.

Chapter Questions

1 When evaluating a desktop system for use by applications with sophisticated graphical user interfaces, which single component would you expect to have the most impact on perceived performance?

   a Backplane bus

   b Video card

   c Host adapter

   d Disk drive

2 Which type of benchmark workload generally gives the most realistic estimate of a system's performance?

   a Application

   b Kernel

   c Synthetic

   d Database

3 What of the following is not an important aspect of developing a benchmark?

   a Workload size

   b Quality of random number generator

   c Application selection

   d None of the above

4 Which averaging technique would be most appropriate if categories of items are being compared?

   a Arithmetic mean

   b Median

   c Mode

   d Geometric mean

5 Which averaging technique is most appropriate when the sum of the data values is a meaningful number?

   a Arithmetic mean

b Median

c Mode

d Geometric mean

6 Which kind of system settings can always be easily and accurately determined by the performance analyst?

a Hardware switch defined

b EPROM defined

c Software settable

d None of the above

7 Meaning the performance of a system from "warm start" state means:

a Using the system for awhile before beginning the benchmark run

b Turning the system on for an hour or so to reach thermal equilibrium before beginning the benchmark

c Defragmenting the test disk before running the benchmark

d Running a fixed workload on the system before running the benchmark

8 Which of the following parameters would it not be necessary to record when doing performance measurements on a Sun Sparc based computer?

a BIOS version

b Operating system name and version

c Benchmark version

d Processor type

9 It is useful to repeat a given run several times because:

a It provides a more accurate estimate of the quantity you are measuring

b It allows you to determine confidence intervals for the quantity you are measuring

c Both a and b

d It increases your chance of collecting time and a half overtime pay

10 The formula $\sqrt{(1/(n-1))} \, \Sigma \, (x_i - \bar{x})$ is used to calculate:

    a The sample mean

    b The sample standard deviation

    c The confidence level

    d The statistical correlation of the sample

❒

14

Single User (Desktop) Benchmarks

What This Chapter Is About

Single user systems, also called desktop systems because processor cabinets are usually small enough to fit on desktops, dominate the market. Because of their typical uses and relatively simple configurations, they require very different benchmarks from those used by the traditional multi-user mainframes or servers. This chapter describes some of the most popular desktop benchmarks, while the next describes some popular multi-user and server benchmarks.

Desktop Attributes

Because there is only one user, I/O is usually limited to one or two disk drives, a floppy drive and perhaps a CD-ROM. Also, usually only one application runs at a time with very little concurrent I/O. Concurrence amounts may soon increase, as newer multitasking operating systems allow background applications to run concurrently with a foreground application. But for now, one application at a time is the rule, and these benchmarks are designed to simulate that environment.

Core Test

Overview

Core test is a simple disk performance test which at one time was quite popular. It is easy to run but is a highly artificial synthetic test, which simply reads as fast as it can from one group of disk blocks. Core test is now considered obsolete, and is no longer available, but many copies still exist and are still used for performance measurements.

Core Test Features

- Service tested: Maximum transfer rate from the disk

- Test results: MBytes per second

- OS: MS-DOS

- Network: None required

- Type of benchmark: Synthetic

- Test patterns: Fixed reads of varying block sizes, all starting at the beginning of the disk

- Required test setup: PC with disk drive running MS-DOS

Comments

Core test reads out of a fixed group of sectors on the disk. For example, if you specify a read size of 8 sectors, it will read sectors 0 through 7 over and over again. Since these sectors will all be stored in the drive cache after the first read, transfers will occur at the maximum rate the host adapter, host, and operating system can handle. While rather unrealistic, it does indicate the maximum drive to host transfer rate possible, allowing some measure of comparison.

Adaptec SCSIBench™ Software

Overview

A fully synthetic benchmark, which reads various size blocks of data from SCSI hard disk or CD-ROM. The starting point of each read can be fixed, sequential, or randomly selected. The SCSIBench program is part of the EZ-SCSI package included with Adaptec SCSI host adapters.

SCSIBench Software Features

- Service tested: SCSI disk accesses using ASPI calls

- Test results: MBytes per second

- OS: Windows 3.1 or higher

- Network: None required

- Type of benchmark: Synthetic

- Test patterns: Fixed, sequential, and random reads of varying block sizes

- Required test setup: PC capable of running Windows and at least one SCSI host adapter and disk drive

Comments

The test only does reads, so data already on the drives is not affected, but write performance is not measured. The test will only work on SCSI drives with ASPI based device drivers loaded.

Ziff-Davis PC Bench 95

Overview

The PC Bench 95 benchmark is a fully synthetic benchmark which runs under DOS. It has separate sections which measure processor, disk and video subsystems. A subset of the tests are based on profiles of typical DOS applications and are executed as part of a suite which also computes an overall score. Copies of the PC Bench 95 benchmark suite and user's manual may be obtained by writing to Ziff-Davis Benchmark Operation, One Copley Parkway, Suite 510, Morrisville, NC 17560.

PC Bench Features

- Service tested: Execution of desktop applications

- Test results: Normalized score of weighted test execution times

- OS: MS-DOS 5.0 or higher

- Network: None required

- Type of benchmark: Synthetic

- Test patterns: Disk Mix, random and sequential disk accesses, Graphics Mix, graphics primitives, CPU performance

- Required test setup: PC with 386 or greater processor, VGA display card, disk drive with at least 34 MBytes of free space, and at least 2 MBytes of memory

Comments

Because the test is oriented towards DOS applications, it may not give a good indication of the performance of Windows applications. PC Bench contains a wide range of benchmark programs, including many simple single component ones. But a subset of the benchmarks are modeled after a set of real applications, and these are used when the DOSMark suite is executed. The set consists of seven applications which are currently the biggest sellers for DOS. The same seven applications are profiled by all of the tests which use profiling.

This is the only Ziff-Davis benchmark that attempts to directly measure CPU performance. A number of CPU intensive benchmarks are included, but the *16-bit protected mode large mix* is designed to mimic the behavior of the suite of real DOS applications. According to Ziff-Davis, the mix "uses a PC's bus, CPU internal cache, CPU cache interface, external cache, main memory, and instruction set in the same way as leading DOS applications."

Among the disk tests, PC Bench contains a *disk mix* test which executes from a script based on disk accesses logged by the suite of popular DOS applications. Finally, PC Bench contains a number of video benchmarks, including a pair, called the Video Mixes, which executes from a script designed to mimic the way the suite of DOS applications uses the video board.

In general, synthetic benchmarks which are modeled after suites of real applications give a more accurate prediction of expected performance than more arbitrary synthetic benchmarks. Ziff-Davis does not reveal the details of their profiling processes, but claims that comparisons with the original applications have yielded similar performance.

BAPCo SYSmark93 for Windows

Overview

SYSmark93 for Windows is a desktop computing benchmark from the BAPCo industry benchmarking consortium. This suite consists of a copy of Microsoft Windows 3.1, and the binary for each of the

selected business applications. The applications cover word processing, spreadsheet, desktop publishing, database, desktop graphics,
and desktop presentation. The benchmark executes each application
using scripts based on actual usage, and computes the final score
based on the approximate time each application is used by typical
business users. Information about, and copies of, the SYSmark93
benchmark can be purchased from Business Applications Performance Corp., 2200 Mission College Blvd., MS RN4-21, Santa Clara,
CA 95052.

SysMark93 Features

- Service tested: Execution of desktop applications

- Test results: Normalized score of weighted application execution times

- OS: Windows 3.1 (provided)

- Network: None required

- Type of benchmark: Real

- Test patterns: Actual applications executing from scripts

- Required test setup: PC capable of running Windows 3.1,
  printer loop-back plug

Comments

BAPCo uses extensive user surveys to determine which applications
to use, their weights on the final score, and the scripts used to drive
them. They include some configuration checking features to help
prevent test rigging. The suite can take many hours to run, depending on your processor and video board performance. Because the
applications are heavy users of the video display, the results are
very sensitive to the video display adapter's performance. But, this
probably reflects what most Windows users experience anyway.

The scripts do not include any think time, so they operate at the
maximum rate possible. As mentioned in Chapter 13, this can distort
the results somewhat. But overall, it is a well designed benchmark,
even including "standard" releases of the operating system and
applications software. Thus, differences in score from one machine
to the next reflect actual hardware differences, and are not clouded
by software version differences.

Microsoft CD-Test

Overview

Tests performance of CD-ROM drives. Checks to see if they can maintain their rated transfer rate, and reports the percentage of CPU utilization taken by their drivers. The Benchmark is distributed with a Microsoft CD-ROM Developer's kit. Contact Microsoft for more details.

CD-Test Features

- Service tested: CD-ROM reads of large sequential files
- Test results: Throughput and CPU utilization
- OS: MS-DOS only
- Network: None required
- Type of benchmark: Synthetic
- Test patterns: Sequential reads from the CD-ROM
- Required test setup: PC with a CD-ROM player

Comments

Attempts to measure the ability of your computer system to run CD-ROM based multimedia applications. The program is given a transfer rate, in multiples of the basic CD-ROM transfer rate, and measures the ability of the CD-ROM subsystem to keep up with that rate, as well as the amount of "left over" CPU cycles that are available to run the rest of the application program. It depends on the DOS timer and the fact that DOS is single threaded to compute the CPU utilization, and hence will give misleading results under any variant of Windows. Because DOS is single threaded and uses blocking IO, the CPU utilization is mostly made up of time spent transferring data from the CD-ROM, even when DMA is used and the CPU could theoretically be doing other work.

Ziff-Davis WinBench 95

Overview

WinBench consists of two parts, one which measures the performance of the disk subsystem and one which measures the performance of the graphics display system. The tests are synthetic and attempt to mimic the behavior of real applications with respect to disk and graphics. The usage patterns are based on "profiles" of the applications used in Winstone™ 95. Copies of the WinBench 95 benchmark suite and user's manual may be obtained by writing to Ziff-Davis Benchmark Operation, One Copley Parkway, Suite 510, Morrisville, NC 17560.

WinBench Features

- Service tested: Disk subsystem and graphics subsystem

- Test results: Normalized score of weighted test execution times

- OS: Windows 3.1 or higher

- Network: None required

- Type of benchmark: Synthetic

- Test patterns: A distribution of disk operations and a distribution of graphics operations, plus some optional disk and graphics tests which test specific operations

- Required test setup: PC with at least a 80386 processor, 4 MBytes DRAM, 41 MBytes of free disk space

Comments

The benchmark includes a variety of disk and graphics test suites, but two suites in particular attempt to model the behavior of real applications. The two suites, called Disk WinMark and Graphics WinMark, are based on profiles of the operations performed on these two subsystems by the Winstone benchmark of 13 applications programs. It appears from the documentation that the profiles are used to create statistical distributions, which are then used to create service requests during the benchmark runs. Details of the statistical modeling process are not given.

The WinMark tests should give much more realistic results than the other, more artificial tests which are also included. On the other hand, the DiskMark test's service request distributions will change from year to year, whereas the other tests have remained constant for many years, allowing old test results to be compared to new. Depending on how you plan to use the results of the tests, one or the other test approach may be preferred.

Ziff-Davis Winstone 95

Overview

Winstone 95 measures the time a PC takes to execute a set of application scripts that exercise 13 of the best-selling Windows 3.x applications. Winstone weights the individual script execution times using the unit market shares of the applications and reports results normalized to a reference machine. Copies of the Winstone 95 benchmark suite and user's manual may be obtained by writing to Ziff-Davis Benchmark Operation, One Copley Parkway, Suite 510, Morrisville, NC 17560.

Winstone Features

- Service tested: Execution of desktop applications

- Test results: Normalized score of weighted test execution times

- OS: Windows 3.1 or higher

- Network: None required

- Type of benchmark: Application based

- Test patterns: A set of 13 Windows applications is run from a test script

- Required test setup: The computer under test, with adequate hardware to run the Windows operating system and all 13 applications in the test suite

Comments

The Winstone benchmark is targeted at general office tasks. The 13 Applications are divided into four categories: Business Graphics/ Desktop Publishing, Database, Spreadsheet, and Word Processing. Each application is executed from a script, and the running time of the script/application is recorded. When calculating the final result, a ratio is formed from the measured run times and the run times of a base machine. These ratios are then combined in a weighted harmonic mean, with the weights based on market share of each application.

The tasks and task sequences represented in the scripts are based on survey data from PC Magazine and Microsoft's usability lab. Thus the scripts are modeled after actual usage patterns. It can be argued, however, that basing the scoring weights strictly on unit sales is misleading, as some applications may be much more heavily used by purchasers than others. Still, this approach is better than one which does not use weights at all.

Winstone supplies the executables for all of the applications. The user supplies the operating systems, DOS 5.0 or latter and Windows 3.1 or Windows for Workgroups 3.11 or later. Thus the scores will reflect both the underlying hardware speed and the performance of the operating system in use. If only hardware comparisons are desired, then all of the hardware platforms must be running with identical operating system software.

❐

15

Multi-user Benchmarks

What This Chapter Is About

In the personal computing world, multi-user systems are typically the server portion of a client/server system. However, high-end PCs are also used as time-sharing "servers" where the users interact through traditional terminals. Thus this chapter begins with descriptions of several popular client/server benchmarks, and then describes three popular time-sharing benchmarks. While oriented toward time-sharing, these benchmarks do measure many aspects of a system which affect performance in a client/server system. However, it should be remembered that a server workload can be very different than a time-sharing workload, so caution should be used in interpreting the benchmark results.

Ziff-Davis NetBench 3.0

Overview

NetBench is designed to measure the throughput of file servers. File read and write requests are sent to the server from clients running the NetBench software and the resulting data rate (in bytes per second) is recorded. Any server operating system and network can be used, so long as they can support DOS clients. Copies of the NetBench 95 benchmark suite and user's manual may be obtained by writing to Ziff-Davis Benchmark Operation, One Copley Parkway, Suite 510, Morrisville, NC 17560.

NetBench Features

- Service tested: Remote file access

- Test results: Bytes per second delivered to clients

- OS: The clients run under DOS while the server may be running any operating system

- Network: Any network can be used

- Type of benchmark: Synthetic

- Test patterns: Application mix derived, sequential read, sequential write, random read, random write, random read and write, network interface

- Required test setup: File server under test, one test control computer, one or more client computers, and a private network segment

Comments

The most significant addition to NetBench from earlier versions is the Disk Mix test, which attempts to emulate the remote disk traffic which would emanate from typical office applications, such as editors and spread sheets. The clients do not actually run the office applications, but rather scripts based on profiles of the applications.

The other tests in the benchmark place highly artificial loads on the server, though they are useful for pinpointing particular subsystem bottlenecks. The network interface test is particularly useful in determining when the test results are being network limited, as it tends to indicate the peak achievable bytes per second with an ideal disk subsystem. When the network is the bottleneck, the other tests may not be very useful as measures of disk subsystem performance.

Ziff-Davis ServerBench 1.1

Overview

ServerBench is designed to measure the performance of the server under a synthetic transactions processing workload. Transaction requests are sent to the server from clients running the ServerBench client software and executed on the server by the ServerBench server software. The clients measure the number of completed transactions they observe during the benchmark run. The final results are presented as a composite rate of transactions per second. Copies of the ServerBench 95 benchmark suite and user's manual may be obtained by writing to Ziff-Davis Benchmark Operation, One Copley Parkway, Suite 510, Morrisville, NC 17560.

ServerBench Features

- Service tested: Remote transactions

- Test results: Transactions per second delivered to clients

- OS: The clients run under DOS while the server may be running SCO UNIX, NetWare, or Windows NT

- Network: Any network can be used

- Type of benchmark: Synthetic

- Test patterns: Simulated transaction execution by processor, sequential read, sequential write, random read, random write, file append, network (client to server), and network (server to client)

- Required test setup: Server under test, one test control computer, one or more client computers, and a private network segment

Comments

ServerBench emulates a client/server system, such as is typical of a modern server based database application. ServerBench consists of multiple clients, each consisting of a PC running ServerBench client software on MS-DOS, and a server running ServerBench server software on either SCO UNIX, Microsoft Windows NT, or Novell NetWare.

The ServerBench clients run scripts which generate a mix of transaction requests designed to mimic those a real client might generate. The requests are sent one at a time, with a new one sent as soon as a reply from the previous one is received. Since in a typical on-line transactions system the clients generate transactions at a much lower rate, one ServerBench client can generate the workload of several real clients.

The server runs a synthetic transactions processing application supplied as part of ServerBench. This application has eight build-in stress tests, divided into three groups:

- CPU: One test which performs a set of database operations on an in-memory database

- Disk I/O: Five tests which transfer data between disk and main memory, consisting of sequential read, sequential write, random read, random write, and append tests

- Network: Two tests which transfer fixed size blocks of data between the clients and the server's main memory over the network in the client to server direction and the server to client direction

Several test suites are provided, some of which just test specific subsystems. There are also several *Blend* test suits which test all three subsystems, combining all eight tests in such a way that they mimic a typical transaction processing system. In the Blend test suites, each transaction requests one of the eight tests, and representative workloads are obtained by generating transactions for each test in the appropriate proportions. Thus to emulate a real TP system, you might send a transaction to do a burst of network input, followed by one requesting a burst of random disk reads, then one requesting a burst of processor activity, one requesting a burst of random disk writes, and finally one requesting a burst of network output. Since each burst does the work of several typical real transactions, the reported TPS rate of these five partial transactions should be similar to that of five real transactions doing a similar amount of total work.

ServerBench has an advantage in testing storage subsystems in that it places much lower demands on the network, and so should be much more sensitive to disk subsystem differences. Yet the full server system is still being tested, not just the disk subsystem. However, as faster disk subsystems are used, the CPU may become the bottleneck, limiting further improvement.

IOBench

Overview

IOBench is a Netware Loadable Module (NLM) used to measure the performance of the disk subsystem. It does not use the network and bypasses the NetWare file system, so it can concentrate on the disk subsystem. The benchmark is available free of charge from Symbios Logic, Inc., 3718 North Rock Road, Wichita, KS 67226.

IOBench Features

- Service tested: Disk subsystem of NetWare server

- Test results: IO operation rate and throughput

- OS: NetWare 3.11, 3.12, or 4.01

- Network: None required

- Type of benchmark: Synthetic

- Test patterns: Sequential, fixed, and random; mixed reads and writes

- Required test setup: Server running NetWare

Comments

IOBench produces the typical access patterns of simple disk subsystem benchmarks. Such patterns are good for comparing the raw performance of different disk subsystems, but are not very representative of real workloads. Thus, when using IOBench to compare servers, be aware that its results may not be indicative of overall system performance differences. However, for I/O subsystem comparisons, the fact that the network and the file system are bypassed means that the disk behavior is not masked by slow networks or efficient file caches.

CLARE

Overview

Clare is a new server benchmark that was recently developed by IBM, designed to measure the throughput of file servers. File read and write requests are sent to the server from clients running the CLARE software and the resulting data rate (in bytes per second) is recorded. The access patterns are based on those of the following applications: WordPerfect, Lotus 1-2-3, cc:Mail, Foxbase, DOS COPY UP, DOS COPY DOWN. The CLARE benchmark was developed by the IBM Boca Raton Laboratory, 1000 N.W. 51St. Street, Boca Raton, FL 33467.

Clare Features

- Service tested: Remote file access

- Test results: Bytes per second delivered to clients

- OS: The clients run under OS/2 while the server may be running any operating system

- Network: Any network can be used

- Type of benchmark: Synthetic

- Test patterns: Application mix derived

- Required test setup: File server under test, one or more client computers, and a private network segment

Comments

Clare clients run under OS/2, which supports multitasking, potentially allowing each client machine to emulate several "virtual" clients, producing more realistic request patterns. The documentation indicates that the Clare clients are using traces from the execution of actual applications to generate their requests. Thus, the file server should receive a traffic mix as realistic as would be obtained by a set of actual applications running from "keystroke" scripts on the clients.

Transactions Processing Council (TPC Benchmark A, B, and C)

Overview

A set of benchmarks which test the performance of transactions processing applications and the hardware on which they are running. More information about the TPC series of benchmarks can be obtained by contacting Shanley Public Relations, 777 North First Street, Suite 600, San Jose, CA 95112-6311.

TPC Benchmark Series Features

- Service tested: Online database transactions

- Test results: Transactions per second (A and B), transactions per minute (C)

- OS: Any

- Network: None (B), any LAN or WAN (A, C)

- Type of benchmark: Real, with input from transactions scripts randomly selected from a weighted distribution

- Test patterns: Varies by benchmark

- Required test setup: A network connecting a set of terminal emulators to the system under test is required for A and C, just the system under test for B

Comments

The TPC benchmarks are developed and administered by the Transaction Processing Council, a non-profit industry consortium. The benchmarks are intended to represent typical transactions processing workloads. The present benchmarks are modeled after a simplified banking scenario (A and B) and an order entry system (C). Two additional benchmarks are being developed to model other common uses of online transactions processing. It is anticipated that online transaction processing will continue to become more pervasive and handle more complex applications in the future, requiring the continuing development of new benchmarks.

TPC A and B are very similar, except that TPC A requires a set of terminal emulators connected by a network to the system under test, while TPC B provides a transaction generator which runs directly on the system under test. Hence, TPC A is considered to be more realistic, but TPC B is much easier (and cheaper) to run. The transaction workload produced by these benchmarks is considered to be too simplistic to be representative of many of today's online transactions systems, so the TPC-C benchmark was developed. It requires a network with terminal emulators, like TPC-A, but models an order entry system with a mix of transaction types rather than the single type used by TPC-A and TPC-B. The TPC-C transactions are also more complex than the TPC-A and B ones, and result in much higher CPU loading.

While the rate of transactions processing is the key metric for all three benchmarks, the benchmark reports are required to include cost figures for the system under test (and terminals and network for TPC-A and TPC-C). The cost figures are used to derive a dollars per transaction figure, which provides a more meaningful measure for typical system purchasers.

AIM Benchmark Suite

Overview

This is a suite of synthetic UNIX benchmarks developed by AIM Technology. The suite includes tests to measure CPU integer and floating point performance, disk I/O performance, memory speed, system call and library function performance. The component tests are grouped together into suites which attempt to duplicate popular usage patterns, such as file server, single user engineering, or general business. Metrics of peak and sustained performance and price/performance are reported. The AIM benchmarks are maintained by AIM Technologies, 4699 Old Ironsides Drive, Suite 150, Santa Clara, CA 95054.

AIM Benchmark Features

- Service tested: A variety of intra box computation, I/O, and communication functions

- Test results: Appropriate performance metrics for the given test

- OS: The computer under test runs UNIX

- Network: No network involved

- Type of benchmark: Synthetic

- Test patterns:

  - Disk: Disk copies, sequential and random reads and writes, directory searches

  - Floating point: Single and double precision adds, multiplies, and divides

  - Integer math: Short and long integer adds, multiplies, and divides

  - Library routines: Memory, sort, numeric, trigonometric, and string functions

  - System call: System memory allocations

- File system: File creations and closes, directory operations

- Interprocess communication: Shared memory operations, TCP/IP messages, stream pipe messages, and others

- Algorithmic function: Linear equation solving and others

■ Required test setup: Computer system under test

Comments

The AIM benchmark has an advantage that it runs stand-alone, without requiring separate clients. As mentioned in the introduction to this chapter, it is specifically a UNIX time-sharing benchmark and not a client/server benchmark. However, it tests many key system components and should give an indication of expected server performance. In particular, it has I/O subsystem tests that could be useful in comparing I/O subsystem performance.

Neal Nelson Business Benchmark

Overview

The benchmark suite consists of thirty tests. Five of the tests use synthetic workloads which approximate the activity generated by real applications such as Office Automation, Database, Software Development, and Transactions Processing. Benchmarking products may be rented from Neal Nelson & Associates on a monthly basis. Contact them at 330 North Wabash Avenue, Chicago Illinois 60611-3604 for more Information.

Business Benchmark Features

■ Service tested: CPU, Memory, and I/O subsystems as well as mult-user batch processing of typical business applications

■ Test results: Total time required for each of 30 test scripts

■ OS: Any that can run programs written in "C"

■ Network: Any network can be used

■ Type of benchmark: Synthetic

- Test patterns: Specific patterns to stress subsystems as well as simulated applications

- Required test setup: System under test

Comments

As mentioned in the introduction to this chapter, the Neal Nelson Business Benchmark is not a server benchmark, but rather a time-sharing benchmark. It tests many key system components and should give an indication of expected server performance. In particular, it has I/O subsystem tests that could be useful in comparing I/O subsystem performance.

◻

▼▼▼▼ Bibliography

Paul Massiglia, Editor, *The RAIDbook, A Source for Disk Array Technology*, Fifth Edition, Raid Advisory Board, St. Peer, MN. Available from:

> Joe Molina, RAID Advisory Board Chairman
> c/o Technology Forums
> 13 Marie Lane
> St. Peter MN 56082-9423 USA
> (507) 931-0967 (Voice)
> (507) 931-0976 (FAX)
> 0004706032@mcimail.com

Novell, Inc., *Novell NetWare 4.0 Concepts*, 1993

Terry Dettmann, *DOS Programmer's Reference*, 2nd Edition, Que

Steven Simrin, *MS-DOS Bible*, 3rd Edition, 1989, The Waite Group, Howard W. Sams, 1989

The Waite Group's MS-DOS Developer's Guide, 2nd Edition, Howard W. Sams, 1989

Robert Jourdain, *Programmers Problem Solver for the IBM PC, XT, and AT*, 1986, Brady Books

System BIOS for the IBM PC, XT™, AT® Computers and Compatibles, Phoenix Technologies Ltd.

The Winn L. Rosch Hardware Bible, 3rd Edition, Brady Publishing, 1994

Frank Van Gilluwe, *The Undocumented PC*, Addison Wesley, 1994

Michael Abrash, *Zen of Code Optimization*, Coriolis Group Books, 1994

Peter M. Ridge, *The Book of SCSI*, no starch press, 1995

Friedhelm Schmidt, *The SCSI Bus and IDE Interface*, Addison Wesley, 1995

John M. Goodman, *Hard Disk Secrets*, IDG Books, 1993

Hard Drive Bible, Corporate Systems Center, 1994

Hard Disk ToolKit Owner's Manual, FWB Software, Inc., 1991

IDE•ATAPI•SCSI Forum Conference Proceedings, ENDL Technology Forums, February 21-22, 1995

Ray, "Design Goals and Implementation of the New High Performance File System," *Microsoft Systems Journal*, September 1989, p. 01

Thomas W. Martin, "1394: High-Performance Serial Bus For Desktop and Portable Computers," *Computer Technology Computer Review*, Spring/Summer 1994

Dal Allan, *Is it ATA? Is it IDE? Is it Enhanced IDE?*, ENDL (408)-867-6630

Dr. Robert Selinger, I/O Interfaces—What to Use Where, Adaptec presentation

The Zadian SCSI Navigator, Zadian Technologies (408)-293-0800

Understanding the Small Computer System Interface, NCR Corporation, Prentice Hall

Western Digital Enhanced IDE Implementation Guide, Revision 5.0, November 10, 1993, Western Digital Corporation

Adge Hawes, *Serial Storage Architecture—A Low-Cost, High-Speed Serial Connection for Disk Subsystems*, Document Number AJH\C:\MISC\SSAART12.SCR, IBM Storage Subsystem Development, IBM Havant, June 24, 1994. Reprinted on pages 163 through 175 by permission from International Business Machines Corporation, Copyright 1994

IBM Corporation, *Technical Reference, Personal Computer XT*, 1984

IBM Corporation, *Technical Reference, Personal Computer AT Version 2.02*, 1983

Raj Jain, *The Art of Computer Systems Performance Analysis*, John Wiley & Sons, Inc., 1991

The Benchmark Handbook for Database and Transaction Processing Systems, Edited by Jim Gray, 2nd edition, Morgan Kaufmann, San Mateo, 1993

Helen Custer, *Inside Windows NT*, Microsoft Press, 1993

Helen Custer, *Inside the Windows NT File System*, Microsoft Press, 1994

Andrew W. Wilson Jr., *Hierarchical Cache/Bus Architecture for Shared Memory Multiprocessors*, 14th Annual International Symposium on Computer Architecture, Pittsburgh, PA, 1986

Understanding and Using WinBench® 95 Version 1.0, Ziff-Davis Publishing Company, 1994

Understanding and Using Winstone™ 95 Version 1.0, Ziff-Davis Publishing Company, 1994

Understanding and Using PC Bench™ 9.0, Ziff-Davis Publishing Company, 1994

Understanding and Using NetBench™ 3.0, Ziff-Davis Publishing Company, 1994

Understanding and Using ServerBench™ 1.1, Ziff-Davis Publishing Company, 1994

Unix System Price Performance Guide, Summer 1994, AIM Technologies, 1994

"IBM 1993 Server Systems Performance White Paper, Version 2.3," IBM Boca Raton Laboratory, 1994

BAPCo Report, Business Applications Performance Corp., Vol. 2, Issue #2, 1994

"PCI Local Bus Specification—Production Version," PCI Special Interest Group, Revision 2.0, 1993

◻

▼▼▼▼ WWW Bookmarks

Given the importance of the Internet, we include a WWW Bookmarks section.

Benchmark Information

http://www.zdnet.com/~zdbop/

http://www.yahoo.com/Computers_and_Internet/Hardware/Benchmarks/

SCSI Information

http://www.adaptec.com/

http://www.yahoo.com/Computers_and_Internet/Hardware/SCSI/

RAID Information

ftp://ftp.mcs.com/mcsnet.users/llangevi/VSE/text/RAID.FAQ

Generic Information

http://www.yahoo.com/Computers_and_Internet/

http://www.stpt.com/

CAM Information

http://www.symbios.com/x3t10

Other I/O Information

http://www.peer-to-peer.com

❒

▾▾▾▾ Index

T

About Adaptec

Overview

Adaptec, Inc. (NASDAQ:ADPT) designs, manufactures and markets IOware solutions to eliminate performance bottlenecks between microcomputers, networks, and peripherals. Solutions range from simple connectivity products for single-user and small-office desktops, to intelligent subsystem, high-performance SCSI, RAID and ATM products for enterprise-wide computing and networked environments. Adaptec I/O solutions are incorporated into the products of virtually all the major computer and peripheral manufacturers around the world.

Founded in 1981 and headquartered in Milpitas, Calif., Adaptec is a recognized market leader in high-performance I/O technology. Adaptec currently employs approximately 1,800 people, and with its global distribution network, serves customers worldwide.

Adaptec's World Wide Web home page address is *http://www.adaptec.com*.

Additional Detail from Adaptec's 1995 Annual Report

When the first desktop PCs emerged early in the last decade, Adaptec was already pioneering I/O solutions to improve system performance. From the beginning, Adaptec took a total system approach, addressing I/O challenges on both sides of the interface in peripherals and hosts. As PC technology evolved with more powerful CPUs, multiple architectures and operating systems, and more sophisticated software applications, Adaptec refined and improved its technology.

From its earliest innovations, such as the first multitasking disk controllers more than a decade ago, to pioneering ASPI software standards as a common interface for operating systems and peripherals, to the recent breakthroughs such as the first affordable ATM network interface cards, Adaptec continues to build on its heritage of innovation. By continuously broadening its expertise, expanding its strategic relationships with major software and systems companies, growing its distribution channel, and strengthening its brand franchise, Adaptec helps insure its ability to attain long-term business success.

Today, input/output not only remains a critical issue for system performance, but has also grown into a complex, multi-faceted market. Adaptec's experience supports a growing family of IOware products, comprised of host adapter cards, custom ASICs, and software that improve overall system performance by speeding data transfer rates between systems, peripherals, and networks. There is no substitute for experience, and Adaptec's industry leadership is founded on a comprehensive background in I/O technology, putting it in a class by itself as the leading industry supplier of I/O solutions.

Because of its broad perspective and expertise, Adaptec is not limited to any single I/O technology. Consequently, Adaptec is able to lead the important and expanding SCSI market, yet still have the resources to address other significant I/O solutions. By staying involved with every new generation of microcomputer technology, architectures, and bus standards, Adaptec develops IOware products that span all industry standards—from SCSI, EIDE, and PCMCIA, to ATM, infrared, and serial technology.

Experience with multiple technologies also gives Adaptec the capability to enhance performance and connectivity within a variety of environments. The market has embraced the company's IOware solutions for high-performance workstations, for client/server throughput and redundancy, for enterprise-wide networking, for the mobile computing market, down to the small business and single user on desktop PCs running the latest games or graphics-intensive applications.

Adaptec corporate headquarters is located at 691 South Milpitas Blvd., Milpitas, CA 95035, U.S.A. Corporate telephone number is (408) 945-8600. Adaptec's home page is *http://www.adaptec.com*.

About This Book

Copies of this book are available from Adaptec sales representatives by requesting Stock Number 511048-00.

"This book is desperately needed. I hope everybody involved with I/O for PCs reads it. PC I/O is chaotic and suffering from years of architectural neglect. I applaud anyone who tackles these problems."

Gordon Bell, Senior Researcher, Microsoft

"I/O subsystem performance is inseparable from LAN server performance. This book illuminates and integrates many complex considerations NetWare exploits to achieve maximum I/O subsystem performance."

Robert Frankenberg, Chairman, Novell Corporation

"This is an excellent overview of the I/O system for industry standard computers. I/O subsystems are just as important to overall throughput of the computer as the processor and memory systems. They all need to be balanced in an optimized architecture."

Gary Stimac, Senior Vice President, General Manager
System Division, COMPAQ Corp.

"I've read enough portions of your book to state that it is a job well done!"

Joe Molina, Chairman, RAID Advisory Board

"*Understanding I/O Subsystems* is an encyclopedia of the PC and workstation storage subsystem. It covers the technology, hardware, software, architecture, availability, and reliability of these systems in a manner that will satisfy all but the most experienced storage architects. Good reading!"

James T. Brady, President and CEO, MatriDigm Corporation
Former IBM Fellow and IBM Academy of Science President

"A high-impact I/O subsystem overview in the finest tradition of Adaptec's technology leadership."

Larry Boucher, Chairman, Auspex Corporation
Author of original SCSI Specification
Founder, Adaptec, Inc.

To Order Copies of this Book

This book is available by contacting Adaptec directly at:

800-442-SCSI (7274) or 408-957-SCSI (7274), Monday through Friday, 6:00 a.m. to 5:00 p.m., Pacific Time.

Book stores, dealers, and libraries contact:

Peer-to-Peer Communications, Inc.
P.O. Box 640218
San Jose, California 95164-0218, U.S.A.
Phone: 408-435-2677
Fax: 408-435-0895
Email: info@peer-to-peer.com
WWW: *http://www.peer-to-peer.com*

❒